MY MOTHER'S MIRROR

A Generational Journey of
Purpose, Resilience, and Self-Discovery

By
SABRINA SOFFER

858.255.0207 ◆ MMM@BYSABS.COM
WWW.BYSABS.COM/MYMOTHERSMIRROR

A JOURNEY OF TRANSFORMATION, EMPOWERMENT, AND PERSEVERANCE

My Mother's Mirror is a transformation journey of a woman relentlessly searching for her purpose, passions, and principles as she faces inner conflicts, identity crisis, and contentious relationships. At twenty-three, she experiences an earth-shattering moment as she faces herself crying hopelessly in the mirror. This moment, rather than breaking her, emerges in a lifelong commitment to being honest with herself and others in search of purpose, fulfillment, and joy. She pursues each obstacle as an opportunity to know herself by taking responsibility and communicating assertively. Each extreme emotion serves an indicator of beliefs and paradigms to accept, reject, and change toward self-repair and inner peace.

My Mother's Mirror inspired by true events and intents to empower women around the world. Social changes have turned women's lives upside down, and many struggle to balance their personal needs with societal demands. Through this generational journey, readers will gain insight about tools for success in their adolescence, single lives, relationships, marriage, parenting, and beyond as they shift from one role to the next.

DISCLAIMER

Library of congress control number:
ISBN: 9798787796858
All Rights Reserved to IQNet, Inc.

Dedication

To my mother

She planted me in the eyes of pure sunlight

Watered plenty

Nourished endlessly

Unconditional care, love,

Unwavering protection

To sprout and blossom in the right direction

Standing tall in a crowded field

Among all walks of life who try to slash, to manipulate,

Or cut through

She remains a shield, she stays true

So her seedling flowers

With wisdom, strength, and ambition

Rays shine, they glow with power

Never with fear nor affliction

Her character, her actions

Hold not a single contradiction

Authenticity and confidence,

She holds powerful tools

To mold minds, to traverse tides

To garden groves, to conquer coves

Uplifting those she nurtures

Feeding them knowledge, values, compassion

With class and composure

An inspiration to me—her baby seedling

Whom she planted in the eyes of pure sunlight

Envisioned was an image of her

A soul immune to fright

A mind with no boundaries in sight

So I could become

A mirror, a reflection

To personify this stroke of beaming beauty

She shaped me in her steps

Leading a life with principles and purpose

Just as she lives

A life with no regrets

~ Your Daughter, Sabrina

A Message from the Author

Summer, 2020.

As a 2020 high school graduate new to the adult world, I've long reflected upon the principles driving my passions in pursuit of the road ahead. Taking a gap year before college amidst the COVID crisis seemed unfortunate, but there was a silver lining of opportunity: An invaluable time to bond with my mother.

During endless quarantine walks, I grew curious about my mother's roots and upbringing. She shared the story of my grandmother's marriage at thirteen to my grandfather who was twenty-four by tribal tradition. She shared her story of marriage in the Orthodox Jewish Community and her divorce. She shared endless dating stories that made us laugh and reflect together. She told me about her transition into motherhood and shared stories from my early childhood. All these narratives shared one commonality— moments of epiphany that fostered life-changing paradigm shifts which enabled my mother, and eventually myself, to gain personal power and strengthen relationships with myself and others. My fascination with my mother's emergence from confining cultures to her stance as the confident entrepreneur and activist she is today is everlasting.

My Mother's Mirror is my memoir paired with my mother's, uniquely styled with tools for value-based decision making, empowerment, and building confidence. The book comes alive in eight parts, beginning with my experiences as a teenager, then looping back to my mother's roots where she tells her life story in full.

A visceral urge to break away from taboos, normative inequality, and suppression drove the moral imperative of my mom's life journey.

'Know thyself' was her goal so she could understand and later manage the behaviors driving her actions, reactions, and outcomes of certain situations. This journey of rebellion, resilience, and reform through personal and cultural extremes is staged on an international arena: It begins in a mountain-top village on the Russian Caucasus, shifts to Israel, between the Boro Park and Wall Street communities in New York, and finally, to San Diego, California.

I was raised under a traditional roof fused with a collaborative parenting style. This shaped me into a hybrid between my grandparents' culture, my father's traditional ethic, and my mother's liberating paradigms. As a child, I was never punished but rather guided with principles, processes, and practical tools to take personal responsibility in all situations. This enabled me to transform obstacles into opportunities growing up, emphasized as a central theme in this book. The events I recount in my section illustrate how my mother's paradigms influence how I search, seek, and strive toward purpose. My mom's staunch activism inspires me to follow in her footsteps, too. She has taught me to confront conflicts collaboratively and head-on with compassion, all of which cultivate my character and help me learn from each situation.

This book is dedicated to women of all ages around the world who seek a fulfilling, enriching, and empowered life. I strive to help women uncover their own inner strengths and use them by providing them tools to navigate their independent lives, professional lives, relationships, and parenting so they can author their own destiny. I've surely built confidence in my own skin with my mother's guidance, and I hope to pass such principles onto others so that they can do the same.

Table of Contents

PART · I

Daughter's Reflections

2015 - 2022

1

Advocate for Your Kids so They Can Advocate for Themselves

It seemed all too innocent. We were just eighth graders. Sean's calculator fell under my chair during class, and he instinctively reached down to pick it up. I hardly noticed that his skillfully concealed hand had just snapped a photo beneath my skirt. Days later, I learned that mine was among the hundreds of photographs of my female peers' underwear and crotch humiliatingly exposed.

Shockingly, the abuse had been an open secret for some time. Several friends, fearing embarrassment and backlash, refused to file a complaint. Despite their abstinence, I was adamant to do so anyway. My mother had always taught me to speak up when my safety was compromised. It seemed like a no-brainer: This perversion needed to stop. A classmate of mine, Melissa, also agreed with me. We wasted no time in reporting the offense.

School officials seemed receptive at first.

"We'll take care of it, don't worry," they assured.

The next day, Melissa and I were called to the office for a meeting.

We were simply instructed to sit down in front of Sean, who was already there. He had an apology written for us.

"Would you like to read the letter you wrote to the girls?" The principal asked him compassionately. He unfolded the crinkly sheet of yellow paper and read, "I'm so sorry for what I did. I do-do-don't know why I did it. I just don't know. And-and I-I won't do it again." Tears escaped him. I couldn't take him seriously.

"Is there anything you want to add?" the principal turned to me, and then hinted at my classmate, "What about you, Melissa?"

Mine and Melissa's stricken eyes locked, trying to conjure up what we could possibly "add" in this sticky situation. I froze.

It was clear to me that the case was being shoved under the rug to avoid a scandal. Sean was never disciplined; I would've expected at least suspension. My peers and many parents were outraged. In meetings to follow, the principal suggested that my allegations were exaggerated:

"It seems like every time you step into my office, you're just making the issue bigger than it is," he said, "it was only one picture, and it's deleted now."

Lie. A male friend of mine had informed me that there were 200-some pictures in an album on someone's iPad. And whether it was one picture or 200, it didn't matter. Bringing this up resulted in yet another dismissal.

"With all due respect, I think he needs to have consequences. He'll never learn from his mistakes if he's not disciplined. I think suspension for a few days would be the right punishment." I replied firmly.

"That's not possible, I'm sorry."

The principal's unapologetic gaze irked me.

Cowardice, Courage, and Consequences

While presenting myself assertively on the outside, I was crumbling on the inside. *My friends were right. I should have never spoken up, they told me the school makes things worse.* They were upset that I insisted on reporting the issue: Now that I did, and messed things up more, I feared that nobody would be my friend anymore. No wonder Melissa didn't follow through. Betrayal.

One Monday morning, a close friend of mine confronted me during art class. "Why did you tell-on him? You're such a tattletale. Not cool, Sabs." After two weeks of episodes like these, I'd call my mom begging her to pick me up from school almost every day. She always did. Upon arriving home, I'd run up to my room and lock the door (I'd usually do my homework in the kitchen downstairs). My mom often barged in to check on me, only finding me sobbing into a pillow with piles of math homework thrown on the floor. The more I told her to go away and leave me alone, the tighter she pulled me into her arms. "Everything is going to be ok. You did the right thing," she'd say.

My isolation morphed into self-destructive behavior, self-questioning and doubt pushing me deeper into a dark hole. *Why was I, the victim, being hurt more than the initial pain that was caused to me? I have no friends, my teachers don't care about me, and the principal thinks I'm a liar.* Spiraling into a deep depression, the nickel-sized bald spot on my scalp was growing, growing, and growing. I'd peer down from my bed side to see strands of hair— like my sense of hope— pulled out, fallen, and stranded beneath me. *School is a dangerous place. Trust no one.*

"Why did you tell me to speak up!? You always told me to, and I trusted you, so I did! And now look at what happened, look at what you did!" I cried to my mother amid a teary tantrum. Months later, she told me that these were the words that drove her to fight for my justice no matter the cost. She pledged to model the behaviors she had preached, demonstrating that advocating for oneself is always the right choice. The alternative— sitting in silence with festering shame— is far worse.

My dad, on the other hand, was standing on the sidelines and minimizing the issue: "Boys will be boys, I used to peep when I was a kid too. It's normal." Sometimes he echoed the school principal too: "Are you sure, Sabrina?" This really didn't help. Our household was polarized, and yet again, the empty patch on my head was exposed. Therapy was no longer an option.

I hated to admit this at the time but going to therapy changed the course of my life. My therapist advised me to wear a Pandora bracelet with collectible charms which I could fidget with when I felt the urge to pull my hair out. It sounds trivial, however, made a significant difference in my behavior. Until this day, each charm added to the collection symbolizes something meaningful, marking a certain milestone or a passion of mine. When I look down at my bracelet in moments of distress, each charm reminds me of how far I've come. *Sabrina, you don't deserve to hurt yourself.*

As my mother kept advocating for me and insisting that the school incur justice, my dad still refused to step in. Ongoing disagreements pushed my parents to see a family therapist to diffuse the situation. Within thirty minutes of our first session, the therapist posed, "Do you think this is a gender issue?" My dad was speechless. Leaning toward him, she continued, "This is not about your childhood or how you feel about the situation. This is your daughter's childhood, and she's clearly expressing how she feels about it."

As the conversation evolved, she asked whether the school reported this incident to Child Protection Services. "They are mandated reporters, and it's illegal to take up-skirt pictures in this state." She insisted that my dad call the school and inquire as to whether they reported the incident and to whom. Once he finally called the principal, that's when the school's administration relented. A gender issue indeed.

Reflection, Repair, and Resolution

A bulwark in this battle for my dignity, my mother never let me down. As one to encourage unrelenting self-advocacy, I would have deemed her failure to support me as hypocrisy. And hypocritical is something that she is not. Over the next five months, my mom would engage in endless email communications and meetings with the school, whose dismissive administrators exacerbated both my anxiety and hers. It was like punching a wall that never breaks, but she'd fight until their fort fell. My mother demanded that they issue an apology to me, run a workshop on proper use of phones for students, and amend handbook policies to ensure a transparent conflict-resolution process for all stakeholders.

This all happened around the same time that USA Gymnastics Dr. Larry Nassar's trial broke news headlines. My mom was glued to the TV day and night.

"You wake up and fall asleep with Larry Nassar! What's going on with you?!" My dad and I would make fun of her. But soon, I'd understand why she was mesmerized with these proceedings. Her purpose is always in mind.

So, while to a lesser extreme, my mom researched the parallels between the USA Gymnastics case and mine. My school, like many other institutions, was deliberately covering up to protect their prestigious reputation and shield themselves from liability. She went on to publish a report titled the Underground Practices that Normalize Child Abuse as the foundation for her book, Act Responsibly, and developed innovative technology platforms, Let's Speak Up and ICIARA.

My mother's whole-hearted investment in me and passion for justice inspired me to ally with her. Together, we researched the legal ramifications surrounding my case and brainstormed what an adequate resolution could be. We discovered that the school had failed to file the formal CPS report, a state mandate for minors in any private entity. We also discovered that upskirting, a form of voyeurism, is a criminal act in California.[1] While school handbook policy was clear about the handling of such matters, the administration opted out from following it.

Being inappropriately photographed was no longer the source of my anxiety. My distress was intensely induced by the school's perverted actions. To ensure that others who encounter similar issues would not endure my same experience, my mom and I were determined to bring awareness and broaden policy to include transparent communication, genuine apology, positive repair for victims, and education for offenders.

Meanwhile, the school was still refusing to suspend Sean and fulfill their fiduciary duty to protect us, victims. My mom suggested a

---

[1] Cal. Pen. Code § 647(j) (1872) is the California Penal Code that cites crimes of invasion of privacy by secretly using an object, such as a device to view or photograph a person in a private area.

disciplinary method which she exemplified at home, effective in both doing justice to us girls while teaching him a lesson.

"Maybe he can do a project about proper cell-phone use and present it to the class or some community service, so he learns from this situation," my mom proposed.

"Do you want to humiliate him? I cannot allow that," the principal replied. My mother and I were incredulous.

About six months later, I was mailed a letter of apology from the principal and the dean. It came far too late. But eventually, and not without setbacks, the fight paid off. My mother made a condition with the school: They would amend the handbook to include a new safety policy, including the report of the incident to all parties involved and the mandatory filing of the CPS report among other precepts. This was first presented through a newsletter to the parents and was explained to students in an assembly that we pushed for later that year.

While justice was not granted directly to me, I was honored to have played a role in transforming school policy for the safety of my peers. Mine and my mother's bold impression on the administrators restored my eroded self-esteem. I took pride in becoming a voice for the voiceless— for my fellow classmates— regardless of how they treated me.

To Speak Up or Sit in Silence?

In years shortly following this incident, I circled back to weighing risks and rewards of speaking up or sitting in silence. Powerful emotions like fear and shame conquer all, and understandably, most people cannot face them. Is speaking up worth the repercussions I faced as a young teenager? Or would avoiding the anxiety by remaining silent yield greater mental distress of regret and shame? The faith I've gained in my principles grounds me to embrace my fears, eliminating any prospect of shame in pursuing truth and doing what's right. So what if I'm scared? What's the worst thing that can happen? Remaining silent would have been the worst thing. Silence is a plague that devours the weak.

Although I initially resented my mom and myself for speaking up, I reap the rewards of my courageous actions today. My experience, while with grave consequences, left me stronger than ever. It confirmed my passion for human rights, advocacy, and leadership. Therefore, I continue and will continue to speak up against injustices in my view. I hope that by doing so, as my mother did for me, I can inspire others to do the same.

2

The Dawn of High School: Decisions, Decisions.

Freshman year of high school is when most kids, if they ever do, choose to move schools. Due to my distressing experience in eighth grade, my mother asked me if I wanted to start afresh. This would mark my sixth move.

"No, I don't want to move again. Plus, I have some good friends and teachers are supposed to be great. I think high school will be better. I want to stay." In my eyes, moving from this school would have let Sean and the administration win. I couldn't let myself lose: Moving would paint me with weakness. Weak: That's one thing I'm not. Weak is one thing I refuse to ever be.

My freshman year set-off to a great start: The middle school administration was different from the high school. I did not share a single class with the boy who violated me either, but when passing him in the halls, we could hardly look at each other. Despite some discomfort, I ventured to new friendships. My mental health improved as confidence trickled back to me, knowing-well what my principles were, that I resiliently held on to them, and who I was. Without even moving, I felt fresh.

A couple of months in, things rolled downhill again. Contrary to my assumption, my teachers were awful: Some didn't know their material, some put me to sleep, and some acted borderline abusive. I felt violated and, yet again, worthless. This was a stark contrast from middle school where my teachers radiated with positivity and tried to lift me up out of my dark hole. Maybe I just got unlucky.

My mother's days were reminiscent of the previous year— interrupted by my persistent messages and calls begging her to pick me up. And of course, she always did: Unconditional support, care, compassion.

By spring, I was desperate: "Mom, get me out of here, I can't stand it anymore." I couldn't fathom three more years at that school, especially high school where grades and extracurriculars meant everything. Besides, if my experience was so miserable, it wasn't worth driving forty minutes every day or paying thousands of dollars for an elite private school that carried a brand but was not catering to my needs. My mother agreed to explore a few different options.

Our local public high school, just a mile away from home, was ranked among the top in the state. Academics have always been my priority, and I sought intellectual stimulation from quality teachers in challenging classes. The new-student tour bought-in my move for sophomore year. This decision did not fly so seamlessly at home.

My dad was adamantly opposed: "You just got unlucky with one year of bad teachers. You can't just leave when you don't like some aspects of a place. Besides, the private school environment and a tight-knit community are a better fit for you, trust me."

Debates back and forth lasted from spring through summer until my mom and I finally convinced him. How did we manage to do that? Good old grinding.

Grinding to the Core

My mom and I joke that it takes seven times until my dad considers any ideas we propose. He is often skeptical of ideas or solutions deemed outside the box, requiring 'grinding' of those ideas several times before influencing him to say yes. It's true: A few years prior, my mom and I determined to make my dad aware of his notorious habit. He didn't believe us. To prove him wrong, my mom proposed a family challenge. She created a chart that tallied the number of times each person said "no" in the span of a week. My dad's count tallied to about fifty-some; my mom and I came to about twenty. He couldn't believe himself.

There are many skeptical personalities like my dad out there: Getting a taste of how people like him operate and learning how to manage them is essential. The first time you present my dad with a new idea, his answer is always no. The second or third time, you can pepper in a bit of your reasoning, but it's still no. The fourth and fifth time, he asks you questions to understand the suggestion from your perspective. He usually concludes with, "I'll think about it." The sixth or seventh time, your wish might be granted if you're lucky.

This grinding technique must be executed artfully and methodically over a period of weeks or even months. It requires patience and emotional buttress to endure the push back, but it also requires practice in persuasion. To me, debating comes easy because of my many years of training (with him, mostly); I find great joy in it. The one thing you **don't** do in any argument is give up. So, when my dad says "no," I've learned to keep pushing a little bit at a time. His rejection presents opportunities to ask him questions and understand his boundaries, risks, challenges, and concerns. It also serves as a clue to shovel up stronger arguments and shape them differently until he gives in.

When my dad shut down the idea of me switching schools, my mom and I brought up new reasons each time and repositioned our arguments to diffuse his opposition. We began with how my current school was impacting me first emotionally, and then academically. Then, we transitioned to how moving me could benefit him:

"You won't have to pay or waste time in the car schlepping forty minutes each direction," I added. Over many days and weeks, we'd garnish each conversation with positive details about the local public school and how it compared to my current private school. Our hands got dirty in the process, but I finally got my way. Unfortunately for me, my dad was right this time. Perhaps I made the wrong decision. Regardless of my regrets, I'd eventually transform my high school experience into an opportunity to learn about myself through this environment.

3

Fifty Shades of No Shame

I've always enjoyed tagging along on my mom's outings with her friends and attending her women's leadership workshops. I relish in adult conversations over an array of mature and intellectual topics— from philosophy to current affairs and even taboo ones like politics and sex. The tough transition to my new school glued me to my mom's social group. She'd often organize girls' nights out with her friends to go watch a movie and grab dinner afterward. I rarely declined an invite.

One Friday night was the debut of the third movie in the Fifty Shades of Gray series. Some of my mom's friends were planning on going to see it, so she thought it would be fun for a whole group of girls to watch it together and mingle afterward. My mom always encouraged me to join the ladies, and I'm open to learning about anything. I knew little about the infamous trilogy at the time, just that it involved sex, whips, and some red room. Ok…. sounds interesting! I'm in!

Before the movie, I read summaries of the two films prior so I could understand what was going on in the third. Although a bit confused, the harmony between pleasure and pain intrigued me. *How could a human being inflict such pain on someone they love?* Among the many questions that crossed my mind, I wondered how realistic this story was, or could be.

Even when sex was vanilla, both characters were easily aroused by just minutes of intercourse in the movie. Obviously acting is dramatized, but I began to reflect on all the other movies or TV series I had watched: In every single one, these short moments seemed to bring people into a whole new fantasy. *Can something so invasive really feel **that** good? Is sex really like in the movies?* Hmmm…I guess I'd find out eventually.

The ten of us plus me, "the kid "(that's what my aunt calls me when I tag along with the adults), sat down at California Pizza Kitchen after the movie. My mom's friend group ranged from early thirties to seventy plus. No age requirement excluded anyone. Sometimes, my friends from school came along too! We squeezed in at a long booth at the back of the restaurant. After placing our orders, my mom embodied her de facto role of facilitator.

"What did you think about the movie?" was the first point of discussion. Considering how long these women have been friends, they wouldn't hold back from expressing their opinions. *This is going to be a very interesting dinner.*

One woman, Helen, aged sixty-eight was seeing a fifty-year-old guy who she had met dancing tango at a bar.

"I just love sex. I mean, I won't date someone if they don't know how to touch me. You've gotta find that chemistry, something that turns your partner on, ya know, I think he gets turned on when I send him videos of me walking in red stilettos," she shared confidently, twirling her jet-straight brown hair. Everyone cried tears of laughter. I could hardly contain myself, nearly choking on a bite of grilled cheese dipped in tomato bisque.

The conversation took more serious turns as each woman shared her sexual experiences and dates through various relationships. Some were recently divorced, some were still single and looking, and some were going through a rough patch in their marriage.

"I could relate to when he left her without notice in the movie because even when I fly to go see Andy, he does that to me too sometimes. I get really hurt, I don't know why he does it, and I don't know what to do," shared another woman in her mid-fifties currently dating long-distance.

Other girls, mostly the younger ones, talked about their sex lives— their likes, dislikes, and desires. Fifteen-year-old-me found this rather odd, but I was content to listen in. I felt valued seen as an equal member of the group despite my young age. One to usually contribute to the conversation, I was a bit limited this time.

On the car ride home, my mom and I talked about the movie and dinner discussion. I had one lingering question. Since my mom and I have a very close relationship, and we can talk to each other about anything and everything, I decided to go for it.

"Is sex really like in the movies? Li-like does it really feel that good? It seems kind of— I don't know— invasive, painful."

Stopped at a red light, my mom turned to me with a big smile, trying to hold back her laughter. "Sabrina, let me tell you the truth. It may burst your bubble. Sex is not like the movies. Sex can be exciting and passionate but having sex with a guy your age who is inexperienced can be disappointing. You might regret it. If it's with a 15-year-old boy it's going to be seconds of 'uh-hum uh-hum,' and just, hmmm, how do I say it? It will be over before you know it and you'll have gooey coconut cream splashing all over you! Then you'll be running to the shower, scrubbing your body, and then you'll ask, 'is this really sex!?!'"

"Coconut cream?! Ah!!!" Muscles in our faces and stomachs contracted, struck by unabated convulsions of laughter.

We rolled up the driveway and my mom parked the car. "Listen, Sabrina. I'm not against you having sex. I just don't want you to have regrets, so I want you to know what to expect the first time you do it. Before you have sex, we have a showerhead with a bunch of different water streams. You can use it to explore your body in a clean way. And when the right guy comes into your life, you must first develop a true friendship, get to know him, and make him invest in you equal to your investment in him. You know, having similar values, interests, and an emotional connection is where it all starts."

My mom proceeded to tell me about her friend Lazuli, whom she had met through her mother while living in Brooklyn. "I learned from her in my late twenties. She told me that I didn't need to be in a formal relationship to experience pleasure, so you can discover your own body and then guide your partner to touch you the way you want. I am giving you the power that she gave me, but just know that sex is much better when you have an intimate relationship and really love the guy."

"Ok, makes sense." I didn't think much about it but figured that she was right.

My Friends Prove That My Mom Was Right About Sex

A few months later, my mind couldn't help but circle back to that post Fifty Shades of Gray car ride conversation.

"How was your day? How are your friends?" my mom asked when she picked me up from school one Wednesday afternoon. I threw my binder to the back seat as usual and buckled up: "Today was good. I think I did fine on the Chem quiz. The girls and I got Chinese food for lunch after. And, well, we had a really weird conversation." I paused, then continued to share, "Mckayla said that she had sex for the first time, and she totally regrets it now because the guy didn't know what to do. She said it really hurt."

"That's a shame.... remember when I told you to really think about who you're having sex with before you decide to do it. This is why I told you what I did, Sabs. I want you to explore, but I don't want you to regret it and be torn up. It's something you can't turn back. And if you need advice, never hesitate to ask me," she assured.

I knew that none of these girls talked about their relationships at home. Some even hid them from their parents. Understandably, not all parents are the type to have those sorts of discussions with their kids; inevitably, teenagers are curious to explore. But honesty is always the best policy. Without openness and clarity, streams of regret never cease to flow.

Before starting my homework that afternoon, I made a commitment to have a solid friendship with anyone before starting anything physical or sexual. I'd set my boundaries and make them clear to avoid misunderstandings. Misunderstandings, although many times insignificant, can fracture what was once a beautiful relationship. To me, maintaining that beautiful relationship involves reserving sex for someone I know I love and trust.

While exposed intellectually, I held on to my sexual innocence for the time being. Because of my values, and due in part to my rather conservative upbringing, I've stayed out of the boy drama at school or any promiscuous affairs. I hadn't even thought about any of that yet and felt too young to engage in such activities. All the while, my maturity has enabled me to analyze and understand them.

Further reflection made it impossible for me to leave the rest of the Fifty Shades of Gray series unfinished. "Ewe! You're reading that?! It's like porn! That's nasty!" My friends exploded when I pulled the book out of my backpack. While self-conscious at first, I realized that there was nothing nasty about it. In fact, anyone can relate to it, and there are a handful of lessons to learn from.

Fifty Shades of Grey isn't really about BDSM (sexual activity involving bondage, discipline, sadism, and machismo) or sex per se. The erotic flavors spice up the story line with unique flavors unlike the thousands of other romance novels out there. What the story is **truly** about is the connection between lovers. It's about how men and women express their love and want to be loved, where women often seek more emotional bonds while men tend to display their affection physically. Finally, the plot reveals how any couple can bridge gaps dividing them to build a healthy relationship. My thoughts reaffirmed my long-standing belief that a physical relationship cannot blossom without intimacy through common values and trust.

To prove my point and share my experience, I wrote an article and posted it on my blog site, https://bysabs.com. BySabs would emerge as the residence of many other pieces I'd write to share my thoughts on topics I deemed important and interesting. Writing would become my most valuable tool to express myself, bring awareness to necessary issues, and influence those around me. Besides, word art (as I like to call the styling of words) is therapeutic for me. I just love it. Through this portal, I can help peers of my breed— those who crave hard intellectual discussions— to feel safe having them. If the subject is addressed properly and people engage constructively, taboo topics don't need to exist— even if they invite a splash of coconut cream!

Part I Daughter's Reflections

4

Converting Passion to Action

There's something about the artistry of writing that satisfies me; as I said, "word art" is my therapy. There's something about telling stories, whether mine or not, that makes me feel as if I'm making a difference— it's fulfilling. Instant gratification. There's something about the flow of a narrative that molds each one into a unique masterpiece— it's stylistic, it's creative, it's unique. So personal, so powerful.

You can have knowledge and you can have passion; you can have skill and you can have talent. *But what's it all for?* Because writing requires talent, and your stories are the only thing that nobody can take away from you, I was driven to master this craft and use it to accomplish how I felt about doing it— as if I was making a difference, because that's what it's for.

The Jewish Talmud (book of rabbinical teachings), says that "to have changed one life is as if having changed an entire world." I wish this was true: I know that I alone cannot change the world, and I also know that I cannot change people. The only thing I can do is influence, and indeed, to have influenced just one person sets precedent to influence many. I strongly believe that societal growth and change can only prevail through mass dialogue and personal connection, along with the spread of knowledge and innovation. The combination of these elements fosters wisdom— the application of the knowledge you gain to life itself.

Through my deep research of the Holocaust, I discovered how education could gear ideologies for generations and change the course of history. *But what if all those horrible things hadn't been preached? What if, rather, ideas of how to accept differences and bridge similarities had been? How would our world look today if we stood up to injustices in our view?* Our society would be far better-off if we used negative situations as opportunities to develop, grow, and improve oneself and society: Love not hate, peace not war, and tolerance for one another.

My studies also revealed that human capacity can hold so much hate, but I was wrong to think that the hearts of the hateful are filled only with pent-up disdain. Their hearts are plagued by suffering, pain, and scarcity longing for love, compassion, and joy. They come to hate themselves, and hatred of oneself becomes the greatest sin: A person cannot love another if they hate oneself. Individuals cannot open their minds to new ideas when harboring rage and anger. Hateful actions are rooted in the belief that other ethnicities, religious groups, or minorities stripped one from opportunities to thrive and prosper.

We can and should be upset with perpetrators and criminals for the harm they cause. However, in the end, we must pity them because they lack the skills to love themselves and heal. So, just as much as they should be held accountable, it is essential that compassion be infused into the accountability process so that they **can** heal. Healing can only occur when a person understands the situation and how to cope with similar ones through healthy behaviors that better oneself. This sort of healing can prevent future offenses because one can wire their brain to formulate positive change. Negative emotions should be signals to strengthen oneself: Through pain, one understands weaknesses, strengths, opportunities for progress, and methods to cultivate better relationships.

My purpose is to help others gear their minds' settings toward a growth mentality through the art of writing. Narrating stories in an effective way— evoking emotion to bring authentic awareness and passion— leads one to shift paradigms with a tolerant outlook and act with respect and compassion toward each person they encounter.

Interwoven

The more I interacted with Holocaust survivors and posted their stories online, the more I was inspired to broaden the range of topics I wrote about. Like them, I had my own stories which also held important lessons for my peers and even adults. At the time, I had already been documenting my experience with upskirting for my Deeds by Kids book project. There were so many angles to it, and I couldn't help but write pieces that piggy-backed from it ranging from institutional betrayal to mental health. Through my research, writing, and discussions with friends and family, I've found that the generational gap between parents and children is the source from which many issues spring. However, my mom always says that the generational gap is easy to close if we are willing to listen, understand disparities, accept differences, and cultivate collaborative solutions via controversial ideas.

While my blog houses a diversity of themes, lessons from history (more specifically the Holocaust) remains the backbone of my work. I believe that using the past as a reference for the present can foster repair in the future, just as generations renew themselves by mere reflections in the mirror. But so often, like humans repeat our own mistakes or those of our parents in everyday life, history repeats itself as well.

There came a point where tragic historical patterns couldn't hit closer to home. Just twenty minutes south from my home, kids were being torn away from their parents at the US-Mexico border. A couple of years later, a shooting occurred at my grandmother's local synagogue in Poway. Before I knew it, my website was filled with articles about these events and others, warning of the dangers as related to history.

At school, I'd find a way to apply my classwork to a particular blog post I was working on. I'd find myself researching and writing during lectures. I'd often use my lunch breaks to edit and finalize my work. My mom once told me that when you can do something for ten hours a day and the clock doesn't faze you, that's when you know that you've found your passion. While some feelings can lead one to the conclusion that passion has been discovered, don't close-in on one direction. Most important is getting comfortable with the idea that passions or intended career paths can shift at any time. What you wish for will fall into place eventually so long as you continue doing what you love and are working hard with a balanced routine. Embrace challenges with an open mind to embark on new journeys and seize opportunities when they arise. While your journey may turn to an unexpected path, hold on to purpose and core values to overcome obstacles so they don't break you. Obstacles are always the road to building strength.

Passion: A Path to Profession

Imagine someone else sketching your self-portrait that you've been waiting years to paint. A blank slate was never even provided to you. Many parents make the mistake of framing their kids into an image of what they want them to be before giving them a chance to stare at the easel. This can be due to financial situations, culture, or simply out of genuine care. Although with good intent, some parents mold their children into robots mechanized to execute excellence and implant the idea that some sport, career, or activity is their true passion. However, they brush over the fact each human being is their own engine geared with different settings, and what sparks one may not ignite another.

I have many friends who have been raised this way. They whine, "Ugh, I don't want to go to tennis today, I want to quit" or "I hate science but I'm taking seven STEM classes because my parents want me to go to Medical School." Forced molding depletes a young adult's motivational battery. The energy a person holds to propel forward is drained when feeling enslaved to something or someone rather than blossoming through the work for the sake of learning. Fatigue is real, but time to rest and recharge enables us to proceed. Our batteries may exhaust when we realize that what we've devoted our entire lives to is not our passion at all. Now we're stuck. The anxiety, the doubt, the emptiness— drainage into the gutter. But it's not a gutter: It's a ladder to climb upward to new heights of potential.

When someone shows extreme feelings about something, it's a clear indication that they care about it. Transforming interests and passions into a profession is a potential path toward a career or business aspirations. This process begins with immersion in a particular field, for example attending weekly gatherings, classes, programs and connecting with experts to confirm or reject one's passion. I am fortunate to not only have had endless experiences to explore but to have been given the tools and freedom to pursue all my interests. Growing up, my parents signed me up for a wide variety of classes, camps, and summer programs. I was able to try out different sports, tinker around in a variety of subjects, and meet influential people in those areas. This way, I could expand my interests, and thereby determine my true passions. Passions should emerge naturally, not by force.

Through my teenage years, I've taken the initiative to open my own doors like my parents did for me. Through those doors are inevitable obstacles that could hinder me from opening the next. However, obstacles are rough patches that we can all overcome with proper tools and support. Parents: Don't penalize or crack the whip if your child is struggling. Find and offer ways to help them by asking what the source of their obstacle is so you can help them transform it into an opportunity. Whereas the recipe for resentment is pushing a child without considering their point of view, the key to success is fulfilling needs. And success— aside from high-achievement— is doing what you love and executing every action with heart.

5

"Why Don't You Have a Little Fun?"

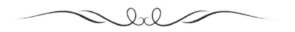

I met Mia in my senior-year math class. She one of the main partiers at my high school. She was also a great athlete but couldn't play soccer that season due to alcohol-related health complications. Over the course of an entire semester assigned to the same table, we became good friends. One chilly December morning just before winter break, we were discussing our plans for New Years' weekend.

"Oh my goodness, Sabrina! You're so pretty, you can get so many guys! I can hook you up with some at my party on Saturday, and we can get sooooo drunk! We can smoke, get high, it'll be a great time! Common, you're always studying, why don't you have a little fun?"

I thanked her for the compliment and invitation but was totally turned off by her offer. "I'd love to meet some of your friends, but partying and getting drunk isn't really my idea of fun."

"Why not? What's fun for you then?" She tilted her head sideways and squinted her eyes, examining me as if I was some odd breed.

"Well, losing total control of yourself and poisoning your body isn't really my thing. Learning about things I'm interested in is fun for me, writing, playing tennis, working out, reading, cooking, having dinner, shopping with friends...don't worry about me! I have lots of fun!"

"Really?" She slapped me playfully across the shoulder, "Come on, Sabrina!" We chuckled.

That day after school, Mia and I grabbed our favorite Mediterranean salad bowls from the shopping center across the street.

"I still can't believe you don't party. You're impressive, girl!" she praised.

"It just never appealed to me. I went to one party, and I felt uncomfortable with the drinking and the drugs. Besides, I wouldn't be able to function the next day, and I need to keep up with my studies and training for tennis. I am happy in the present. No need to escape," I giggled, and took a big bite.

Mia shoveled a spoon-full of tabbouleh and shrugged her shoulders. "Well, kudos to you, your body is a temple then!"

"A temple? I'll take it! But let's get ice cream!"

Despite our differences, we enjoyed each other's company. I invited her to come shopping with me the following week.

The Impacts of "A Little Fun"

While parties are a great way to socialize and alleviate stress, much of the activity that ensues is destructive. Substance abuse has become ingrained in teenage culture, whereby temporary happiness through frequently getting wasted and drugged escape is 'cool.' Peer pressure, coupled with anxiety and depression in school environments enables this culture to thrive. This has made the overuse of drinking and drugs a ubiquitous norm, where more and more teens are falling into this destructive trap. They don't even think twice. Sadly, the need for escape— especially considering its harmful effects— points to dissatisfaction with life in the present. There's no higher passion to live for, no purpose to keep them on track. There's nothing to lose.

It's inevitable for every child to feel hopelessness and despair at least once, if not many times in their lives. These issues are often exacerbated because one attempts to control situations that are out of their hands but find themselves at complete loss when they try. Seeking to avoid the problems that foster these feelings is important, knowing that they will arise again. That's why it's essential that parents teach their kids how to react and emerge stronger from them. They must also introduce them to healthy coping mechanisms so that they can alleviate stress— a constant with an eternally changing source.

I faced my breaking point in my junior year of high school. While my health was compromised due to tremendous anxiety, after much-needed reflection and guidance from my parents, I found healthier ways to cope rather than resorting to partying, drinking, and drugs— something I have never tried, and never will, for two reasons: First, I've never had the urge to, and second, the risks greatly surpass the rewards, if any.

My method involved channeling my passions into my coping mechanisms so I could relish and benefit from my escape, or in what I considered 'therapy.' Months of agony would endure until I'd find the keys to unlock my natural high, but it was all worth it. So, how do we know what gives us our high? Well, we don't know until we try, fail, and try again. It's a never-ending process. If we know the potential risks and losses of trying and failing, and we do not compromise our health or physical well-being, it's ok to push the boundaries a bit at the time to gain tenacity for better outcomes. Even drinking a little bit and safely if you want is totally ok, just don't overdo it or associate it with a coping mechanism! Enjoy it with family at holiday celebrations or on special occasions. Be intentional, make it meaningful. That's how you should construct your coping mechanisms too: make them mean something to **you**.

New experiences elicit happy moments through different stages of life. Reactions and feelings, like my mom says, are the greatest indicators of our likes and dislikes, comforts and discomforts, along with our strengths and weaknesses. Taking the time to evaluate the origins of these feelings dictates one's decision to continue or change the experience. That way, we can find linked activities or alternative ones to help us through certain situations. Kids (and even adults!) need mentors— from parents to teachers and even a large circle of friends— to provide them the insight and tools to assess their experiences and spearhead future actions in a healthy way.

6

I Burned My Bridges. Don't Do That.

Many of my passions had come alive by my sophomore year of high school. With a chance to prove herself at a new school with a diversity of top-notch programs, the ambitious Sabrina aimed to pursue them all. I enrolled in advanced classes, joined an array of academic clubs, and played on the varsity tennis team. Through my sport, I was fortunate to befriend a group of girls who embraced me with open arms. The six of us would eat lunch together every day, study together after school, and hang out on the weekends. I was happy and really couldn't complain.

As my schedule intensified and I met other students in classes, I felt that the time spent with these friends was a complete waste. When my mom would ask me how my day at school was, I could no longer hold back:

"Do they have anything else to talk about!? All they talk about is boys and their parties… and then it's all about drama, and more drama. I can't stand it!"

"I understand it's hard, but maybe try changing the subject," she advised.

"I tried! So many times! It doesn't work, they just go back and talk about the same stupid thing!" I raised my voice. What bothered me most was that one of the girls insisted on setting each of us up with her guy friends (I made it clear that I wanted no part in this plan). While each one of these girls was incredibly kind, my tolerance plummeted after a few months.

My place at our usual table moved to the end, where I sat in silence with my nose in a book or completing homework assignments out of sheer boredom. *Why am I here?* I figured that instead of wasting my time during lunch, I could be studying in the library or asking teachers questions about the lesson. And sure enough, that's what I did. I gradually distanced myself from social circles, and even began turning down invitations to get-togethers. My belief: The rewards of hard work will make me happy. Or at least that's what I thought would make me happy.

Naturally, I no longer received invitations to parties and events. I was initially hurt but soon thought it to be better that way:

"Geez, I can't be around Sabrina anymore, she is so high-strung," I heard that an old friend of mine gossiped to another. Clearly, my "high-strung" personality and discomfort in social settings made people around me uncomfortable. My philosophy: if they didn't like me, so be it— I didn't care. Yet another degree of separation from social life.

At the tail-end of my sophomore year, I came to associate school only with schoolwork. When I was in school, every action had to revolve around my studies. I reserved my slivers of free time for friends from my old school, whom I missed dearly. If you came over to my house, we had to be productive. Because many of my good friends at the time were focused on academics too, they didn't seem to mind. No time to waste.

While my weekends involved at least one social interaction, my attitude changed completely in class. I was mute, totally unlike the spunky, argumentative girl people knew. I didn't talk to anyone unless required of me. I didn't even wave to my peers in the halls. Understandably, I was agitated and needed time for myself, but this didn't justify this behavior toward them. Leaving my friends in the dark, wondering what they did that made me keep my distance, goes against my character. Anxiety had overwhelmed my rationale.

What I should have done was communicated my grievances and explained why I removed myself from gatherings to my friends. My second mistake, and worse yet, was removing myself from the group completely. These girls did nothing but extend themselves to me— I was the one who had issues with myself. It was I who failed to maintain my relationships at a different level. It was I who failed to appreciate the gifts of warmth and embrace these girls brought to my life. I burned my bridges and was stuck on a cliff— self-alienated, lonely, totally sad.

Never burn your bridges: Build new and different ones to walk across with those same people. Try engaging in other activities with them, tell them you need some air, but most importantly, keep the friendship alive. Every individual comes into your life to contribute it in some way or teach you something new. Whether intellectual or not, everything matters. Nothing is a waste of time: It's just the way you think about things and how you apply them that counts.

The person who considered herself intelligent and well-rounded still had much maturity to gain. Differences in values and priorities caused me to unreasonably break my bonds with others. This was a grave mistake because, in part, this was a reason that I would break too.

7

Plunging Into the Pressure Cooker

A couple of weeks before my sophomore year ended, I discovered an after-school program that seemed to align with my interests. It was also directed by my favorite teacher. Yes! This will pin me with the 'perfect student' star— great for college! Besides, I'd find more like-minded people to engage in heated debates and intellectual discussions with! *What more can I want?* I'd come home daily raving about the Humanities Conservatory and planned on applying for the following year.

This perfect plan wasn't so perfect after all. It so happened that any student who chose to join a conservatory program couldn't play on a school sports team. I was now torn between my two greatest passions on opposite sides of the spectrum. Giving up varsity tennis was unfathomable, but the humanities program seemed like such a unique and enriching opportunity. *Can I do both? Maybe the school will let me.* My parents and I tried to convince the head of school and the teachers managing the programs through several meetings. No luck.

A decision had to be made— one that would impact the next three years of my life. Not long in perspective, but since every day moved at the rate of three, it mattered to me. A lot. My mom and dad supported me unconditionally, and never pushed me one way or the other: "It's totally up to you. We will support you either way." They suggested that I weigh the pros and cons of both and talk to people in the conservatory to get primary source accounts of their experiences. So, I did just that. Here's a snapshot of my mental schematic:

- I can play tennis independently after conservatory or during my free period.
- Tennis is just something I enjoy, and maybe I'll play in college. If I want to compete, tournaments are available year-round.
- Whereas varsity tennis is something that all schools offer, Humanities Conservatory is unique to mine.
- Friends wise, I can just socialize with the girls on the tennis team. We play for fun on the weekends. Plus, I can easily make new, and probably better friends in the conservatory.
- I have a great relationship with the teacher that manages the program, so I can get personalized attention and secure my letters of recommendation.

I deduced that the Humanities Conservatory was the right choice. It would make a far greater impact on my college application than tennis would since I am not interested in pursuing tennis professionally. What colleges want comes first; I'd brand myself to the tee to fit their type.

In the last week of tenth grade, I auditioned for the program and was soon notified that my spot was reserved for the following year.

The summer between my sophomore and junior year was

overwhelming. My three-month break from school fledged with a two-month academic adventure to sharpen my writing skills. I began in Oxford England with the New York Times, then traveled across the British countryside to Cambridge, and concluded my journey with a course at Columbia University. Each program was run by top authors, journalists, and professors— total immersion into all fields of writing. It was intense and highly demanding but confirmed my love for this craft.

A love for something can be easily destroyed by something or someone, but you might just ruin it for yourself. My heavy workload began piling up with additional schoolwork in preparation for the Humanities Conservatory and an online bridge course in French, a prerequisite for the two advanced French courses which I was to take in my junior year. Several AP classes were also in plain view, and I had just started SAT test prep (I brought that thick book with eight practice tests on my trip!). This may sound weird, but I was actually excited to conquer it all and eager to conquer it early. My high expectations however, induced self-imposed stress that left me as the only person to blame for the mess it created. Love not only for writing but for life, and even myself, were withering away.

During my trip to England, my anxiety began to manifest itself in tormenting stomach pains. I couldn't seem to digest anything— both mentally and physically. Mental reflux causing physical indigestion. Eating, something I used to love, became a struggle: Even a bowl of white rice, known as the ultimate tummy fix, left me curled up on my bed in tears. I'd facetime my mom almost nightly as I watched my friends laughing in their canoes on the River Cam, wondering why this nightmare began and when it would end.

"I can't even get up, I couldn't go to the activity tonight, I don't know what to do anymore."

"You will be ok, trust me. Take some time off from working and go for a walk with your friends, even if it hurts. I know it's hard, but you'll feel better after. I'll see you soon, and we will figure this out together."

Despite my mother's loving words of encouragement, everything seemed impossible in those painful moments. The knots only tightened— emotional distress from physical symptoms shocking my body further. I was clueless that a settled stomach required a settled mind. Who knew that the gut was a second brain?

The first few days of my upper-classman status and membership to the Humanities Conservatory felt amazing. My classes were challenging and engaging; I couldn't have been luckier with teachers. Nonetheless, loads of homework required staunch concentration. And lots of coffee— maybe four or five cups a day. Who cares? Just ace the tests, check the boxes, get into a good college.

I was trying to make myself believe that I thrived under pressure, which could be true to a certain degree. Pressure propelled me to live efficiently and obtain satisfaction through completing all necessary tasks. But I went too far. That perception of fulfillment and boost in self-worth would eat me alive.

Each and every day was structured to the tee. I became the master of routine. Wake up at 5:00 AM sharp to study before a morning exam; go into teachers for questions during lunch; go to conservatory after school; arrive home in the late evening to finish up any pending assignments; have a snack, shower, and sleep— just maybe on the sleep. On lighter days, I'd use my block between 5:00 and 6:00 AM to go on a 20-minute run, a substitute for team tennis practices that year. Light days were rare. Routine became a toxic obsession. If there were any abrupt changes to my perfectly planned schedule— uh oh. You don't want to know…

Rigidity and Rudeness Result in Regret

One evening, my mom and I went to the movies. It was the Friday before finals week. I was set on starting my review for AP US History so I could finish by Sunday. I drew miniature charts in my planner with time slots for every day, marking every activity for every hour— there was always a plan. Our cinema outing had been penciled in for a week now: 7:00 PM to 9:00 PM.

On the way back from the movie, my mom asked if we could grab a quick cup of coffee at the mall, across the street from the theater.

"Are you kidding me? I have to study! No way!" I snapped.

"You're ridiculous! Relax!" she shouted back.

"Mom, I already made plans to study, seriously, I want to go home. I'm super stressed out!"

Mall averted. Grumpy girls drove home in silence.

Upon arriving home, I bolted out of the car, grabbed my textbook, ran upstairs to my room, and locked the door. I jumped on my bed and started reading. I couldn't focus. *I really hurt her feelings.* I know the coffee didn't matter; it was my selfishness that blew her off. *My mom would go out of her way to do anything for me!* This brought me to tears. I planted my face into a pillow and cried myself to sleep.

How ironic! My inflexibility, designed to save time, cost me more of it! Instead of deviating from my plan for ten minutes, I wasted a whole night's worth of review sulking. Changes in my behavior were baffling me. *Why am I acting this way? My character is kind, giving, loving—*

what am I doing?! Who am I becoming? These negative thoughts were indicative of a spiraling depression that would shadow me through a dark junior year.

I could have saved much energy and tears if I simply paused to relax for moments at a time. It's ok to go with the flow, and it's even better to break routine when you're anxious. After a spontaneous activity, one feels refreshed, ready to conquer their tasks with a clear mind and revitalized energy. My mom had always told me this, and despite being upset, she always addressed my poor behavior with compassion.

The next morning, I awoke to find a sheet of paper on my bedside table: 'Just let go. Never give up the things you love when you're feeling stressed. Be kind to yourself, always, then kindness to others will come.' From this short note, a series of letters would ensue that infused compassion and hope in me with tools and guidance: 'Do not quit on your dreams because of others! Bottom line, with commitment, focus, and perseverance, you will achieve them. Turn obstacles into learning opportunities.' She tried to convey that my anxiety was rooted in overwhelming care to achieve and succeed: 'It's ok to fear the unknown, but never let it compromise YOU.'

Although I carefully read her words of wisdom, my mind wouldn't budge. I refused any outside advice consumed by the belief that I, alone, could achieve better and more than anyone else. Just push harder. Achieving, however, would not mean succeeding because I, alone, would fail: The worst failure of all being that I failed myself.

Prioritizing Yourself is Not Selfish.
My Well-Being Comes First.

My parents witnessed my well-being deteriorate before their eyes. I was jittery, pale, and weak inside and out. I was isolated— a once social butterfly deteriorated into a helpless hermit. Nervous breakdowns. Pain. Sickness was wrecking me. But I sought strength. I sought any outlet that rewarded instant gratification.

Movement. I was desperate for it. If you know me, you'd know that twenty-minute runs would fall short of satisfying this essential need of mine. I longed to feel the satisfaction of pounding the tennis ball with all my might. The sound. A click of assurance that everything would work out in the end. A sound that assured me that I'd be ok. I longed for the warm spirit of my team, the confidence that came from being a part of something you loved with people you loved. The warmth that fills your heart with a sense of belonging. While some of my teammates were in my classes, we no longer spoke. They didn't want to hang out with me anymore. Sheer loss overwhelmed me when girls varsity tennis team victories aired on school announcements. *I could be playing in those matches. I shouldn't have given up tennis for humanities.*

Afternoons at the Humanities Conservatory were dreadful for me. The projects didn't really pique my interest. They surrounded the artistic side of the humanities more than politics and human rights. I didn't feel like I was learning much. All I could think about during those hours were upcoming assignments and tests. My stomach sent pervasive signals. Something would have to change. But I said nothing. I hoped that things would get better. I hoped that my decision would prove me right.

After two weeks, I couldn't hold back anymore.

"Mom, it's so boring. I thought it would get better, but it's not. I don't know what to do." She suggested that I drop it.

"What? Are you crazy? I can't do that!" I exclaimed. The rational thinking behind the principle of 'what's the worst that can happen?' escaped me.

She echoed that exact question: "Sabrina, what's the worst that can happen? What's the price you'll pay if you drop it?"

"You just don't get it! It's too late now! It's the best for college anyway! If I drop, I won't get a letter of recommendation. Plus, the teacher will think I'm a failure!" I began to cry. I felt like a failure in my own eyes, backing out of a program I was adamant to join.

In late September, my parents insisted that we meet with my teacher.

"No! You guys just talk to him! I'm not going!" I fought them until the very day of the meeting. I didn't want to face my melting self, nor admit to my favorite teacher that I wasn't enjoying his program. However, looking at yourself in the mirror to recognize what you're going through and what's needed to move forward is non-negotiable.

"Sabrina Soffer, to Mr. Steve's class promptly at three o'clock," rang on the loudspeaker. No choice now. My parents began by expressing their gratitude to Mr. Steve for creating opportunities for students to engage in various humanities projects. Then, they dove into the vast commitments each project takes, and how I had taken on more than I could handle.

"She has too much on her plate, we are just very concerned about her mental health and well-being," my dad said.

I tapped in, "I know that Humanities is great for college. I want to be involved— it's just that— I-I-I just have too much going on and I can't do all these projects to the best of my ability." My eyes swelled. Holding back my tears I suggested, "M-Maybe I can do an independent project aligned with my blog to contribute to the conservatory, since I'm doing that already and there are similar themes?"

Mr. Steve said that unfortunately, there was no way to integrate this as a part of the program, but that continuing my project was a stellar idea and a great addition to my application. His words comforted and resonated with me:

"I won't hold it against you, I won't think of you differently whether you stay or not."

My mom turned to me and added, "Your education is for you to discover your passions. It shouldn't be compromising you. It should only give you knowledge, curiosity, and skills."

"Ok," I murmured peering down at my shaking hands. This affirmation of my self-worth from people who I knew thought of me highly provided me the ability to look at the outside from within. I had to step back to prioritize my well-being to keep excelling in my studies and athletics. Stepping back is not always a selfish move or one of failure. Remember— you live for yourself, not anybody else. My decision had been made.

I Now Understood the Word "Opportunity"

Childhood is designed for experimentation— trying, failing, learning, and trying again. Although emotionally taxing, teens must be permitted to make their own decisions under their parent's roof. It's a recurrent mental exercise imperative to learn and improve through each lived experience.

Each adversity is an opportunity to guide, infuse values, and train children to make wise choices from a young age. Doing this early on is essential because decisions can become life-altering in adolescence and adulthood. Unless children's safety is at risk, parents should be present to show their kids **how** to make a choice, not which choice to make. If the decision yields poor outcomes, parents should help the child examine the outcomes by highlighting what the child did, has learned, and devise an alternative action plan for next time. Pushing boundaries of comfort, a bit at a time, is key to building resilience, tenacity, and future success. Children will fail initially, but they must have their parents to fall back so they can guide them through second, or even third chances.

A second chance came my way, and junior year did improve for a short while. However, my free hours after school were replaced by individual tennis training, writing blog posts, AP exam studying, and of course, the college search, testing, and application process. The spring semester served as an opportunity to ace this second chance. I experimented with diverse options and solutions to break out of my depressive cycles— from studying with friends, exercising before school, and even coming home for lunch sometimes. But these were just band aids I was placing over the bullet holes in my heart. To truly heal, I had to stitch these wounds with threads of love and compassion toward myself. I had to realize that it wasn't **what** I was doing that needed to change, but **how** I approached life that did.

8

Is the Ivy Brand Really So Grand?

W hat comes to your mind when you think of the word, college? Harvard, Stanford, Columbia, Princeton; campus life, city life; sororities, fraternities, parties, football; major, double major, minor. What do you seek in your college life? A warm community of students, rigorous academics, passionate professors, vibrant city life, and internship opportunities. These were the first two questions my college counselor posed in our initial meeting together, and the answers are what I imagined college to be. Today, these answers lead me to the conclusion that all these words surrounding 'college' compose nothing but a brand with varying levels of prestige.

College, like clothing, is a nationalized branding mechanism: The label you wear defines and builds other people's perceptions of you. We live to fit the brand so we can climb the ladder of self-esteem and common society. However, the pressures packaged with shaping life around this brand may break us. And for what it's worth, nobody should pay that price.

The competitive culture surrounding the college application process influenced my approach to selecting schools. Since freshman year, I was set on Columbia University. Why Columbia? Well, it's in New York (my favorite city!), has a great pre-law program, top-notch professors, and a stellar community of students. It's top-tier in academics— for the intellectual elite— and I want to be up there with them. But don't other schools share these qualities too?

"If you can replace the name Columbia with any other school for your reason in choosing it, then you must look deeper," my college counselor challenged me.

I didn't really know much else about the university other than what I experienced the previous year during my summer program there. I hadn't researched beyond that yet. *What's there not to like? It's an Ivy League! The best of the best!* After much discussion with my counselor, she broke the bad news.

"I know you love Columbia, and you can still apply there if you want. But in my honest opinion, I don't think Columbia is the school for you. Trust me, if you don't enjoy the robotic method of studying and the stress that comes with it, you're not going to enjoy a school like that."

Eventually, I discovered the flaw in my reasoning: status was the driver while my needs were in the back seat. So, the following week, my counselor and I formulated a new list of schools that I had researched thoroughly. While some consisted of the nation's most reputable schools, none of them were Ivies. *Am I not smart enough?* was my first thought. *No! You are smart enough!* Just because it's branded, doesn't mean it fits. Just because the tag looks good on paper, doesn't guarantee success. And just because there's one way to go about your future— undergrad, grad school, internship, job— doesn't mean you have to follow it. There are alternative routes to success, avenues with endless opportunities that don't have to stem from the traditional path. This was something I still had to learn.

Many high schoolers see college as the beginning and end of their lives. I certainly had this perception. Today, however, if someone were to ask me what comes to my mind when I think of the word 'college,' I think of a bridge. College is a path upon which one traverses to transition between their adolescent and adult lives. So, if we're on a bridge, why would we try so hard to walk across it in fear of what others think? The more we tread in distress, the shakier that journey will be. The only way to cross that bridge smoothly is to remain true to ourselves, prioritize our well-being, and savor the experience. If not, we get nervous, we panic, and shake the bridge. We fall.

Unfortunately, this epiphany came late in my process. I had spent endless hours trying to master the SAT and AP tests. My study habits were fueled by unabated cycles of caffeine and anxiety. I couldn't even take exams properly. I'd shake or freeze in the middle and leave half the questions blank. I tried everything— from test strategy therapy to hypnosis, and stress-relieving exercise to drinking Calm, a magnesium-based elixir with relaxing effects. Nothing worked. My SAT scores barely improved, and I could never perform as expected. I was like a pigeon caged in my own head— unable to communicate my agonies freely, plucking out the feathers of my well-being. Helpless and hopeless.

The combination of helplessness and hopelessness had a dawning effect on me. I saw the sunshine when I stopped caring so much. *Maybe testing just isn't my thing, and that's ok.* Knowledge and potential are not necessarily dictated by exam scores and grades, but by a deep understanding of the material, the ability to apply it, and the resilience to push through challenges. A larger portion of the pie is socio-emotional intelligence— from interpersonal skills to conflict resolution strategies— and they don't test that in school! Stressing over the numbers is useless. Do your best, display your grit, absorb what you can, and love to learn. My mom tried to explain this countless times: "Wherever you end up, you will do great. If you change your attitude to see the value in yourself, you can be successful anywhere. Look at the world's most successful people! Howard Schultz, Abraham Maslow, Anne Rand...Some of them came from modest means and didn't graduate from college!" I've often wondered how I could be like them, how I could use their path to model my own.

Success does not have to be a product of an Ivy League school or even a traditional college education. So often taken for granted are the various avenues one can take to personify this universal term: 'Success.' Although we use it ubiquitously, we must see success through our unique, individual lenses. The application of the knowledge one gains through their unique journeys— experiencing people and experimenting endlessly— imbues an individual with more wisdom than any institution could ever offer. Successful people are resourceful even when resources are scarce. Successful people seize obstacles as opportunities, push themselves through any challenge, and learn from their failures by noting them as mistakes to never repeat. Failures present chances to repair and improve just as rejection brings liberation to do something new.

While all these opportunities to explore and experiment are offered in college, it's up to **you** to make the best out of your experiences to author the future that **you** want. College may help you achieve your dreams but will not define the path to your success. Success is what you make of it. It's what fulfills you, what makes you happy day in and day out. Ambition, audacity, passion: It's attitude— needs and beliefs that influence behavior—that makes all the difference.

Study Smart, Not Hard

My attitude through high school was to study hard because hard work reaps rewards. That may be true. But I've learned that rather than studying hard, one should study smart. Yeah, it's cliché, but I've interpreted it from a more personal lens rather than a generic time management and habit standpoint:

To study smart is to study yourself first. Begin by examining your purpose, and then evaluating the most efficient and your preferred methods to achieve your purpose. Once this methodology is ingrained in you, the hard work begins. Part of this 'study smart' strategy is understanding your needs: How often do you need breaks to continue being productive? When do you like to study a certain subject— in the morning or at night? Which assignments should you work on individually or in a team? Answering these questions before beginning any task enables one to complete the work in a timely, effective manner and provides the flexibility to design a daily roadmap based on needs. Examine how you feel while carrying out tasks, and if it helps, take notes so you can later use them to build an optimal schedule. By shifting paradigms to embrace any challenge, have fun with it, and learn something (even if it's something you hate) enables one to cope in a healthy way. Don't give up, but most importantly, never give up on yourself.

Finding the brand that fits **you**, not anybody else or the standards society places, is the avenue to success. A blind loyalty to societal standards is an approval-seeking behavior that enslaves and entraps one's soul in tireless servitude to others instead of being true to one's own principles, values, objectives, and needs. We are taught to believe that the traditional path to greatness is marked by certain credentials or accolades— from where one goes to school or works. I've found that greatness does not necessarily come from the brand you wear— it's about how you wear it. And when you wear **your** brand with pride, you can project confidence and results will soon speak for themselves.

9

The NYU Blues

I opened my laptop within a minute of settling at my desk in senior year AP Government class on that crisp Wednesday morning. Boom— there it was. Finally, an email from NYU with the subject line 'Your Application Decision is Ready.' *Do I really want to open this now?* Chills overwhelmed my entire body. My hands were shaking above the keyboard. I could feel the cold sweat accumulating under my white long-sleeve shirt: A teenage girl's worst nightmare, pit stains in white or gray. I didn't bring a jacket. My stomach began to knot in that way it always does. I curled closer into the desk until my arms cusped around my belly.

"Hey, Sabrina are you ok?" whispered one of my classmates.

"Yeah, yeah, I'm ok," I nodded fakely, trying to brush away unwanted attention. *I'll just open it, there's no use in waiting. No expectations.*

'We regret to inform you that your admission to NYU has been declined.' My face flushed. I was still shaking. No tears shed. Frozen.

I excused myself from class and ran to the restroom. My only thoughts were *why? Why don't they want me? Was it my flunked SAT? My essays? Was it because I'm Israeli and Jewish?* Everything went into that application— my time, my heart, my identity, my life! I looked into the fingerprint-stained mirror, seeing my face as one of those dirty blemishes. *Where did I mess up?* Stop thinking about it. Bad luck. I peered down at my charm bracelet and dangled it around. *You still have tennis, piano, writing— you are still you.* Deep breaths. At this very moment I had forgotten my mother's mantra: "We don't have control over other peoples' decisions. We only have control over our reactions, actions, and our ability to influence others."

I came back to class twenty minutes later as if nothing happened. Ms. Banks, my teacher, gently escorted me into the back hall.

"Where were you? That was a long bathroom break, are you ok?" she asked concerned, rubbing my shoulder. We had a close relationship: She was one of the most understanding and compassionate teachers I ever had.

"Yeah, I'm fine, I-I just got rejected to NYU, but umm—" saying this out loud made my eyes water. "But I'm fine."

"It's ok, Sabrina. You will do great no matter where you go. You land where you do for a reason. I know how much you wanted to go there, but maybe NYU just isn't the right school for you." She hugged me. I came to believe that maybe, she was right. The school that embraces me as I am— my identity, my character, and accepts me despite my sub-par SAT scores— will be the right one.

"Thank you, that really helps, I appreciate it." I returned the hug helplessly, and in great gratitude, began to cry again.

Today, the more I think about "you land where you do for a reason," the more it proves true, and the more it sticks. In earth-shattering moments where emotions conquer all, this philosophy may be difficult to accept. But by training your mind with this resilience-building psychology, you can embody tenacity.

After my conversation with Ms. Banks, I returned to my desk and texted my parents. It was best to tell them now. *Just hit send.* I couldn't even fathom what disappointment I'd bring to these patrons of my education, my extracurriculars, and my achievements. For a while, I struggled to reject the notion that all the money, support, and resources they invested in me did not pay off. *It's all my fault. I didn't work hard enough; they'll never be proud of me.* My warped belief system would be the only source responsible for their loss of pride in me. Worse yet, it was I who had implanted this belief system in myself while my self-worth was eroding.

Some hope was restored when scrolling through the list of schools I awaited responses from. Of course, I was still feeling down and knew that I alone couldn't get myself out of this funk. From experience, I knew that being alone after experiencing something so major is a recipe for disaster. I called my mom after school as usual.

"Hi mom," I tried to stop sniffling. *Stop crying.* "I'm driving home right now, but can we go on a hike?"

"Of course, let's do it."

Wandering in nature with someone who loved me unconditionally was the antidote I needed. As my mom and I ascended the cliffs overlooking the seashore, she tried her best to comfort me.

"I know that you feel awful, but you just have to know that you did your best, and you can't do anything about it now."

"Honestly, it sucks. It's fine, I just want to know why." I told her the truth.

"I'd want to call the dean. I want to know too! If we paid to send the application, we should know why you didn't get in!" My mom burst with a smile. We both laughed and gasped for air as we climbed to the peak. In plain view was the wide ocean, a symbol for the wide world ahead of me. A fresh start, no matter what ship I'd sail on, would land me on an island to build my life upon. We sat on a lone bench, gawking at the crashing waves in appreciative silence for being together and coming this far.

After a few minutes, my mom got up and said, "You know that if you have passion, motivation, and determination— which you do— you'll succeed anywhere, right? It took me eight years to finish my undergraduate degree. I didn't take the traditional path, and no one has to take it to be successful. I built my life by being resilient, positive, and working hard no matter what comes my way," she said, still searching for words. "If NYU doesn't want you, it's their loss. They're losing a great student, and the school that takes you will be so lucky," she lauded, "You're not only a star student, but a person who can enrich any university community. You'll succeed wherever you go, and remember, the college selection process is so luck-of-the-draw."

"Thank you." I muttered, peering down at my dusty Nikes. "Don't just say that cause you're my mom!" A slight grin crept on my lips. We both leaned in for a hug.

Look at the Bright Side: Inner Light

As the sun set that afternoon, I reflected upon how lucky I am to have such a great mentor in my life. My mother is someone who can light up any moment no matter how dark it seems, reviving my self-esteem by illuminating the value in me to me. This conversation with my mom let me understand that my struggles emerged from a flawed understanding of the purpose in my higher education. I had perceived the hours of hard work poured into my schoolwork and extracurriculars as a leg-up into college rather than an investment in my growth. College itself became my purpose, rather continuing to learn for the sake of learning and cultivating my passions.

To rekindle my confidence, I had to view all the activities, exams, and classes having served their purpose in teaching me things that I didn't know. The unknown is the greatest tool for knowledge, growth, and personal development. Invest in **you** because you are the greatest project you'll ever work on. You're the only project that you cannot give up on.

I remembered when my mom told me about her epiphany at twenty-three, where she cried before the mirror wondering what she was missing to secure her happiness. She had shared that rather than anything external, there was a void inside. Her internal void, surfacing from living for others, had to be filled with self-knowledge and self-commitment. Committing to herself required internal awareness of values, feelings, and emotions to guide actions. From this moment on, my reflection serves as a promise to mirror her introspection as I'd approach adulthood and author my future.

10

Graduation

In the March of my senior year, I was ecstatic to receive my acceptance letter from George Washington University. There couldn't be a better place than Washington, D.C for me to pursue my passion for human rights, politics, and justice, which had grown since my college search process. You land where you do for a reason.

The complexity of the human mind enables us to see the same road through different lenses. Our reactions to each hump and curve along the way are indicative of our approach to life. To appreciate life in full, one must look through each lens and acknowledge their contributions to our being— whether it be situations or relationships. Graduation became this moment of acknowledgment for me: It was the first window I peered through as I reminisced over my treacherous high school experience. In my rearview was an unconditional team of support— ranging from my family and closest friends— who lifted me out of the sandpits that swallowed me along the way. My approach had shifted from obstinate independence to accepting support, an attitude that my parents had tried to encourage over the past four years.

While graduation is deeply personal and a major milestone, I also saw it as a great accomplishment for both my mom and dad. My high school graduation was representative of their success in raising and guiding me until this point. They deserved a gold medal, and I felt some moral obligation to express that. Since writing has always been my preferred method of expression, I decided to address them in a unique letter paired with parenting diplomas:

From the University of Parenting: Congrats, Mom and Dad!

On this momentous occasion, I'd like to present you with your diplomas from the University of Parenting. I can say with full confidence that you have, indeed, graduated. While your exam scores did fluctuate on occasion, both of you will receive this certificate of completion with nearly perfect GPAs— as valedictorians. It will be, in this letter, my distinct honor to explain why:

I cannot begin relishing my own commencement without thanking you both. Although it sounds cliché, I'm going to say it anyway: I have the best parents in the entire world, and I couldn't be prouder to say I am your daughter. Without you both, none of this would have been possible. Your unwavering support has been the backbone of my success. Your dedication and investment in me have established my platform to thrive.

When my journey through adolescence began, I asked myself why I had to be so different from the other kids. Why did I have to be the 'new girl' every two years? With maturity and my evolution of self-respect and identity, I began to realize that being the 'new girl' or the 'one who didn't fit in' was a virtue: Unparalleled perspective, profound awareness, and dignity.

Six schools and many years later, I feel as if I've graduated from all of them, taking away gems that were precious to me from each. In Hebrew Day School, I found a friend who, after all these windy years of life, remains my truest and best friend at heart. I was also acquainted with my roots, and unknowingly, developed a deep love for Israel and the Jewish people over time. SDJA and Chabad brought me to my senses, enabling me to make connections with diverse members of the Jewish community. Academically, I had to decide if a more well-rounded, secular education was more suitable for me. And yes, as I resisted but you insisted, I was immersed into a melting-pot of personalities, classes, and extracurriculars at Francis Parker: The bonds with teachers and the knots of friendship I've tied have never lacked substance, and their impact on my life has been momentous knowing they will last. My passion for history, languages, and academics began with National History Day but transitioned to a pressure cooker of stress and opportunity.

My determination to push myself into an intense academic environment and escape my struggles at Francis Parker left me at CCA. Emotionally draining and mentally exhausting, I am glad to have faced the challenges I did. Spending time with myself and battling through mounting anxiety made me my biggest cheerleader. Being so close to home, I fully came around to understanding how integral good parents are to wellness and success. I can never thank you nor repay you enough for walking along this journey with me every step of the way.

While reading and taking notes from a textbook is considered 'learning,' you both always promoted the idea of 'learning' as a culmination of experiences. And outside of my formal education, you both encouraged me to never stop. Since childhood, I've been afforded the privilege to participate in boundless extracurricular activities. From banging on the piano at the age of four, horseback riding to soccer, and gymnastics to tennis, these sports have ingrained in me qualities of resilience, perseverance, grit, and the one I dread most of all: patience. But research and writing, of course, also require patience: an unabated cycle of reflecting and refining, revision after revision.

At programs in Oxford, Cambridge, Columbia, Harvard, and Mouratoglou Tennis Academy, loving the process became a reality for me. I failed several interviews, wrote piles of mediocre papers, and yes, I even ended up coming home early from a top-tier university. But, despite all the matches I lost against others and the ones in which I lost myself, I committed myself to always take another shot: the real failure would be abstaining from doing so. Whether it be hitting serves painfully from my knees planted on red clay or spending hours on a mediocre paper to maximize my full potential, in the end, it's all worth it. To love what you do and do what you love: only with passion comes good work ethic, and good work ethic brings authenticity. And never, in the past seventeen years, has authenticity been drowned by the superficial.

Besides a stellar education, you've raised me on ethics and values: the virtuous tenets of life. "Children are a reflection of their parents," is a statement of yours that has always resonated with me. Today, I couldn't be more honored to prove it true. I've been surrounded by two sharp minds overflowing with intellect, knowledge, and wisdom. But some of the greatest minds battle each other in the arena of personality. With mom at one end and dad at the other, your behaviors oppose each other like two daggers at polar ends of a double-edged spear. However, your values are the steel keeping the metal bar connecting you unbreakable.

While chaos erupts and heated moments emerge, it is in these episodes where I discern who I want to be: How would I react in this scenario? Would dad's logical and traditional way of thinking be appropriate? Or would mom's adamant advocacy be more effective?

Aligning priorities with emotions in every situation, I follow the guiding principles upon which I've been raised. Regardless, the fire always extinguishes, with a hearty resolution and an intimate learning experience for each one of us. Your love for me is always a magical ingredient, always having my best interest at heart, no matter the cost. True love and authenticity, toughness graced by compassion: I have chosen my path this way thus far, and it is how I will continue to do so throughout my career and the rest of my life.

This milestone, in which your daughter moves on to the next chapter in her life, also marks the beginning of a new phase of yours. For seventeen years of my life, you've demonstrated that this family never backs down. The bond between us is sacred— our construct never lacks stability. Like pillars of a magnificent temple, this family builds me up, sustains me, and even in ruins, still stands.

The journey continues, and new adventures await.

~ Sabrina

Another Degree of Dedication

I decided to look at graduation through the window of my friends and fellow students as well. As the COVID crisis chopped off what would be the most memorable portion of my classmates' senior year, we were left with no prom, no grad night, no in-person classes, and worst of all, no real graduation (well, a drive-through).

I kept myself on a balanced and enjoyable schedule during quarantine, but many kids my age verged on depression as lockdown orders intensified. Witnessing my friends resorting to bad habits as their boredom took over broke my heart. Some were sleeping or staying in bed watching Netflix until 2:00 PM, and not even stepping outside for fresh air for days at a time. Some were drinking and partying in secret, night after night. I was astounded that they were taking their health for granted, especially in a pandemic era where health is critical.

As for me, I knew that to critical to my health and happiness, I'd need some daily routine (a flexible one) balanced between social, intellectual, and physical activities. I wrote an article about how I planned my days and even shared an ongoing list of books that I recommended. After completing a book, I'd post what I learned from it on my blog. When I met up with my friends, I'd try to motivate and guide them, but most didn't change their habits. Because you can't change people, only influence them, knowing that I tried my best was good enough.

I didn't mind skipping the graduation ceremony so much. However, I could understand where my peers' feelings of devastation were rooted. Since words hit differently on paper, I sought out another method to lift their spirits. On the morning of our to-be graduation, I wrote the following blog post which I spread all over social media and sent to my peers:

Graduation: My Dedication to the Class of 2020

Heavy clouds loom over the rays of sunshine meant to propel us toward our bright futures. A vivid moment in our lives now rests in the hands of a cursed, invisible enemy. The aura surrounding graduation emanates anything but brilliance: This years' commencement projects gloom and austerity. Mere disappointment saturates us as we take steps closer toward the end, where an unfortunate reward awaits. No senior prom, no senior week, no hugging our best friends, no personal farewell to our favorite teachers. My senior t-shirt even reads, '2020: The ones who got quarantined.' No scribbly signatures in our yearbooks concluding with "HAGS," because we know COVID-19 has already plagued our summer plans. Even our freshman year of college is up in the air, potentially compromised by this contagion. Trapped in our homes and muzzled by surgical face masks, it just seems like everything has gone down the drain. There's too much to sulk about.

Most of you, especially my peers and classmates, feel exactly like this. Senior year of high school is, indeed, supposed to be one of the most fun and memorable years of a teenager's life. We've worked tirelessly like robots, mechanized by a system that esteems numbers over humanity— exam scores reign over mental health, and what may be perceived as success over personal character. The culmination of our sacrifices, the proliferation of our achievements, and the realization of our journeys ahead ignited sole sparks of joy. Now, euphoric sentiments of reward are suffocated, with six feet distancing us from these feelings of warmth. When all we want is to finally embrace each other and surrender our battle over what we deem as success, another war is imminent. Coming to our senses after years of intense competition marked the beginnings of viral division.

Losses inflicted by destructive conflict never impact everyone equally. But in times of agony, I have learned, it is important to frame yourself in the position of others. Understanding broadens your horizons, providing empathy instills comfort and hope. In this time of distress for many of you, although I am not heartbroken, I do feel your pain. I have experienced despair, self-defeat, and am still torn by scars of regret. It's been easier for me than for others only because my community is dispersed. I've moved schools several times, having attended six schools from the beginning of my academic experience. All with diverse cultures and groups of people, I was compelled to expand my social circle beyond school. Sports, academic activities, and family dinners enabled me to befriend people of all ages and demographics. Although I consider myself independent, self-motivated, and routine, time with friends is precious to me. Isolation is never the answer: interconnectivity is key to human nature and happiness. But also necessary to us individuals is adaptability: making the best out of any given situation gives us a platform to thrive on personal growth. And when we think about what this means, graduation is the only word that comes to mind: overcoming and learning from adversity **is** *graduation.*

While I am not heartbroken by the prospect of empty chairs facing me as I obtain my high school diploma, a new pain emerges. The probability of deferring from my freshman year of college seems high; even higher is the pressure that torments my thoughts over this decision. Like many of you, I want out and I want to start anew. The moment GW became a reality for me, all I've wanted is a one-way ticket to D.C in August. High school, notably my junior year, was unbearable: ill memories of mounting depression flood my mind when I reminisce over the past four years. Despite my trauma, I triumphed from the quicksand of anxiety that drowned me in misery. I promised myself I'd never repeat my high school mistakes, that in retrospect, I am thankful to have made. Sealing my maturity with a fresh mindset, I am more ready now than ever before, to embark on a new journey. But once again, our world is unpredictable. My decision stands currently as unresolved.

Storms of chaos often leave us vanquished by doubt. But in fact, these challenges do everything but confine us: as we put things in perspective, they bring unprecedented windows of opportunity. Speaking from experience, the two worst years of my life empowered and instilled resilience in me. I took hold of my life to become the best version of myself that I could be. My bold, type-A personality is a direct product of navigating through waves of adversity.

*Quarantine has challenged me emotionally on various fronts. I've experienced disappointment in some of my closest relationships. Your bond to your class, to each other, and, yes, to this graduation is just as legitimate as one between you and a loved one. Being locked in our cars at commencement is most certainly an obstacle. However, quarantine has fostered moments of self-reflection that have enabled me to align my priorities with my emotions. What and who are **actually** important to me? What are my **real** priorities? What is **really** worth fighting for? Day after day, I notice myself evolving, maturing, and learning to answer these lingering questions in the back of my mind.*

To see clearly and to be seen clearly is a principle I live by. My parents, since I was a little girl, urged me to build relationships, travel around the world, and read a wide variety of books and newspapers. With each friendship, a new connection was sparked; with each exotic journey, my blind spots crystallized; and story after story I read, gems of knowledge filled the treasure box in my mind. And hence, my passion for history: when we can see clearly into the past, we can understand our present, and predict our future. Having studied historical events and the capacity of humankind, I understand the consequences of my actions. History has proven that leaders willing to hold themselves accountable tied ropes of trust between themselves and their people. For this reason, I'm a proponent of being seen clearly while it comes at a cost: transparency yields vulnerability, and it leaves us fully exposed. But as we know, narratives only begin at the exposition.

2020 is in fact, the class of vision: No, not just vision, but perfect 2020 vision. We are living witness to an era ravaged by social and public health crises. COVID-19 forced an international reset on social, political, medical, and economic fronts; the cold-blooded murder of George Floyd exposed the omnipresent racism lurking in the shadows of American society. Wasn't 2020 supposed to be the perfect year? It sure sounded like it. But perfection never lasts, nor does it materialize. All things that are seemingly flawless, are oftentimes dangerous. Life is filled with paradoxes, provoking us, playing with human psychology. This paradox we are living— a perfect year in a disordered world— was meant to be for this new generation of students. Everything happens for a reason.

*Our class will not go down as not the unfortunate and doomed. It is the one whose eyes have been fully opened to the stark realities of our world. Isn't **this** what it means to graduate? A rite of passage, elevation, moving forward. But on the other hand, to have graduated means to have successfully completed. Putting the two together, our diploma serves as a license to spearhead motions of change in a backward society. The world is crying for change, pleading for ethical leaders and social* *justice. And this generation has been summoned to seize this moment. Our class has graduated with more weight than any other. Our diploma carries an obligation we are privileged enough to be responsible for.*

Since childhood, I've dreamed of repairing the often indifferent and unjust world we live in. My profound study of history has taught me that positive change is, indeed, the hardest to foster. My adventures through adolescence have made me realize why: we keep trying to fit the system. Most of us won't question it, blinding us from seeing clearly and being seen clearly. So, to implement REAL change, we must follow the advice of the revolutionary entrepreneur Howard Schultz. He tells us, "Don't do things the way they've always been done. Don't try to fit the system. If you do what's expected of you, you'll never accomplish more than others expect."

2020, we don't seem to fit the system: Our graduation certainly isn't normal. This year, despite all odds, we graduate untraditionally with renowned strength balanced by grace— this fuels our passion, our purpose. Let's use our impeccable vision to veer off the path of the expected to accomplish more than the world expects of us.

From a 2020 High School Senior.
~ Sabrina Soffer

The lessons I learned in high school will forever change how I engage with life. I now question what purpose can be extracted from unprecedented and undesired outcomes rather than seeing them as pure setbacks. If we take that same logic and apply it to 2020 itself, we'd be puzzled as to why tragedy after tragedy continued to ravage our world. It began with the raging Coronavirus, piled upon by the wildfires, the cold-blooded murder of George Floyd, followed by global riots, and beyond. The slew of events left us wondering, *what is happening to our planet?* Many challenges struck my personal and family life as well.

When we shift our mindset to discern what good can come out of the bad, we combine resilience and strength with joy. That is graduation: To flip through the pages of the past, learn from your mistakes, and begin a new chapter through a different window. Each page we turn is a symbol of our growth, a stair above where we once were, and guides us to receiving gifts from life every step of the way.

11

The Gift of Gap Year

Endless trial and error helped me construct my optimal and balanced routine. Sunny summer days were balanced with physical, intellectual, and social elements— integral to staying stimulated and fulfilled. Every morning began with my much-needed workout followed by making brunch, then reading and/or writing in the afternoons, seeing a friend, and to close the day, dinner with my family. My routine was open to shifts unlike before, and I enjoyed spontaneity. While admittedly a bit OCD with my spiral-bound planner which transformed into my color-coordinated google calendar on my new laptop, I found no harm in being organized. I felt happy.

Over quarantine, I had learned to be flexible with my schedule, which was much easier now being stress-free. School ended, and I no longer needed to crank out tedious assignments. Having struggled with virtual school for the last portion of my senior year, I knew well that it wasn't worth starting college that year if it remained remote. Once the announcement was official, I sent my deferral request to take a gap year.

During my year off, I'd devote much time to reading books of my choice and writing my blog posts. My mom also asked me to help her finish our Deeds by Kids projects and edit some of her pieces, including her <u>Make Your Thanksgiving Meaningful</u> book. At the same time, she was launching her technology platform, ICIARA, along with <u>Act Responsibly,</u> which needed content. The company's mission is to stop sexual misconduct from the onset, which I am also passionate about, so I wanted to help my mom develop some material. With different perspectives on the subject, other writers and members of her team were more than willing to collaborate with me and provide their feedback. I was gratified to work in a team of adults who valued my contributions and saw me as an equal.

Besides bonding with my mom via working together, we also bonded over our many, many, many walks together. Since gyms were closed, we usually walked about three times a day, totaling to over ten miles sometimes! Besides getting our daily steps in, those hours sparked many conversations about current events, philosophy, psychology, relationships, and more. These deep discussions brought forth stories about her childhood, her twenties, and life before I knew much about her. Each story she shared helped me understand a particular concept or navigate a conflict. It was like listening to a live lecture, personalized podcast, or Ted Talk.

"In a way," my mom told me, "This time in quarantine is a blessing. We're spending time together that we are unlikely to have again." A blessing indeed.

Inspired By 'Unorthodox'

Quarantine also blessed me with some relaxation after many many months of stress and anxiety. I had deleted Netflix from my devices during school to avoid distractions (not recommended if you have self-control! Balance matters!), but now had all the free time to indulge myself in binge-worthy series and films. My mom and I got hooked on the TV show, 'Unorthodox.' We finished it in two nights.

"I can't believe that! How do some Jews NOT support the state of Israel!?! That can't be, I just don't get it!" I vented the next morning on our walk, "Is the show actually accurate?"

My mom told me that while she didn't share those exact experiences, there were different sub-cultures within Boro Park and the series' portrayal of the Hasidic community stayed close to the truth. I started researching the topic avidly and was able to connect my new knowledge to the stories my mother had shared about her early life during our walks. Then something clicked: If Unorthodox was a national hit, my mom's life story could be one too!

I came downstairs bright and early the next morning eager to present my brilliant idea. My mom was already at the kitchen table sipping on her first cup of coffee with a dark chocolate peanut butter cup on the side.

"Mom, you write so many articles, blogs, and even books, but you should write a memoir! You've had such a complex life that people can learn from!"

"I've tried. I have pieces, but I don't have the skill to put them together."

"Well, if you're not going to do it, I'll write it for you. Seriously."

Part I Daughter's Reflections

12

The Author's Journey

The dynamic duo began as it had been— walking and talking, sharing and bonding. But now I was recording my mother, transcribing what I gathered, and researching missing pieces. Foreign to much of her early life in Dagestan, Israel, and Boro Park, I interviewed a few family members and flipped through photo albums to form clear images in my mind so I could describe them in words.

Authoring my mother's memoir is one of the greatest projects I could have ever pursued. Although my admiration came across through creative birthday and Mother's Day cards, my reverence could be enriched through connecting our lives in boundless words and using our relationship to help others. Our sacred time together enabled me to understand how my mother became the strong-willed, determined, and compassionate woman she is today. Our bond has inspired me to radiate my energy with these same traits.

A life through cultural and personal extremes is one that forces an individual to transform. For some, like my mom, it bestows a duty to help others do the same. Empowering people, from teens and single women to parents, became a lesson in personal empowerment. I was able to apply some of the tools my mom and I dissected from each story and use them in my relationships or to guide friends. I've been raised with support and to support, so there is no greater gift than using our stories to connect with others and empower them to be their best selves.

Human connection sparks a domino effect, prompting us to share findings or breakthroughs with family, friends, and neighbors. Just think about how much power one domino holds: Learning something, bonding over it, and spreading the knowledge can generate a flight of change. With introspection, courage, and grit, **you** can be that domino and influence a movement. My mother is the domino that moves me to model her character and work as she does, in tribute to truth seeking and justice via her passions. She always says, "Sabrina, my daughter, is my inspiration— both my masterpiece and my master." I cannot conclude my section of this book without saying that she has been and will always be mine.

Mother's Preface

1991

The Quest to Know Thyself

Who am I? The day I looked at myself in the mirror with red puffy eyes and tears streaming down my cheeks, all I saw were shattered pieces of a broken woman. *Am I a traditional Tat Jew? Am I a married Orthodox woman who is supposed to blindly serve her husband? Am I an Israeli woman who was given the courage to question everything with confidence? Am I assimilating into the liberated American girl?* I was ridden with shame, confused about my identity or what I was living for.

My first marriage ended at twenty-three. I could no longer tolerate the vicious cycle of shouting matches, physical aggression, and emotional flares. Over time, my resentment toward my husband and his family festered and turned back at me. Skirting around confrontations void of accountability intensified the cycle and exacerbated my mental, emotional, and physical well-being. My loyalty, perception of love, and submission to his power stripped me of self-respect. A toxic whirlpool swallowed me.

At this crossroad was a doomed fate— one I would have never foreseen. *What's the worst thing that can happen? Do I break these norms and stain my reputation? Or should I idly stand by? Should I continue enduring humiliation, abuse, and distress?* Most women in my place would, but not me. I could not continue a life in constant questioning of my existence and self-worth. My end game was clarity within, paired with some purpose to strive forward. I could not allow myself to live my mother's destiny— one of self-sacrifice for life. I needed the confidence to act, the courage to grow, and the tools to flourish.

My mother's suffering and pain were rooted in her submission to suppressive and duplicitous rules. Married at thirteen into a tribal traditional culture, my mom had no other reflections to mirror but her mother's and those of the women surrounding her. Imprisoned by the authority of her husband, his demands, the sake of her children, and social norms, she had no alternate route to take. Her unyielding attempts to please everyone became her sacrifice— living for others rather than for herself. No matter the price I'd pay, I refused to mirror her destiny of tremendous weakness and pain.

Since the age of five, I waged a war on conformity: *Why should I stop fighting it today? Do I deserve this fate? What am I lacking?* I am beautiful, bright, highly ethical, and have been endowed with many talents. But it just occurred to me that I was just like my mother— allowing a man and his family to destroy my essence. This was the moment where I looked in the mirror and was committed to taking control of my life. To reclaim my dignity, self-worth, dreams of a fulfilling life, I had to build a stronger relationship with myself first: "Know thyself" became my mantra. Values and principles emerging from this commitment formulate my rule book to lead life with confidence. The power resided within me to determine my destiny, not anybody else.

Growing up, my parents endowed me with strong morals and ethics that still shape each decision I make. Many of these principles come from biblical stories, Judaic teachings, and influences from Muslim culture embedded in my heritage: Don't lie, don't steal, don't take credit for something you didn't work for. Be kind, honest, and help others; be there for each other, and share everything you have; treat everyone with respect. We deserve what we earn; never back down; never give up. These ethics resonated, but social norms and rules did not apply equally.

Many societal rules and taboos seemed confusing and contradictory when I applied them to relationships. They seemed artificial and lacked integrity: I couldn't bear being treated as subpar to my male counterparts. I couldn't bear being shamed upon while I was morally upright, and others were praised despite their hypocrisy. *Why should I remain loyal to others in the face of disrespect? Why should I preserve family honor or privilege the community when I am being disgraced and abused?* This simply did not make sense.

While throwing fire at fire was the nature of my childhood, I've followed my parent's values of hard work and persistence to achieve my needs and goals. I used the same model to fight conformity until the rules broke: In some cases, I succeeded, and in others, I failed. Until this moment, I was clueless as to why it worked when it did and vice versa. I questioned the worst-case scenario. *What are my limits?* To truly liberate myself, I was the one who had to break first. If that's what it would take to reclaim my identity, self-worth, and being, I was prepared to break again.

From Shattered to Mastered

Today, I see many women struggling to free themselves as they endure humiliation and regret. Their strides toward change may shock their social circles or jeopardize their closest relationships. Torn by loss, they are left feeling worthless and empty. They soon begin to live as if life were a chore, consumed by the perceptions of others and seeking approval. They claim that change is too hard and that it's not even worth trying to transform for better outcomes. I deem this mindset a surrender on oneself, an enslavement to others, and a submission to groundless confines. For me, giving up wasn't an option. The alternative: a life of internal death. As for me, I was a fighter and had the will to change, but there was still an enigma to be solved.

My father warned me that my divorce would make me an undesirable woman: "No decent man will ever marry you. You're second-good merchandise. You're stained." This would be my worst-case scenario. I'd destroy my family's honor with it. To my parents, living for the community came first, and failing a life within it was unacceptable. *So what if I never find love again?* These were consequences I was willing to accept: The only person guaranteed to stand by me is me. Only I can be my own true advocate.

At twenty-three, I finally realized that the beliefs and paradigms ingrained in me were confining me in boxes: A man should court a woman, dating for fun is too scandalous, and challenging a man is disrespectful. A woman should know her place— she should serve her husband, attend to his needs, and remain loyal to him regardless of his actions. A woman's needs are secondary. I knew neither my place nor my purpose, but what I did know was that it would not be here, blistered in the Boro's bondage. I knew that life could be better.

My exposure to a different world was not lacking— on the contrary: I had now experienced a diverse infusion of cultures, conflicting beliefs, and opposing value systems. *How could I leap into a new world in a state of self-doubt and disarray?* Distress became my starting point. I began to embrace unsettled feelings, uncertainties, and conflictive paradigms. Understanding the confines placed around me and their impact on my feelings enabled me to balance my needs and acknowledge my boundaries within those of family and community. My commitment to 'know thyself' would lift me out of this rip current of identity crisis and save me from drowning again.

To avoid repeating my mistakes, I resolved to live a life that countered my past. This journey brought many obstacles upon which I'd stumble and trip, but they strengthened my mental muscle. The warrior in me was awakened as I focused on spearheading every challenge with resilience and focusing on learning from each one. Internal progress—behavior that instills confidence— reigns over perfect results.

Although ingrained with incredible values from my family's culture, I was rarely guided in terms of their application nor given the tools to solve problems in a constructive manner. This was something I wished to learn long before I was twenty-three. I wish I knew how to resolve conflicts constructively. I wish I knew how to bring about change collaboratively. I wish I knew to identify that I did not know myself. I wish I had known the process to transform myself. Breaking out of normative binds may have broken me but bolstered my tenacity so I could merge the gaps in my identity. And yes, you can do it too, even if you make mistakes or think that your time has passed. It's never too late.

Fractures in human life are inevitable, just like in all things. What keeps us from completely shattering is using these fractures to rebuild our strength. Change is always imminent. My answers always return to the base of my principles and values. The tenets I was raised on still influence my every decision, regardless of the consequences. My every action is well-intended at heart, hence the cliché, "live life with no regrets." Honesty with myself comes first and foremost, to evaluate what feels right and what does not. My devotion to introspection has crowned me with confidence, and I deem comfort in one's own skin the greatest royalty a person can achieve.

The experiences I share in this book are pieces of MY puzzle, which produced and continue to produce a clear picture of my purpose. My feelings serve as signals for self-examination: *What should I accept, reject, or integrate into my new philosophy toward life?* With each answer, I gain ownership, with ownership I gain dignity, and with dignity I gain pride regardless of the outcomes. My courageous strides forward have become the pieces that shape me and render me proud of my masterpiece in the making. The woman I saw would vow to merge the cracks of her identity back together with integrity. The shattered woman in agony would artfully emerge from the rubble as a mirror projecting confidence for generations to come.

PART • II

Roots

1968 - 1986

Part II Roots

1

Roots Shaped My Attributes and Attitudes

The community, witnesses, and families had been howling night after night for the marriage to be consummated. Where was the blood-stained white sheet? What was taking so long? What if she wasn't pure? What a shame if she wasn't a virgin!

The wedding had taken place just seven days prior. A blood-stained white sheet was to be taken to the groom's family the following morning, who would then deliver it to the bride's family. This precious cloth is the honorary asset exchange between families signifying the acceptance of the bride into the groom's family honor. It would then be used in a ritual of dancing, feasting, and drinking vodka through the night to celebrate the union.

My mother was married at thirteen. My father was twenty-four. Today, he would be considered a child molester! Russian law prohibited marriage prior to the age of eighteen at the time, and the tribal village my dad came from deemed it a stretch. A woman of sixteen years old would have been more acceptable, but he wanted her before any other man would snatch this beautiful and innocent teenager. An easy fix— fake documents: Zipora Suriclov, seventeen years old.

While formerly a part of the USSR, Dagestan, the southern valley between the Caucuses and the Caspian Sea feels nothing like it. The formal language is Russian, but a dialect called Juhuri— a mélange of Parsi, Turkish, and Azerbaijani— is spoken among Derbent villagers. The village was formerly ruled by the Soviets and populated by Persians and Turks.[2] Although heavily influenced by Muslim culture, amidst the Muslim community was a small population of Jews: We're called Tat Jews. Religious differences would seem to cause division, but the strict norms of both coalesced and lived together in harmony.

Gender roles were distinct. A woman must marry young, have many children, serve her husband, her family, and contribute to the community. In social events, a woman's place was in the kitchen while their husbands lounged on the sofa playing backgammon and chess. It was customary for a woman to serve men food, drinks, and tea. Their role had no place in manly affairs. A woman's duty entailed attending to their husband's wants and needs— to treat them like kings. A woman could not work outside of the home. A woman could not be seen alone in the company of a man outside her family circle. Women primarily engaged in conversations among themselves about cooking, village gossip, holidays, and their children. My mom was unique in that while she lacked a high school education, she was an avid reader. She yearned for an outlet to discuss literature with her friends, but none were as intellectually savvy. The conversations she longed for remained an internal dialogue until my

---

[2] For more information about the Derbent region in Dagestan, Russia, see the following source: Britannica, T. Editors of Encyclopaedia. 2015, May 4. Derbent.

sisters and I grew older.

My mom, Zipora, grew up in the same village as my father. Her family was educated in the city. My dad, Ariel, was born and raised a wealthy countryman. His family managed prime property and cattle in the village. He was also in the military. Upon retreating from the fronts of the 1956 Russian-Hungarian War, it was time for him to find his mate. Ariel fell head over heels for Zipora, bewitched by her radiant beauty, delicate kindness, and youth. She, on the other hand, was intimidated by his bold presence and was infatuated with someone else— her uncle's son, Dimitri. At the tender age of twelve, Zipora's concept of love resided in Russian romance novels; her love for Dimitri was the only love she could attach to boundless pages of literary fantasy. Unfortunately for her, blood-tied marriage was prohibited, deemed to breed unhealthy children and family complications. Her mother was also sick at the time, so she sought to secure her daughter's future by marrying her into a well-to-do family.

Despite Zipora and Ariel's differences in status and niche, both sets of parents considered the arrangement to benefit their families. The marriage between my mother and father was arranged; marriages in that region are still arranged until this day. Prior to marriage, a woman must be untouched. A virgin. Her destiny, too, is predetermined: Zipora had nowhere to turn. Any efforts to protest and escape failed. A young female voice could never be loud enough.

Days leading up to the wedding were dreadful for Zipora. The marriage could not be consummated until the blood-stained white sheet was in the bride's parents' hands, with the whole community as a witness.

This ritualistic transition sealed the marriage with preserved honor. When I reached my late teens, my mother told me, "How could I have sex with someone I barely knew? At thirteen?! I was petrified!"

The Surielov ranch was large enough to accommodate hundreds of community members. They would be served food and drink daily until the blood-stained white sheet was in the witnesses' hands. Families and neighbors congregated in the household, drinking and feasting away their anxieties in the waiting. Rumors circulated: "What if Zipora destroys the Surielov family's dignity? What if she ran away with Dimitri? What a shame that would be!"

Six days passed filled with soapy gossip of witch-hunt stories. Ariel's patience was wearing off and he sought a return to normalcy in the village. Without a doubt, he'd get it done. On the seventh night, my father forged a pact of secrecy with my mother: "Zippa, I am sick of these people. I have a plan. I will make a cut on my hand to stain the sheet with blood and show it to the family. This will be our little secret. Let's get rid of these people." This incision of compassion and patience sprouted seeds of Zipora's love, care, and respect for her husband. Until the day he died, the scar on my father's left hand ceased to fade.

On day eight, a sigh of relief spread like a wave among the villagers. The sheet was delivered, and everyone dispersed to their homes. With blessing upon the new couple, village life could continue as it had. Zipora would soon give birth to seven children, two of which passed away. Raising three girls and two boys with an alpha husband by her side would eternally seal her fate as a subservient wife.

Blindness to Boundaries is Not Blissful

I was not raised a religious Jew. However, the norms in small-town Derbent closely matched those in the Orthodox Jewish community. During my first marriage, I noticed parallels between my relationship with my husband and that of my parents. My mother was a dog on my father's tight leash, just as I was tied to my husband's. *How can anybody be happy this way? This is not freedom. This will not be my life.*

I've always had the visceral urge to speak my mind without anybody controlling my speech, questions, and beliefs. This is one of the freedoms I cherish most until this day. The diversity of opinions fosters discussion, opening doors for progress and innovation. *How can societies improve when rules aren't understood but are conformed to?* In my eyes, blind conformity is a surrender of one's self-respect and society at large. Self-respect is personified questioning any curiosity in plain view, catalyzing self-growth by learning from others. The progress of a community always starts with the individual.

Many who are raised in tight-knit communities think differently than me. They find comfort in boundaries that maintain order, tradition, safety, and provide a sense of belonging. Pushing those walls breaches comfort— a personal security— whereby challenging the status quo manifests as messy confrontation. As common society chooses security over freedom, I reverse this saying and ask, *who feels secure when their freedom is taken away?* No one does.

Only later, through my activism efforts, did I recognize that people who fight for change are willing to endure the consequences associated with breaking barriers. There is great risk, but those who decide to take that risk are well-aware of the dangers that conformity yields. While a minority, their efforts prove them mighty.

Going against the grain has always broadened my understanding of rules and expands my liberties. If a boundary is placed on me, greater comfort is in the explanation of it. The greatest comfort of all is knowing exactly what our freedoms are and how to exercise them effectively toward desired outcomes. So, I push my boundaries until their logic is clear to me. However, within conservative communities such as those I grew up in, the logic behind restrictions is rooted in tradition. The reasons 'that's how our ancestors did it' or 'because it's God's way,' never cut it for me. You'll see how that worked out...

2

Born in the Caucasus

A pparently, I emerged from the womb so ugly that my parents and older sisters questioned where the "little beast" came from. Rather than disregarding her unattractive baby, my mother graced me with the most glamorous names to uphold my worth.

Ludmila and Gulçiman were the names I was given at birth—Ludmila as my formal Russian name, and Gulçiman as my tribal name. Ludmila was the name of her favorite actress at the time, and Gulçiman means 'beautiful flower' in our dialect.

My behavior as a child was nowhere near that of a graceful actress or the serenity of a beautiful flower. My eldest sister recently reminded me that I never washed a dish at home. I was the middle child, and my sisters were already tasked with house chores: folding clothes, preparing meals, and sweeping the floors. At the end of our conversation, she confessed her resentment toward me growing up: "You did all of these crazy things too and were never punished at all!"

My family jokes that I was born a wild horse that nobody could rein in. I spent my days kicking soccer balls in the grassy fields while my siblings worked tirelessly. My father focused solely on his two eldest daughters and could care less about my whereabouts. There wasn't much my mother could do, or even wanted to do. In fact, she lived vicariously through my rebelliousness. She found the power stripped from her as a young girl in me.

Waging a War on Conformity

"Sit down in this chair, upright posture!" My Russian kindergarten teacher would dictate every morning, "At ten, we break. At noon we eat. At one we nap. Your parents come at five."

The list of orders was overwhelming and agitating. *Why do I have to sit in THIS chair? Why do I have to eat when I don't want to? Why do I have to sleep here? No way. I'm not sleeping here.* I'd swing my legs back and forth under the table with boundless energy. I'd toss and turn on the thin mattress during our siestas, compulsively picking at the loose frays on the dirty rug. I wanted to burst.

"Please, I don't want to go to school," I'd vent to my mom on our daily treks to and from school, "It's so boring. I want to stay with you at home. I hate it. I do not want to do the same thing every day. The teacher makes me take naps. I hate it!"

"You know that's impossible. School is good for you. You must go," she'd reply in her soft, endearing voice.

A month in, my frustration reached a new level. Rebelliousness was innate and I had a plan: My mind programmed itself to retrace the exact route my mother, siblings, and I walked each day to and from school. It was an hour walk each way; it was one of the narrowest and mountainous paths in our village. I began escaping from school during nap time and ran back home along that windy path. Sometimes I'd trip over the rocks protruding out of the unpaved cobblestone, but got right back up, dusted myself off, and kept running. I gazed up at the comforting blanket of trees above me, forging ahead as adrenaline rushed through my every stride. Never look back.

Upon returning home, I'd leap into my mother's arms. She never scolded me; her tone was loving.

"What are you doing here? What happened at school?"

I looked at her with puppy eyes and a mischievous smirk, lost for words. Without further questions, my mom clasped her hand around mine gently and walked me right back to school. Of course, I raced back home again!

My teacher eventually called my mother worried about my sporadic absences.

"We cannot keep her here. She runs away daily. She is not happy here, and it's a hassle for us to go out and try to find her every time."

"I agree. I am sorry but nothing can be done. Gulçiman is a bit wild," my mother replied, then asked, "Can her older brother take her place? Please, he is a very sweet boy."

The arrangement was made. I stayed home with my mom and baby brother. I enjoyed spending days with my family and galloping in the fields.

At twenty-five years old, my mother was raising five children from ages between one and ten years old. Starting motherhood as a teenager, she did not have the heart or the tools to discipline and guide her children. She did, however, understand that there had to be a reason behind my rebellious pattern of behavior. While the sibling-exchange solution was not ideal, my mom's compassion towards me established lasting trust and love between us.

From Punitive Discipline to Collaborative Guidance

You're grounded. That's how most parents would punish their kids if they acted as I had. Parents are often convinced that their kids are being spiteful or are trying to manipulate them when they rebel. This isn't always true. Children naturally test their boundaries as they grow up: They are simply curious, uncomfortable in a certain situation, and lack the skills to communicate assertively to express desire for change. It is a parent's responsibility to understand their kids' needs because adults have the maturity and skills that their children lack.

Instead of exemplifying constructive conflict resolution skills to their children, 'grounding' imposes strict restrictions disconnected from the conflict itself. Restrictions with no room for growth infuse resentment and engender a toxic cycle of defiance, punishment, and repeat. To avoid this, I had to see the world through my child's eyes and act as her coach. I would teach her why certain behaviors were unacceptable, how to make compromises, and the way to approach similar situations in the future.

Although I oppose punitive consequences, this is not to say that I do not encourage parents to enforce certain rules and correct their children's behavior. The definition of 'discipline' includes the phrase 'punishment to correct behavior through control and coercion,' [3] which is why discipline is **not** a philosophy I promote. Literal discipline creates a fear-inducing environment ridden with power struggles often leading to secrecy and lies. Children should feel comfortable enough to express

---

[3] Discipline. 1828. In *Merriam-Webster*.

their needs honestly rather than having to rebel to achieve them. If parents strive to gain their children's trust, consequences infused with respect, compassion, and opportunities for restoration are necessary.

My method involves treating the child as an equal and confronting the conflict collaboratively. A parent must be sympathetic toward their children's emotions and needs, no matter how trivial they may seem. Dissecting issues together with your kids is essential to providing the equal status needed to grab their attention. Then, helping them understand the flaws and consequences of the behavior ensures that they know potential risks to such behavior and how to approach similar situations next time. Raising children with solution-based principles shapes their character, identity, and behavior for life. This prepares them to be self-reliant and effective in their future relationships, school, and work environments.

No toddler has the capacity to articulate their feelings or evaluate their choices rationally, but they do have feelings. Their comforts and discomforts are communicated via their senses and emotions. In this case, parents should try to understand the root of their children's behavior just as they'd analyze themselves in a particular conflict. If the situation is grave enough for a toddler, the parent must remove the source of discomfort and find a way to explain the lesson in terms that the child understands.

By examining situations from a child's perspective, a parent can employ their own principles to guide them. A mature decision is one dictated by values, and it is a parent's duty to instill their kids with good ethics so that this transpires. Simultaneously, this approach may broaden the parent's view in a different way. A mature and mutually acceptable solution emerges from validating the feelings of others and explaining outcomes based on values and a risk-reward assessment.

As a parent who assumes the role of a coach and is a certified life coach today, I have developed a collaborative communications method called e-LEADERSHIFT. This platform has been instrumental in creating a safe environment for open and honest communications and developing collaborative solutions that satisfy each stakeholder in a disagreement, from parenting to relationships and professional disputes.

Short Term Pain for Long Term Gain

Short term pain for long term gain is integral to my decision-making process. When a certain situation is intolerable, it is important to find solutions that relieve moments of hardship to achieve a higher purpose. My short-term pain was losing the status of 'the perfect child,' given my rebellious nature. I was never anyone's favorite— neither my mother's nor my father's. I grew to be ok with that. So long as I fought for my needs and satisfied them, I was content. It was indeed difficult to manage the anxiety and pain these fights required.

Short term pain was the hardest to endure when my family and I were viewed as second-class citizens in our new homeland. Long term gain would take much time to materialize. Acting with good intentions and striving toward my purpose in each endeavor I pursued would grant the greatest reward. The uphill battle was more than worth it. It usually is.

3

The Unity in Community

I was five years old when my family immigrated from the Caucuses to Israel. When the Soviets granted emigration permits to Jews in the seventies, waves of Russian Jewry flocked to Israel. My dad, the staunch Zionist that he was, adamantly decided that we move despite the Yom-Kippur War in October of 1973. Theodor Herzl's famous question, "If not now, when?" became my father's. Like Herzl said, "If you will it, it is no dream." [4] Great love for the promised land of Israel overrode any concerns he may have had. My father endeavored to make his dream a reality. The words of the Hatikvah (the Israeli National Anthem) personified his passion: "...within our hearts, The Jewish soul sings....forward to the East, To Zion, looks the eye, To be a free people in our land, The land of Zion and Jerusalem." [5]

My parents, four siblings and I settled in Hadera. The town was raw,

---

[4] Extracted from the following source: "Theodore Herzl- Publications." 1879. Knesset.gov.il.
[5] Cohen, S. 1878. Hatikvah- The Hope. National Anthem. Accessed at: https://m.knesset.gov.il/ EN/About/Lexicon/Pages/National_Anthem.aspx

developing day by day. Community members supported each other in construction endeavors, opening essential businesses, and hosting nightly gatherings. This coastal suburb remains the mecca of Russian Jewry and houses one of the largest populations of Tat Jews in the world.[6]

Like other newcomers, my family was first deposited in the Atlit Immigration Center. My dad worked sixteen-hour days for an income to sustain our family. After seven months, we finally moved into a three-bedroom apartment in an eight-story building, housing a melting pot of Jews from Russia, Morocco, India, Germany, Bukhara, Poland, Georgia, Iran, and Yemen. From floor to floor, we'd pick up random conversations, share stories, and ridicule each other's ethnic differences.

In Israel at the time, Sephardic and Mizrahi Jews were looked down upon because of their inability to easily assimilate into both Israeli and Ashkenazi cultures. Eastern European and Ashkenazi Jews were considered the elite, holding intellectual and professional positions—scientists and doctors among them. Jews who emigrated from the southern part of Russia, or other Middle Eastern regions like Iran, were former tribal members, trades people, farmers, or blue-collar laborers. Language barriers were also problematic, and exacerbated by the differences in values, principles, and ideological clashes between these sects of Jewry.

Ethnic tensions remained a serious issue but we all teased each other humorously in good spirits. The Polish Jews called us "mountain Jews with the knife," and we joked that Iranian Jews would "use the tea bag, dry it, and use it again," because many of them were so frugal. Moroccans

---

[6] For more information about Hadera, see the following source: Britannica, T. Editors of Encyclopaedia. 2009, January 19. *Hadera. Encyclopedia Britannica.*

were labeled "the barbarians."

Israel may not seem to be discriminatory or racist, however, the terminology used back then could be characterized as racist in modern society. Additionally, the privileges granted to Eastern European Ashkenazi Jews were far superior to Sephardic or Mizrahi Jews. They were referred to as triple V: Visa, Volvo, and Villa.

Despite trivial fallouts here and there, there were little cries of discrimination. There was no ill-will against anybody. Teasing each other was all fun and games. Each person focused on settling their family in this new homeland to thrive, prosper, and build community. Our life in Hadera would come together with laughter, warmth, and joy.

4

My Mother's Sanctuary of Warmth

My mother fulfilled her role as a devoted housewife, always striving to make our humble home a sanctuary of warmth. Our kitchen table could hardly seat five of us, but she never turned down any guests. She ushered in each person at the door, spread colorful Turkish rugs outside or across the floor, and brought pillows from our bedrooms and couches to accommodate everyone. Whether or not guests wanted anything, she prepared an abundance of fresh food, overflowing trays of snacks, and brewed tea. "Please, eat, eat. Stay for as long as you'd like," she'd say. I had yet to experience a drastic shift in hospitality culture when I later moved to America.

Although we didn't have much, food was never scarce. My mom cooked twice a day: Every morning, by the crack of dawn, five toasted bread rolls filled with oozing cheese awaited each hungry child. When my siblings and I arrived home from school, the aroma of meat stew had already permeated the entire building. Just follow the smell, and you'd know which unit was ours! And don't even mention her traditional Mejadra, a Dagestani dish of rice and lentils with a side of stuffed cabbage— my favorite!

Until this day, my mother's hospitality is intrinsic in me and has been inherited by my daughter as well. No matter who comes over to our house, the first question we ask is, "Do you want something to drink? Are you hungry?" If they say no or even if they just ate, we prepare tea, coffee, snacks, or even a light soup and salad to enjoy casual togetherness with no special occasion.

5

My Dad's Ethics

Immigration, transitions, and starting all over again posed much difficulty to our family. But my dad was a wise man and knew how to solve any problem. He grew up during the Second World War, a time where his preschool was made a Russian military zone. As a young boy, he balanced his days between school, working on his family's ranch, and helping his mother with house chores. School resumed years after the war was over, but by then, my dad was ten years old. At eleven he re-enrolled and finally cemented basic reading and writing skills. He never completed high school because he was drafted into the Russian army at the age of seventeen.

My dad possessed a strong sense of responsibility and diligent work ethic in anything he pursued. Immersed in the atrocities of the Russian-Hungarian war, he was intent to build his wealth and tend to his family's land, cattle, and wine-making business upon returning from military service. When he was ready to start his own family, he had already fallen in love with my mother, a woman beautiful and young enough that he could mold to his needs.

Although not religious, my father possessed strong faith in God. He believed that God punishes those who harm others and rewards those who are diligent in doing good. My dad instilled in his children that certain values are paramount to living righteously, such as being honest, generous, and never taking anything from anyone that you did not work for. His teachings are rooted in his life experiences, whereby success is achieved by working hard as a unit and sharing the rewards with the team. Before a meal, he would remind us, "Even if you have one slice of bread, share among the five of you before taking a piece for yourself." In his tribal analogy he would ask us, "What is harder— to break one stick or five sticks together?" This was his way of saying, 'you are five, always share and stay together because together, you are stronger.'

6

Luda the Rusty: The Bully Gets Busted

I was five years old when my parents fled Russia and immigrated to Israel. I've always had fond memories of growing up there. My elementary school, Nizanim, was nestled in a high-end neighborhood surrounded by private homes called Neve Chaim, or The Springs of Life. My experiences were certainly different from my daughter, who was raised in the California suburbs. Instead of rummaging through tiaras and princess dresses every morning, I was dressed in t-shirts, muscle tanks, and frayed wide-leg shorts. Even my hair was shaved like a boy. I could have disguised myself as one.

Although I barely spoke Hebrew, I don't recall struggling to adapt. What I **do** recall is the outsider sensation that struck me when I walked into the classroom on my first day: I looked drastically different than the other kids. Uniforms intended to equalize our socio-economic backgrounds, yet I was the oddball with baggy boxers bulging out of my denim shorts to my knees. I didn't think anything of it. I loved school, enjoyed my classes, and had fun with my classmates. I never remembered being bullied. That was poor memory— amnesia of some sort…

During a trip to Israel two years ago, I spent considerable time with my sister, Marina, and childhood friend, Dalia. At our favorite restaurant on the Herzliya waterfront, we discussed the prevalence of bullying in the United States and how it has been escalating in Israel.

"I do not recall any bullying when **we** were in school, what happened?" I questioned.

"You must be kidding! I think you erased those experiences from your brain! You are **so** wrong!" Dalia erupted with laughter.

I was taken by surprise when Dalia shared that some of the boys used to make fun of my clothes and call me names during my first few weeks in first grade. When I walked through the halls, they'd shout "Luda challudah!" meaning "Luda the rusty." I hated that name. At lunch, they'd poke me on the back and run away. As Dalia piled hummus on her loaf of pita bread, she began to tell a story:

"One day, as we were all playing in the sandbox, one of the boys sprayed a bunch of sand on your face. As you got up to shake the sand off, he tried to pull your shorts down. His friends stood by and were laughing, waiting to see the next bad act. Over a sudden, you turned around with an open hand and pushed his head down until he fell to the ground. He fell flat on his face! As he was trying to get up, crying with sand stuck on his face, you looked at his friends that were giggling and ran away." Dalia leaned in and looked at me with all seriousness, "That day marked your image and identity. If you bullied Luda, you'd be busted. No one ever messed with you again. Maybe that's why you do not remember being bullied, my friend!"

Dalia continued sharing stories and recalled that my sister would sit on our second-floor balcony weeping every day during lunchtime.

"Do you remember those days at school? Why were you crying?" she asked Marina.

"Well, I remember that during class, the girls who sat behind me would pull on my braids and poke my neck with their pencils." My sister added, "I was afraid to speak up! It would only cause more conflicts! That's why I didn't complain!"

Marina's classmates repeatedly picked on her until she told my parents about the unbearable situation months later. She was the favorite: She always listened, aiming to please each of my parents' wishes and demands. So, when my dad found out about Marina's situation, it was game over. He asked her to point out the mean girls on the school bus. My dad told the bus driver to tell the two girls that if they did not stop harassing my sister, he was going to cut off their braids. They never laid a finger on Marina again.

7

Role Model Miriam:
My Engaging and Inspiring Teacher

My rebellious character never faded. I continued to defy rules and openly voice my opinions in class. Since Israelis are known for boldly speaking their mind, this was normalized to a degree. I relished the freedom to crack jokes and be mischievous, although I'd get into a bit of trouble sometimes. My favorite teacher, Miriam, tolerated my spunky behavior and encouraged me to express my thoughts. She reminded me of my mother— slender, tenderhearted, patient, and accepting of all.

I took a liking of Miriam's approach to teaching, presenting lessons with applicable themes. She had a certain poise and grace to her style; it relaxed me. I most enjoyed the hands-on education that applied material from the classroom to essential life skills. For example, as a part of our lesson in agriculture, we traveled to farms and learned how to cultivate the earth. We were also immersed in community service for the sick, our soldiers, and the elderly.

To maintain a strong bond among our peers, Nizanim organized various weekly activities. Social hour was my favorite: On Friday evenings, our class would congregate in a circle to sing and share stories before Shabbat. Morah Miriam's interpretations of biblical stories, characters, and their perspectives resonated with me more than any other teacher.

I'd often come home from school and roleplay teacher: "Shalom kita, ani Morah Miriam! (Hello class, I'm Mrs. Miriam!)." I'd stand on a stool and lecture to empty chairs in the kitchen. I stole my sister's glasses, perched them on the tip of my nose, and tied a tablecloth around my waist.

8

Reflect Before You Rebel. Have No Regrets

S adly, Miriam couldn't be my teacher forever. In fifth grade, I had a new teacher named Yafa. 'Yafa' in Hebrew means 'beautiful,' and she was. While nurturing and kind, Morah Yafa was boring in the classroom. Her monotone voice put me to sleep. I was fully focused and engaged when classes were interactive, but I could not focus because she never called on me.

"Luda, you must give the other kids a chance to speak, you talk too much. You overpower conversations sometimes," she told me.

There was no way I could change that. Not many kids would volunteer to participate anyway. I was just too excited! As the class lacked stimulation, I grew restless. I would chat with my classmates or swivel around in my chair, unable to bear sitting still and silent for forty-five minutes.

"Shh! Luda, please, be quiet. You're being disruptive." Yafa had to confront me daily.

If the hall pass for the restroom were a credit card, it would've been maxed out. In today's world, doctors would have probably diagnosed me with ADD or ADHD, prescribing me some tranquilizer and therapy. But in 1970s Israel, disciplinary methods and student-teacher relationships were different. Teachers would build bonds with children and their families, almost acting as a school parent. They would compassionately guide students with values and principles to get them back on track. To put it simply, the system had a different culture and construct.

Yafa had a hard time managing rebellious, energetic children like me. I wanted out.

One day in class, I raised my hand and announced, "Your class is so boring. I don't want to stay in this class. What are my options?" The kids laughed as Yafa's face flushed.

"You don't have any other options. You are required to stay in this class! This is a warning to you. Next time you will have to go to the principal's office!" She warned me firmly.

During the break, my classmates confided in me and expressed their frustration with Yafa's class. I suggested that we ditch the next lesson.

"Let's stay and play, what can they do to us?" I said while climbing a tree. Fifteen minutes later, a fellow student called us to come back to class.

"We know!" I shouted from a treetop, "But class is too boring so we're going to stay and play! Want to join?" I invited her. She ran back and whispered to her group of friends to come too. Before we knew it, half of the fifth-grade class was playing hopscotch during social studies!

Thirty minutes passed until Yafa came to the playground and yelled, "Come back now! All of you! Right now!" The other kids scurried back to the classroom immediately.

"I'm not going to your boring lectures. No." I refused.

"Luda, straight to the principal!"

I walked to the principal, Yehudit Aricha's office, with my head held high. She explained to me that, in life, we cannot always do whatever we want. "Sometimes, we need to follow rules even if we don't like them. But you can always try to change rules peacefully and think of constructive solutions with those who can help you influence change. Maybe you can try writing to the department of education to make social studies an optional class," she proposed.

Quite honestly, I did not know what "constructive "or "influence" meant at the time. She was insisting that I try to compromise with Yafa, discuss why her class was boring, and suggest ways to improve it. But I lacked these skills. All I knew was how to rebel, refuse, and resist, yet to understand how to positively bring about change.

The school called my mother to inform her that I would be suspended for a week. Yafa felt disrespected and was in disbelief of my mischievous behavior, but she had a big heart for me and my family. She wanted to teach me a lesson. "I am sorry that you have to endure this consequence," she remarked, "I understand it's hard for you to focus, but I cannot allow you to disrupt my class and order. I hope you learn your lesson, think about what you did, Luda."

After my ten-day suspension, Yafa called me to her office before my first class back. To my surprise, she handed me a gift— a gift that I carry until this day. I opened the black box to find a small diary with a girl riding a galloping pony on the front cover. The dedication on the inside reads:

Dearest Luda,

In life, we must first think, and then act, so we never have regrets. Use this diary to express your thoughts, so you can reflect before charging ahead.

~ With love, your teacher, Yafa.

9

Girl's Got Chutzpah!
Equalizing the Playing Field

One Thursday afternoon, our dear family friends came over and asked my mom if I could work at their candy store. I used to babysit their two boys regularly, and my sister was good friends with Misha's wife, Laurus. Their store sold over fifty types of chocolate and ice cream among other goodies.

"We need a cashier to attend the shop, help assemble baskets for the holidays, and someone to work part time in the afternoons. We could really use Luda's help," Misha said.

"Luda would want to, and I would allow it, but there is no way her father will. I am sorry, she cannot." My mother turned him down apologetically. It was not respectable for a woman to work outside the home. My face stiffened with disappointment.

At fourteen, I was eager to start shopping for my own things. Aside from clothing, I needed contact lenses which were expensive at the time. My mother only bought me new things on special occasions. Between five children, there was only so much that could go around. I'd steal my sibling's clothing which caused chaos in the household. If I could buy my own things, it would help alleviate the commotion. I decided to take matters into my own hands and ask again. My mom was right.

"Absolutely not! She'll have too much freedom! Chutzpanit! She does whatever she wants anyway, we can't just let her run around this town freely!" My father was enraged. He believed that a young girl with money would have too much independence and sought control over the women in his life to maintain their honorable innocence.

I was confused as to what he was implying: "Chutzpanit" means someone with no shame. *What shame? How is working shameful?* I deem it just the opposite considering my father's emphasis on working for what we earn. I knew I had to fight for it. The freedom to buy things for myself overrode any reservations my dad had. Kids would no longer mock my unattractive appearance or ridicule my thick eyeglasses that looked like a coke bottle. This opportunity would not escape me.

How would I convince my dad to let me work? First off, I needed money to pay for my stuff, and would no longer be using his. Second, it would alleviate sibling quarrels at home. Lastly, I had boundless energy and needed an outlet.

My parent's culture inhibited girls in many ways. The energizer bunny in me was always riled up, which was problematic for me. Even playing basketball or soccer was considered shameful for a girl, unbefitting for a female to play in male-dominated sports. In high school, I asked to enroll in a girls' basketball team. My dad blew up: "What are you, a man? Do you have balls? You are a girl and need to be feminine."

I had a hard time with these double standards, so I defied his orders and continued to play pick-up games after school. I was the only girl in town who played street basketball. This manly domain kept me balanced and grounded.

My father continued denying me of playing ball or working, but I never stopped nagging him. I even asked Misha, the owner of the shop, to talk with him. I guess it took a man-to-man conversation to turn the tables: Soon enough, I was working part-time in the afternoons. Pick-up basketball games between school and work remained my recreational secret.

My teenage years fostered a strength in my personal identity and independence with confidence. Earning my own money and being able to pay for little things empowered me. I felt ready to conquer imminent changes on the journey ahead.

10

The Channel of Change

L ife in Israel smoothly progressed. My father's sixteen-hour days working as a contractor put enough food on the table and a stable roof over our heads. He was soon able to acquire the necessary resources to build a four-thousand-square-foot home in Hadera's high-end neighborhood.

I finally got my own room, but my sister got the room with the balcony. Although a bit resentful at first, I understood my position in our family hierarchy. It was difficult to accept that I was nobody's favorite because I had a lot of love to give, but those who I sought it back from didn't love me back how I wanted or expected them to. While hurt, I soon found motivation and liberty from trying to meet these expectations. I did not need to satisfy anyone, seek approval, or live up to anybody's standards. My actions— working, playing ball, and extending myself to a new social circle— were not hurting anyone. Perhaps I disappointed others when I rebelled or fought for my needs, but no one had high expectations for the anti-status quo rebel anyway. They called me the girl with balls because I broke boundaries that seemed unfair, biased, and hypocritical. I would never stop being me: blunt, bold, and boisterous.

In March, just before my high school graduation, my parents announced that we were leaving for America. The Israeli economy was in shambles. Construction jobs were limited, and over the past couple of years, my dad had traveled between Germany, Canada, and the United States in search of opportunities elsewhere. My parents' friends in Brooklyn promised to help my father find work. In March of 1986, he made his final decision.

My two younger brothers immigrated to New York with my parents. I was to join them after graduation that summer. Since I couldn't stay alone, my eldest sister and her family moved in to look after me.

Betty was an absolute control freak: "Take off your shoes when you come in, be home by ten o'clock, and don't eat in your room!" she'd command. If there was one grain of rice on the floor, the entire house needed cleaning. My sister's rigid, unforgiving style broke her inner spirit as she failed to achieve intended outcomes. Our relationship became a never-ending tug-of-war match. More control meant more conflict, and more conflict meant crisis. Betty would push new rules and I'd pull back. I wasn't used to living this way. My mother rarely enforced rules in the household, nor punished me if I did not follow her orders.

Betty's wrath made me miss my mom more and more; I felt a void without her. Until I was twelve, I'd often sneak out of bed and fall asleep next to her: "Mommy, I'll never leave you, I want to stay with you forever." Now more than ever, I wanted to express these words with her by my side.

While lonely and in the dark, my strength prevailed. I could not allow my sister to exert emotional control over me, let alone physical control. During my free time, I'd keep busy to mask my pain and take advantage of the freedoms my father never gave me. Fortunately, I seized safe and positive opportunities. I continued my routine of working, studying, and socializing, but dramatically increased my engagement in community activities. Israeli folk dance lessons enabled me to connect with friends who enjoyed taking road trips and playing sports on the beach.

I have witnessed those who experience hardship resort to harmful coping mechanisms to escape their pain. They make rash mistakes in the short term that they regret in the long run, with irreversible collateral damage. Throughout my life, I've noticed a pattern of maintaining positive engagement to avoid spiraling into depression. My parents have always been my role models, and no matter how hard or complicated life is, the way up is always pushing towards your goal and happiness in a healthy way.

While having the time of my life outside my home, I felt like a prisoner inside of it. Assimilating into my sister's neurotic lifestyle was possible but I was not willing to play along. Something had to change. I contemplated options to escape her dictatorship. I called a close family friend and explained my situation. Naava embraced me with open arms, and her motherly spirit comforted me. She helped me cope with missing my parents and my brothers who had also just moved to the US. We would walk on the beach for miles discussing her life experiences. She became my mentor for those few months before I moved to the United States and joined my family.

Naava's close bond with her two sons moved me: I observed how they confronted issues honestly and from the onset with a commitment to fully resolve them. They had no secrets between them. Her parenting style intrigued me because in my family, issues were ignored until they blew up.

I realized that when you face a problem when it's still minor, explosive reactions can be completely avoided. This approach to motherhood is the foundation upon which I'd base mine, providing a perfect balance of support, companionship, and freedom. Just like she had, I committed to raise my children to be honest and thoughtful, attentive and authentic, strong and outspoken.

Farewell, Israel

The summer of 1986 finally came. I bid a bittersweet goodbye to my friends at graduation, sad to leave them and the life I had established for myself over recent months. But I looked forward to the new chapter ahead. Packing my bags felt surreal: I had no clue what awaited me on the other side of the world.

Still grappling with who I was and who I had yet to become, I remained a wild horse who could not be reined in. My metamorphosis only began after my divorce, emerging stronger from the confines of another culture ridden with restrictive norms and taboos.

PART · III

Life in the Boro

1986 - 1991

Part III Life in the Boro

1

Landing in the Big Apple

I landed at Kennedy airport in New York City. The Big Apple was bigger than life itself. WOW! Just WOW! While eager to explore this new land of opportunity, I was most excited to see my parents and brothers. I was relieved to be living with them after four months of my sister's dictatorship. My brothers spotted me at baggage claim.

"Luda! It's so good to see you! Finally, you're here!" Aidan exclaimed as we hugged.

"Everything is different here. Let's see how you like it, let's get outta here!" Emilio lifted me up and spun around.

In the car, my parents began to share what life has been like in America. My dad had been driving car service around the clock which kept him busy with seldom free moments. My mother mostly stayed in the house and took occasional walks on the town to buy essentials.

"It's nothing like home, darling, but we are good," my mom comforted me. "Nothing like home" meant to prepare me for the shock I was about to face. As we approached what I would soon call "home," I became increasingly puzzled by the choice of neighborhood. We were

127

barely affiliated with the Orthodox community back in Israel. *Why here?*

The Boro reminded me of the Bnei Brak, an Orthodox quarter in Israel. I recalled that upon moving to Israel in 1973, my family was placed in a Hasidic community for a week. My dad demanded to be moved to a different neighborhood with secular Israelis and fellow immigrants. He was not against their rituals per se: He believed in God and Jewish ethics but refused to adhere to a restrictive lifestyle and religious rules. This time, there would be no outlet for a while— for what seemed an eternity.

This part of my story is where strides toward my personal liberation begins, emerging with difficulty, difference, despair, and disdain. Aside from the ultra-Orthodox lifestyle, the Boro's Jews are predominantly Ashkenazi, originating from Eastern European regions such as Poland or Hungary. While Jewish like them, we were still foreigners with unrefined traditions. For the next many months, I'd feel like a lone sailor in the foreign waters of Boro Park life, and I had yet to flounder through them to find myself in this new world.

2

Floundering Through Foreign Waters

I stood drenched under the Boro Park metro station wearing a spaghetti strap tank top and khaki shorts. It was August: In New York, summers are balmy. Surrounding me were women literally covered from head to toe— tights, maxi skirts, long sleeve shirts, and head scarves— pushing strollers (sometimes two at once!) from one avenue to the next. They wore so many layers that I couldn't even see the sweat on their back. Men too, like the women, showed not even an inch of skin. They wore black top hats, thick coats, and slacks. They looked me up and down, but never in the eye. A group of them walked past me and toward the corner synagogue with prayer books in hand, tzitzit (religious garment worn by Orthodox Jewish men) swinging with every stride.

I headed toward the city center in search of a job. Rabbis and students of all ages flooded in and out of yeshivas, seminaries, and synagogues on each block. Storefronts bore Yiddish names. I was shocked to see businesses purely selling wigs, and vendors selling specialty Judaic artifacts. Grocery store shelves were racked with foods packaged in Yiddish labels. *How will I know what to buy?* The irresistible smell of toasted bread lured me into the deli at the back. My mouth was watering.

"Can-can I have bagel sesame please?" Some odd combination of accents rolled off my tongue. I probably butchered the question entirely. Oops! (Transposing words in English is a problem I still have today).

"Huh?" The shop owner furrowed his brows and glared at me. He called over his assistant, who looked at me the same way. I pointed out the crisp sesame bagel on the bottom rack. They turned to each other and laughed hysterically. I slapped a dollar bill on the counter and took an aggressive bite. So much for a newcomer.

Over time, I found that you really don't need to speak English to get around Boro Park. All the suppliers speak Yiddish, and some speak Russian. While dominated by Jews, only a small fraction of Boro locals speaks Hebrew. I used my Russian when I could. English was my 911, reserved for emergencies only.

During the first few months, I pondered my family's decision. *How can they function in such an extreme community? How could they leave a beautiful 4,000 square-foot home on the Israeli coast for a 600 square-foot shoebox with one window?* My parents had rented a room in some family's basement with the money they had. Five people— my mom, dad, two brothers, and I— were living in a single bedroom with two sofas. My brothers slept together on one, and I took the other. Privacy was an illusion.

The answer to my questions was abundant opportunity: A country where a better life could be hoped for, and dreams could be realized, surpassed any lifestyle inconveniences. *Short term pain for long term gain, right?* For goodness's sake, we made it to America!

Both my parents found jobs: My dad painted homes in the mornings and drove car service through the night, while my mom worked as a salesperson in children's clothing. My brothers also worked after a full day at school. I couldn't continue my education since my parents had no papers for me. And besides, it wasn't acceptable for a woman to go to school in the Boro (unless it was seminary).

Watching my family thrive on the American dream while I cried into my pillow every night tore me apart. The cranking sound of the train awoke me hour after hour, and I lay there awake flipping through memories in my mind— playing basketball after dusk, strolling through Hadera farmer's market on Sunday mornings, and debating philosophy with my teachers and friends. Unlike my life in Israel, each day in this Boro came to an end void of fulfillment, and each morning began with no purpose. I was lonely, lost, and longing for the life I once had, or a life I could have. Just not this one.

Dreams Don't Come True Without Hard Work

Feelings of despair would never break me. Despair motivated me to work harder and push through every obstacle I faced. My electric energy propelled me to find productive outlets. With no friends, no school, no papers, and no special skills, I figured that working at a local store could forge new relationships, fill my days, and introduce me to my surroundings.

Broken English made the job search a nightmare. However, I was able to find work as a salesperson at the local linen shop within a couple of months. Shockingly, my fellow staff were all non-Jews— either Puerto

Rican or Jamaican. While very kind to me, I was bored out of my mind because I was unable to communicate with them or relate to their culture. Business was slow too. The job was monotonous since I hated waiting for people to ask if they needed help, and they rarely did. I missed being on my toes and constantly interacting with customers like at Misha's candy shop back in Hadera. I'd beg the owners if there was anything else I could do; they said no. I'd then retreat to the back of the store, mindlessly folding cloth after cloth and packing orders until sunset. Not what I signed up for.

Before I quit this dreadful job at the linen shop, I needed to find a replacement job. Employment status gave me a sense of security since I didn't have papers. It was my insurance policy; without it, I'd be back in the hole where I started. Digging myself out of that hole took two long months, and I was not willing to sink back in.

Every day after work, I'd trek along 13th avenue on the quest for a new job. In a couple of weeks, my eye caught a HELP WANTED sign on the window of a large and busy supermarket. I jumped on the opportunity. The owners offered me part-time for the first week, from 8:00 AM until noon. The following week, they bumped me up to a full-time position. I absolutely loved it! It was busy, hectic, and intense. I quickly memorized all the prices and packed groceries with an incandescent smile.

Once my post at the supermarket was secure, I quit my job at the linen shop. A month in, I was working 8:00 to 8:00 shifts non-stop for $4.50 an hour. I was ecstatic to find a nexus to the secular world within the Boro Park community. Israelis and secular Jews chatted with me in Hebrew, and I practiced my broken English with no judgments. Even after a full day of ringing up items, bagging them, and exchanging quick

132

conversations, I'd come home feeling rejuvenated.

My First Impression, My First Connection

Ziona was my first friend in Brooklyn. We met at my checkout register. I was immediately drawn to the black ringlets curling around her smiley face. Most women here were blond or brunette with lighter complexions, not dark like me. She was the first woman I came across who wore her natural head of hair. Unorthodox.

After our friendly introduction at the supermarket, I discovered that Ziona had recently moved to New York from Israel after serving in the army. She was born in Yemen and immigrated to Israel at a very young age. Despite being several years older than me, I was glad to have finally befriended someone in this community, and it was a bonus to have connected with someone I could relate to. Whoever composed my social circle— Israeli or American, Jewish, or not— I didn't care. Any interaction elated me, removing feelings of estrangement that plagued me for months.

On an early morning at the supermarket, Ziona invited me to join a singles gathering that her boyfriend, Baruch, was organizing. To my surprise, she was dating a Hungarian-Orthodox Jew. *A Yemenite and a Hungarian, how does that work?* Ethnic and cultural barriers in the Boro would never allow these sects of Jews to mix. Ashkenazim were considered the intellectual elite while Sephardic Jews were considered inferior tradespeople. Through my conversations with Ziona, it was evident that her boyfriend's parents did not accept her as an adequate bride for their son.

"When you're in love, it doesn't matter. It shouldn't affect our relationship, at least as of now," she said.

Single and Ready to Mingle

On that chilly October evening, I rushed back home after work to get ready for the event with Ziona. "Come on Luda, everyone will look at you weird. At least wear a skirt, trust me." She really wanted me to wear a dress. Like in my parent's culture, a grown woman in pants was too seductive or masculine.

"I don't own a dress or a skirt," I told her, "I-I've never felt comfortable showing my legs! My sister always used to tell me that they looked like a football guys' legs because they're so muscular!" I chose comfort over norms, always. Since I had no interest in dating a religious man, I decided to dress secular and classy. Black slacks topped by a silken white collared shirt did just fine.

A smooth orchestra of string instruments sang at the porch of Baruch's house. Vines and roses surrounded the staircase toward the home's main entrance.

"Come in, come in, please." A heavyset Puerto-Rican woman ushered Ziona and me inside through the archway, then into the house. We stepped onto pristine mahogany floors and peered at the furniture embellished with delicate engravings. Behold my introduction to Boro Park luxury.

Our group lounged on forest green sofas in the spacious living room. Baruch's mother greeted us both and brought trays of dried fruits stuffed with nuts on lucent crystal dishes. Minutes later came simmering pots of kugel. The Klezmer music romanticized the scene more than I wanted it

134

to. For me, this was purely a social event: Nothing more, nothing less.

There were about twenty of us— more female than male— and a few couples who were already dating. Most of the men did not wear black hats, and even without ringlets dropping off the sides of their faces. Some women even wore dresses showing their ankles! It turned out that a majority of the group was modern Orthodox. A few had religious families but were disowned because they defied Orthodox rules. I later discovered that most modern Orthodox complied with some religiosity for business's sake.

A young man in his late twenties, Levi, told me that his parents were Satmar Jews, ultra-Orthodox Jews from Romania. They were adamant anti-Zionists, people opposed to the state of Israel.

"You know, if you go to Manhattan on Yom Haatzmaut (Israeli Independence Day), you can see the Satmar Jews protesting and burning the Israeli flag," he mentioned casually.

I was clueless that so many sects of Jews existed, and more so shocked that any Jew could disfavor the state of Israel— a land that gave our people a home, a land serving as a nexus of democracy, innovation, and an infusion of cultures. The Satmar sect also rejects modern technology and culture, from television to the education system. Levi shared that his parents prohibited him from coming back home because he wanted to explore the outside world.

"I'm living in their basement now. It's great— really." He took another shot of tequila.

Most of the girls there were blond, pale, and soft-spoken— classic Ashkenazi. Ziona and I were odd balls— striking bold features, dark eyes, and thick black hair. They knew Ziona but were surprised by the face of the exotic new girl. Since I asked many questions, the favor was inevitably returned.

"Where are you from? How long have you been here? What nationality are you?" A group clustered around me. I bore a magnetic presence.

"Derbent, Dagestan. From the Caucasus," I remarked. When I let the words "former USSR" slip, one of the men furrowed his brows. He knew that I came from the southeastern part rather than the western part. He was probably thinking, *she's too much of a low life for me.*

Mountain Jews are considered second-tier, even below Sephardim in the eyes of the Ashkenazi elite. Nonetheless, I felt comfortable sharing my roots, and I didn't care what they thought of me. I wasn't attracted to any of them: Some had their bellies poking out, a few had long beards, and none seemed athletic. It was just fun to chat and make friends, but after an hour of silly conversations and dry humor, I was antsy to get home.

An announcement aired just as we headed towards the door.

"I have a riddle, and I will treat whoever solves it to a dinner of their choice." The voice was provoking, ringing with intellectual seduction. I turned abruptly to the sight of a slender, tall man with a light complexion. *So handsome!* Emerald green eyes lured me further into the challenge. He presented his question (I don't recall exactly what it was), and after two short minutes, I had an answer. The rest of the group was mind-boggled, rolling their eyes and still finger-counting.

"I have no interest in you treating me for dinner, but here is the answer to your riddle." I scribbled my response on a slip of paper and handed it to him.

"Impressive," he looked at me straight-on with unwavering focus, as if he had never stared at a woman head-on before. "I insist on the reward, please allow me to take you to dinner. My treat. You earned it, smart young lady." He crinkled the sheet of paper and called game over for the group.

"I'll think about it," I smirked.

Ziona drove me home. I confessed my curiosity about the handsome gentleman who presented the riddle.

"That's Mendy, Mendy Wolfson," she said, "His family is very well-off and prominent in Boro Park. They own many delis, restaurants, and properties all over town. Plus, his father is the president of the main synagogue here. I believe Mendy works with his parents to help manage their businesses."

"Cool." I nodded my head and shrugged my shoulders. *Too far out of my league— the way he spoke, the way he looked, his family's prestige...*

"He seemed to think highly of you," Ziona said as I stepped out the car. "Anyway, I hope you had a good time. I'll see you at the supermarket soon, get a good night's rest." She blew me a kiss and drove away.

Part III Life in the Boro

3

First Date: I Resisted, He Persisted

Sundays were my busiest days at the grocery store. After Shabbat, religious families came to restock on food and essentials for the week. I was up for work by 6:00 AM, ready to start my shift at 8:00. By the time evening came, all I could think about was a warm shower, pajamas, and my bed.

One Sunday, I walked out of the crowded supermarket to see Mendy waiting outside looking ordinary as usual. He caught me with a friendly smile.

"I owe you dinner, don't I?" He glanced with sarcastic confusion, then continued confidently, "It would be my pleasure to treat you."

"Not tonight. I'm tired, and my mom is waiting for me. I need to get back home." I tried masking my shock with a grin.

"Let me at least drive you home." He gestured his arm toward the cluster of parked cars afront the store. I agreed.

"I am very impressed with your wit," he said pressing on the gas, "I've never met anyone who could solve that riddle so fast! Where did you learn to do that?"

After a slew of personal questions, we arrived at my doorstep. Time had escaped me. *How did he know where I lived?* I didn't ask, doubting that anything serious would evolve. The social, religious, and economic disparities between us were far too wide; I was assured that he'd steer clear of me after our brief conversation. I was wrong.

"Shall we have dinner Saturday night, when Shabbat ends?" he asked, walking me to my doorstep.

"Ok, sure." *What's to lose?* If only, there was something to gain.

Saturday night came. Mendy picked me up and drove us to a kosher diner off Kings' highway. The evening debuted with riveting conversations about global affairs and politics, then transitioned into philosophy and Judaica. My dates with Mendy always involved intense discussions about famous Jewish commentators Rashi, Rambam, and Ebben Ezra. The dialogue we shared reminded me of school in Israel, where we connected biblical morals to contemporary ethics. Our dinners went on for hours: Just one biblical verse holds infinite interpretations.

"To love thy neighbor as you love yourself, or to love thy neighbor as they want to be loved?" I posed. Mendy was fascinated by the way I reversed this verse among many others. In turn, I was fascinated by a man whose intellectual spark ignited passion in me and who valued mine.

Community Gossip: To Split or to Commit?

Gossip diffuses quickly through the Boro. As word got around about Mendy and I dating, my dad wanted to ensure that I remained pure. Remember, pure? Yes, a virgin until marriage. Uphold the family honor.

Three months in, my father invited Mendy to a man-to-man

conversation at our home.

"If you're serious about your relationship with my daughter, you must ask for her hand in marriage, and if not, you must dissolve the relationship to keep my family's honor," he asserted. Mendy left with a basic ultimatum of two alternatives— take it or leave it.

My dad opposed my engagement with Mendy. He'd repeat, "This boy is not for you. Hungarians are brutal people." My dad was traumatized by gruesome fighting against Hungarians in the Russian-Hungarian war. Rumor also had it that Mendy's father was shrewd and manipulative. My father hated nothing more than dishonest people who lacked integrity. Nonetheless, my dad still gave Mendy the choice.

I was grateful for my father's forgiving attitude toward Mendy. My outings with him allowed me to explore Brooklyn and New York through a unique lens. He filled my life with intellectual stimulation, unconditional affection, and constantly surprised me with thoughtful gifts. I felt loved— a sense of belonging, worth, and comfort that I had never experienced before.

Unfortunately, Mendy's parents were also against our relationship, but for different reasons:

We had minimal means and resources. We didn't eat kosher. My mom did not cover her hair. I didn't dress modestly. We worked and drove on Shabbat. We didn't go to synagogue regularly; we didn't even belong to one. We weren't Hungarian. We weren't Ashkenazi. We weren't Orthodox. We weren't prestigious. We were outsiders. A union between our families would never mesh: Oil and water.

Seeing that my love for Mendy never died out, my dad called Mendy to a second meeting at our home in August: "Mendy, you've been dating my daughter for three months. What's your plan? In our tradition, we don't allow kuchi muchi and then farfuchi (playing games and swinging her around on your finger)." In short, he was saying, 'Do you want her or not? The clock is ticking, and my daughter needs to get married.'

Mendy assured him that the proposal was underway.

Refuse to Submit, Fall into the Pit

Nothing could bridge the sea of differences between my family and Mendy's. Neither could endure pressure from the community or such grave disparities of rules and rituals. We broke off. Mendy's parents sent him to Israel for a month to find a suitable bride of Zakkarpatian (Hungarian/Ukrainian Jewish) descent. Heartbreak devastated me and my self-worth plummeted. I sank into a shell of insecurities, ashamed of my identity and heritage: *I am dark, I am a Tat Jew, and I am lower class. My family has no special yichus* (status). *I am an ordinary girl. I'll never be good enough. I am plainly undesirable.*

I sat on my porch crying for days mired in a quagmire of self-pity. Ziona visited frequently: my saving grace. She shared that she faced similar resistance from Baruch's parents.

"The other day, his dad called me schvartze chaya (a demeaning racial slur meaning black animal in Yiddish). After all this time, I can't believe it!" she exclaimed. Luckily, Ziona's parents were no longer pressuring her to marry since she was already past her prime at twenty-five.

"You're still young, not like me. I promise you'll find the right man eventually. You're not alone, you know I am here for you. We are stronger together." She assured me with a warm hug.

I found comfort in Ziona's empathy and intimate friendship. She taught me that rejection and loneliness are just signs to debunk insecurity and emerge stronger.

"What about we venture outside this pit? What else can we do? Should we take a class or a course and learn something?" I suggested, eager to engage with life beyond this bubble. I was convinced that keeping my days balanced and busy would help alleviate my pain, just like when dealing with my sister back in Israel. We began to toss-up ideas and plan our adventure outside of the Boro.

Be Productive to Alleviate Pain

It was impossible to erase Mendy from my memory. People talked. "How are things with Mendy?" Customers pestered me at the supermarket. Some were just probing, some were curious about the latest narrative, and others wondered how our story would end. "You know he is in Israel. He's dating some beeeaaauutiful, glaaaamorous girl," they'd entice. *Shut up already!* That's the last thing I wanted to hear. Through this gossipy grapevine, I soon learned that Mendy was not interested in the girl from Israel whom his mother had set him up with through the shidduch, matchmaker.

Mendy was already twenty-five, but the pressure to marry young was not as great for men as for women. The pressure upon me was immense, living in an environment where girls marry at seventeen and with a mother who was married at thirteen. I was at the peak: Nineteen. *Get going, Luda.*

My infatuation with Mendy hindered my effort to meet other men. The only way to keep my mind off him was by continuing my normal routine and filling my days with activities. I extended my hours at the supermarket and in the evenings, I'd socialize with my brothers and their friends to avoid being alone. Ziona and I took trips into the city, exploring avenues beyond the Boro's brick walls.

I also reconnected with one of my classmates from Israel who moved to Brooklyn, Alan Step. His family immigrated seeking new opportunities as well. I found comfort playing basketball with him, my brothers, and their friends just like back in Hadera. Nothing would defeat me: There was no way that a man whose family didn't accept me for who I was would. *Emotions are temporary. Forget about him. Love can be forgotten, somehow.* Can it really? *Just numb the feeling, or something.*

4

Love Conquered it All: Changing My Ways

I was waiting outside for Alan to pick me up for dinner in Manhattan on a mellow May evening. I peered down at my chest and lifted my blouse higher to make sure my white V-neck wasn't drifting too low.

"Shavua Tov." A provoking voice spoke. That same one. I recognized it. I jolted my head up and OH MY GOODNESS! *AM I SEEING A GHOST?* I bolted up the stairs and into the house. A drum pounded the inside of my chest, its beat intensifying by the second. Before my mother even had a chance to ask me what happened, Mendy knocked. She opened the door reluctantly.

"Mendy?" Her face turned snow white. "What are you doing here, child?" It had been nearly six months since we had seen him.

"How have you been? What is the honor of your visit?" My mom invited him to come inside and have some tea. My mother and Mendy had a special relationship. They were close, far from the non-existent relationship I had with Mendy's mother who didn't even want to hear a peep about me.

"Well," he began, "I am looking to speak with Ariel. I-I-I want to ask for Luda's hand." His jaw was shaking. My mother could hardly come up with words to say, knowing the toil I was going through over many months.

"Mendy, listen, my child. If you are interested in my daughter, please talk to her first before you speak with her father." She admonished, tilting her head as he sunk into the sofa chair. Here was the gap: In Orthodox Jewish culture, unmarried girls are their parent's property, so permission to marry must be granted by the parents. After marriage, the woman becomes the property of her husband. This norm becomes clearer through various instances and incidents to become apparent later in my story.

I finally came downstairs and sat next to my mother on the couch, across from Mendy. He said, "I searched and searched, but I couldn't find anyone like you. I love you, really, I do."

My heart was melting, bleeding out with mixed feelings. I couldn't believe it. And just like that, with one look, I was back. Yes! A sliver of light would finally return to my life! I knew that strings were attached to this relationship, but I followed my mother's advice: If you really love someone, you follow your man. *What about his parents? Will they accept me?*

Mendy continued, "It will take time for my parents to embrace you into the family. You must be patient and be willing to change your ways." He read my mind. I did not fully understand what this meant at the time but lost all rationale in a moment of uncontained excitement. "Change your ways" was an understatement.

So, he coached me on a few basics: "Dress modestly in public, and please do not drive on Shabbat, or at least not when the neighbors see you. Don't talk like Israeli chutzpanit women. Show humility and modesty." Mendy demonstrated how a decent woman should present herself before family and community members. He was telling me to display myself as an Orthodox girl on the outside, and what I truly believed or thought about on the inside didn't make a difference.

I am always one to refer to my philosophical texts and biblical studies. I remembered the 18th-century Russian-Zionist poet, A.D. Gordon who wrote, "Be a Jew in your home and a man outside of it." To protect the persecuted Jews in medieval Europe, Gordon instructed that Jews in the community assimilate with the outside community and practice their Judaism in a safe space. Today, these same Jews— from Hungary, Poland, and Russia— were blatantly defying modern culture in public and acting as they wished in private. This behavior seemed incongruent to their core beliefs and values. Regardless, I admired the strong display of Judaism in the Boro yet questioned it due to post-Holocaust traumas. But I guess this is why people fled to the United States, in search of cherished liberties— freedom of religion, of expression, and of speech: It's what America is known for! The land of the free. As for me, the wild horse who had to "change her ways," freedom became an illusion.

Attempts to Adapt:
The First Dinner with Mendy's Family

A month passed until I was finally invited to Mendy's parents' home for Shabbat dinner. Since driving on Shabbat is prohibited, I parked a couple of blocks away and walked there. The Wolfsons lived in the corner brownstone, right across the street from the synagogue.

Stepping into their home was like becoming one with darkness. I tiptoed onto the entrance rug and lifted my eyes to meet his father's.

"Good Shabbos," he uttered in a raspy voice looking straight at my feet. I was then greeted by members of his extended family who scanned me up and down. Insecurities kicked in. *They can't even look at me: the disgraceful lower-middle-class, secular Israeli, Tat-Jew.*

"Shabbat Shalom." My accent couldn't have sounded more...me? Yep, me. A mut. Not what they wanted.

I toured their spacious home, peering around each opulent room with my clammy hands clasped behind me. The heavy wooden furniture camouflaged into the room's umber hues and earthy walls. The bookcase was filled with religious books— from the Mishna to the Talmud— all of which camouflaged with the coffee-colored shelf. I was drawn to the short flames emanating light from large silver candlesticks. Baby pink roses flowered out of a crystal vase aside.

We were called to wash our hands before the meal. One cannot speak in between handwashing and before the challah is blessed upon, then eaten. Following the ritual, I was seated across from a man wearing a shtreimel (fur hat). *Luda, stop staring.* Mendy's mother served us each two golf-ball-sized pieces of gefilte fish topped with a pinch of horseradish and drenched in wine. Then came a single cup of kasha with cabbage, something I had never tasted before. The paucity of food on my plate felt insulting and frugal. *It's not like they're poor!* They managed a grocery store, owned a restaurant, and the fridge was packed! (Later on, I learned that serving small portions was Ashkenazi mannerism). My appetite vanished.

In Israel and Sephardic culture, food was always served in abundance— family-style. Your platter could be piled with different meats, grains, stews, sauces, and you'd still be offered more! I longed for home-cooked Shabbat dinners and intimacy of my family's traditions. *Forget it.* I looked at Mendy and remembered his words: Be patient, learn to adapt, and change your ways.

Half-way through dinner, the sermon on the weekly Parsha, or Torah portion, ensued. From what I heard, it seemed as if my notion of God and His place in our lives widely differed. I was intrigued to learn more.

"Who wrote the Torah?" I asked innocently. They said "God." Stupidly, I continued, "So if God wrote the Torah, aren't we all parts of God?" To me, this was a logical formula: The Torah was transmitted orally from rabbis or parents to kids through the generations, and once written form was invented, it was documented by sofers, or scribes. I learned this in school. Eyes shot daggers at me from every corner of the room.

"How could you say that!" Mendy's father broke the second of awkward silence fuming, "What a disgrace in God's name!" All the men began to bow anxiously while davening out of tune. The women sunk their heads into their palms. This was the first time, but certainly not the last, that I'd make a mess in this house.

Mendy was speechless. I don't think he ever imagined that I'd have the audacity to express my unorthodox wit in front of his family. In Israel, no topics were taboo: I was encouraged to challenge respectfully and express all my curiosities. In the Boro, women were not even allowed to read the Torah! I had committed not one offense, but two that night.

The 'act Orthodox in public and as you wish in private' advice was hard for a girl like me who didn't understand the rules and refused to follow them if the reasoning behind them did not make sense. I needed an explanation to reconcile the differences. 'This is the way it works' propelled me to ask the same question until I was satisfied with the answers. But persistent questioning that opposes divine belief is not the way it worked here.

Mindset at Nineteen:
To Be Right or to Be Smart?

At nineteen, I held very strong opinions which I conveyed with passion. Winning arguments was important to me. I dismissed constructive criticism, shut down opposing views, and doubt-filled mind games perpetuated when I couldn't comprehend what was behind a statement or rule. Later, I'd learn that doubt is a demonstration of curiosity and a sign of maturity. Doubt espouses wisdom, and wisdom refines judgment. It was a matter of how I manifested my doubts to certain audiences that drew the line of appropriateness and effectiveness. In the aftermath of the scandal at the Wolfson's Shabbat dinner, I remembered Yafa's words, "think before you act, so you have no regrets."

If I had thought about my purpose going into the dinner, I would have acted much differently. My objective was not to prove my notion of God or to win an argument. *What benefit came out of questioning God in a religious home, especially when their family already rejected me?* None. Adding more gas to the fire doesn't do any good when the pot is already simmering.

To reverse Mendy's family's perceptions of me, I had to win them over by showcasing the most respectable version of myself. Achieving an intended goal comes with tailoring style to the social setting. In the Wolfson household, opposing views and open debate were not welcome— especially not about God, and certainly not when a lower-class woman sparks the discussion. I had to tame myself: Open your mouth only to please their ears. Just sit still, look pretty, smile, and be modest. Aim to please.

Mendy's Circle of Friends:
Put a Woman in Her Place!

As our courtship evolved, Mendy introduced me to his social circle. They joked about methods of 'putting a woman in her place.' "Find some of her faults on your wedding night and slap her." His older friend would make jokes like, "Ah, yes! Then shock her with a bit of aggression!" chuckling and punching his open fist.

I was perplexed by these comments. *Are they just trying to rattle me or are they for real?* It seemed normalized as I heard similar remarks at home among my dad's friends. This experience brought memories of when my father would yell, "I married a young woman to mold her and serve my needs!" Like most Orthodox wives, my mother remained silent. I promised myself to never allow anybody to degrade me in subservience to a man. Silence debilitates me. But at that moment, I froze, just smiling and laughing with them as they launched silly grenades of disrespect and misogyny. Refrain, be patient, change your ways. I was repulsed.

As outings with Mendy's family and friends became more frequent, I wondered how I would maintain my authentic individualism. *How can I balance staying true to my beliefs and communicate them without provoking an argument?* Later in life, I'd figure this out— learning to say things for the right reasons to the right people in the right way with the right message at the right time. Before understanding this, I'd have a long journey ahead.

Part III Life in the Boro

5

Terms of Marriage:
Luda Becomes Leah

O ur parents finally agreed to convene and discuss the terms of marriage. Russian was their only common language. His parents didn't speak Hebrew, and mine didn't speak Yiddish, Hungarian, or English. Mendy's mother insisted that I cover my hair with a wig, wear modest clothing, keep Kashrut laws, and observe Shabbat among the other Jewish holidays.

"You must quit your job and work for us. It's more suitable for a girl like you," Mr. Wolfson demanded. He shifted from staring at me into my father's eyes. "When you come to our home, the women must wear long dresses, and you— Ariel— and the boys, must always wear a yamaka." The terms were one sided. We accepted and had barely any demands in return.

Many rules from their end remained a mystery to us. Wedding invitations had been sent out with my Russian name, Luda Surielov. We had printed over five hundred invitations for Mendy's family, friends, and fellow community members; we hardly invited fifty people. A few days later, Mr. Wolfson was flooded with phone calls from prominent religious leaders in the Boro insisting that I receive a more suitable Jewish name. I had no idea about any of this. Without my permission or my family's, he went straight to the synagogue and suggested the name "Leah" because "Luda" closely matched. I hated it.

"Leah" was one of the four biblical mothers, whose name means 'tired and weary woman.' She also wedded Jacob in her dirty tricks. Her name and character harbored the antithesis of who I was or wanted to identify with. But I let this go and accepted it with more important issues to tackle. We reprinted all the invitations. The wedding was set for October 23, 1987 with 700 guests confirmed in attendance.

The Wedding: The Tip of the Iceberg Unveils the Road Ahead

Minutes before the procession, my family and Mendy's gathered outside the hall.

"You know, Mendy will always be my tatalé (Yiddish for my baby)." Mrs. Wolfson whispered into my ear callously, "He is mine. You are just his wife. He will always be my son." I said nothing. My heart raced. *What does she mean?* The music began. No time to think.

It was finally my turn to walk down the aisle to meet Mendy under the chuppah, or marriage canopy. Not a single inch of my skin was exposed. Even my face was covered by an extravagant beaded veil, double-stitched with lace and silk. I could barely see.

Sitting through hours of ceremonial rituals and Rabbinical blessings was psychological torture for a girl like me who can't sit still for more than half-hour. It was like waiting for food at a restaurant when your stomach is gurgling obnoxiously, just begging for the wait to be over!

Two long hours trickled by until the crowd finally screamed "Mazel Tov!" as Mendy stomped on the glass. A rabbi immediately rushed Mendy and me into a room for Yichud, meaning 'union.' The bride and groom are united in seclusion for at least eight minutes to consummate the marriage. It signifies their first moments alone together. Once the witnesses deemed our Yichud complete, we entered the wedding hall welcomed by waves of guests dancing the hora.

Mendy funneled into the men's side and I into the women's section. My brothers crossed the mechitza (divider) to congratulate and dance with me. Mr. Wolfson caught sight of this obscenity and forcefully pushed my brothers away. I knew that men and women couldn't mix in a religious wedding, but all I wanted was to share this joyous moment with them. I ran toward the back of the hall to find my sister.

"I can't wait for this to be over. Please, Marina, I want to go home. I can't do this. I can't," I collapsed into her arms and burst into tears. Separation from my family had already begun. This distance would only grow.

The First Night, The First Fight

Mendy and I were living in the same corner brownstone as his parents. They occupied the second floor, and we took the third (the family grocery store and luncheonette were on the ground floor). When we arrived home from the wedding, Mendy stayed downstairs chatting with his parents while I rushed upstairs. Infuriated and exhausted, I ripped off the five-pound dress whose heavy train had weighed me down the entire evening. I didn't want to talk to anyone. I curled up on the sofa in an oversized t-shirt as pain in my heart lingered. Mendy finally came upstairs thirty minutes later.

I jumped off the couch and exploded, "What right does your dad have to separate us? Why couldn't he just let my brothers dance with me?!"

"You don't get it, do you?!" he yelled and slapped me across the face.

"How dare you slap me? Wasn't that just your friend's joke about putting a woman in her place?! You are unbelievable!" I yelled harder, almost growling.

Mendy turned his back to me and walked into the bedroom. *Was he expecting me to come after him? Was he expecting me to make love?* Having sex on the wedding night was customary. I refused and stayed on the sofa furthest from the main bedroom. I didn't want to be touched by him, or anyone for that matter. Dreams of being loved and honored on my wedding night concluded with loath toward the man I was longing to be with. All I could think about was my family and the humiliation my brothers experienced. I could not wait for morning— for light, for acceptance, for true love. I couldn't wait to see my mother, yearning for her warm embrace and comforting presence. *What would I say to my father who told me that Mendy was not right for me? Did I have a second chance?* 'Luda, you should have listened, but he is your husband now. I warned that he wasn't right for you, I told you so:' That's what my father would have said. All these thoughts sent me down a spiral of sporadic sleep.

Silence about the wedding debacle was only the beginning of sprouting resentment between Mendy and me. The adjustment was unbearable. Four weeks would pass until I saw my mother. My brothers never came to visit, rebuked by Mr. Wolfson and his strict terms. His rules were so restrictive that my family preferred I come to them.

"Follow your husband. Serve him as your mother served me," my dad encouraged the first time I saw him since my wedding. These words bound me to comply with rules that confined my freedom and mobility. *Change your ways.*

Part III Life in the Boro

6

Married and Buried

I quit my job at the supermarket and began to work for Mendy's parents alongside him. This was a terrible mistake. It would have been a great buffer to work elsewhere rather than spending days in his family's company, but only time would tell until I realized this.

My days began at 5:00 AM and finished at 10:00 PM. I stocked merchandise, helped at the register, served food, and cleaned refrigerators all day, every day. Spare time was dedicated to the store, the deli, and of course, religious gatherings. Saturdays were spent at the synagogue, hosting lunch, teatime, socializing with Mendy's friends, and connecting with other community members. On Sundays I was left alone while Mendy was tasked with his parents' chores.

There was much beauty in the tight-knit Orthodox community— celebrating rituals together, attending events like bar mitzvahs, weddings, and congregating for holidays among other special occasions. As for me, life in the Boro was taking an unpleasant turn: There was no time for the meaningful conversations, fun adventures, and intimacy that Mendy and I once shared. There was limited time for Mendy and me to voice our gripes. No chance to resolve our conflicts. The Wolfson's demands consumed every minute.

Priorities: To Sacrifice or to Satisfy?

I prioritized the Wolfson family above myself. I aimed to please them and adapt to this new lifestyle. Most important tasks involved cleaning the house, entertaining guests, and dressing properly. The maxi skirts and long sleeves were fine but tucking my thick black hair under a wig induced persistent headaches. I opted for hats instead.

"Buy whatever you need, go to the tailor this afternoon. Dress well, be modest. How you appear is very important, darling," he smirked with a sharp wink. I was dazzled by custom fitted blazers, patterned skirts, and karat gold jewelry. I was walking the streets in 2,000-dollar suit dresses and 900-dollar boots. Looking like the Boro Park princess veiled my baggage of undesirable identities. Image is everything.

Mendy's generosity appealed to me. I had never experienced such wealth before. However, over time, I felt as if his gifts were an attempt to compensate for our lack of time together. I knew that he adored me, yet life seemed superficial and centered on material things and day to day minutia. Customers at the shop shared Boro Park gossip, daily chores, and small talk. Nothing profound. I was bored. Frustrated. Trapped.

I had surrendered myself, my lifestyle, and my family to this new life. Maybe I expected too much. *Where is his sacrifice?* Reality began to sink in, but I'd refuse to sink with it. I needed change. Like I always have, I'd search for options to stay productive and alleviate my pain. I began to devise a plan to free myself from this entangled relationship with Mendy's family— one that left me suffocated by taboos, artificial norms, and tyrannical orders. I could not accept such decrees upon me.

But who can help me? How can I liberate myself?

Financial independence was part of the answer. Without my own money, I'd remain dependent on Mendy and his family, translating to enslavement in my eyes. This reminded me of my mother's fate, which scared me the most. A job outside of the Boro would be my ticket to ensuring my safety, security, and sanity. A ticket to freedom.

Part III Life in the Boro

7

Beyond the Boro

I began searching for job opportunities outside of the Boro, specifically those that allowed me to engage intellectually free from the streams of Orthodoxy. Trailing the streets one morning, I picked up the Jerusalem Post. My eyes caught sight of an ad: Ramaz, an elite private high school is seeking an assistant librarian to catalog books, articles, and periodicals. In addition, the duty would include helping students with homework, research, and other administrative tasks.

I applied immediately and was shortly after invited to Ramaz for an interview by the head librarian, Esther Nussbaum. This was my little secret. I told Mendy that I was spending the day in the city. "Shopping, mostly."

The trip from Boro Park to the Upper East Side was extensive. I'd take the F train to Grand Central and switch to Train number 6 heading to 72 street and Lexington Ave. Then, I walked toward seventy-eighth street between park and Madison Ave. Manhattan's streets were so beautiful, so colorful, so diverse— people, architecture, and nature alike. Entering Ramaz Upper School was like entering some prestigious university. I was impressed by the eclectic architecture that fused new and old: marble floors, chrome finishes on dark wood desks, and semi-carpeted staircases. The community was composed of modern-conservative Jews— some dressed like those in the Boro and others not. The sight of boys and girls studying together put a smile on my face emitting vibrance, hospitality, and warmth.

I was directed to the library on the third floor. Two librarians, Esther and Nancy, asked me about my origins and education. They explained the duties of the job and the schedule. I could not contain my excitement.

"I would love to work at Ramaz and help in any way I can. I hope that I am given the opportunity to serve your community and be part of it," I said sincerely. After a lengthy interview, Esther assured me that she would have a decision by the end of the week.

I exited Ramaz and wandered through the bustling streets of Manhattan, imagining how empowering life could be beyond the Boro's boundaries. After a couple hours of exploring, I decided to go see my parents before heading back to Boro Park. I hopped on the B train to McDonald Avenue. When I arrived at my parent's house, my mother and brothers were home. I expressed my misery and need to obtain independence from his family.

"Please Luda, stay a bit longer, stay for dinner," my mom implored. Mendy would be upset, but I couldn't resist the offer to stay out of the Boro for just a bit longer. I still had to let him know.

"Mendy, I'm staying at my mom's place for dinner, do not worry about me. It would be great if you could pick me up later, but if not, my dad will drop me off when we are finished."

"Where have you been all this time? What are you doing out for so many hours?"

I told him that I would share upon arriving home.

Mendy picked me up later that evening. He apologized for not coming upstairs to see my family because his dad needed him to get back quickly to close the store. We rushed back. The car ride remained quiet for the most part until I broke the silence.

"I applied to a job in the city, I need a life outside of Boro Park."

"Where?! What job!?" He braked hard at the stop light. My head jerked forward. I couldn't lie. I told him everything. He was quiet for the rest of the drive. I suspected that he felt equally relieved, and that perhaps this would be a solution to alleviate pain for all.

Librarian Esther called me on Friday morning: "The position is yours. You can start as early as Monday." A proud smile crept on my lips as I opened the curtains and stared beyond Brooklyn to the Manhattan skyline. I felt as bright as the sun shining upon me, knowing well that I was planting the seeds of my independence.

8

Grappling With Hypocrisy to Demand Authenticity

While I could escape the Boro during my work hours at Ramaz, I was still bound to Mendy and his parents. His family dynamic perplexed me. The hypocrisy and double standards were unsettling. On Shabbat— each Friday night to Saturday evening— turning on any sort of electricity is prohibited. During this sacred time, Mendy would watch TV while he'd command, "Don't do laundry on shabbat, don't cook on shabbat!" Then he'd scoff, "Should I really tell you again?! No electricity on Shabbat!"

"So what?! You can turn on the TV on Shabbat, but I can't do laundry, cook, or turn on the light? How does that make sense?!" I was infuriated! Nothing I did or said was good enough: I was criticized for every inappropriate word, question, or action perceived as controversial and disrespectful in public. As a teenager at home and among my friends, you said what you thought, and you did what you said. No duplicitous rules, no hypocritical acts, and no communication that tarnished authenticity or integrity.

On Boro Park's grounds, the game was played with antics over ethics and image over morality. What pretentious prestige! The deception irked me. These double standards fostered a double betrayal— one by Mendy's family onto me and one by me onto myself. The more I'd accept these deceptions and illusions of morality, the more I'd distance who I was from myself. *Why have I been willing to play along? Is it worth exchanging my well-being for prestige and wealth?* Forces wrestled in my mind until I decided to play the game my way. But my pawn only advanced so far. I had dug a hole so deep that my chances for victory tanked as I tried to find my way out.

With minimal influence on stirring Mendy's attention towards my needs, I realized that my actions were all I had full control over. Conducting myself in a fashion that enabled me to rise from these choppy waters would guide me toward a better future. The Boro would not be my final destination, but rather a passage toward success wherever I'd land outside of it. It was upon me to continue opening doors for myself, forging new connections, and enjoying my days to the fullest.

9

Shanda, Shanda! Shame on You!

Expanding beyond the Boro's boundaries lit up my world with a whole different perspective. I spent most of my days working at Ramaz, reading stimulating articles, forming friendships, and learning much from fellow librarians Esther and Nancy. My life back in the Boro was far more bearable with my new job at Ramaz which kept me engaged and promoted my personal growth.

Mendy's parents seemed skeptical of my new job yet satisfied that Mendy remained loyal to them. He was a perfect son— always dropping everything for their needs and demands. I envied their relationship. Deep down, I hoped that Mendy would be available to me as much as he was to them. My animosity would soon manifest into actions and mark me with a scandalous reputation.

On a cold November night, I finally returned home after a full day of work and my hour-long train ride back from the city. It was 7:00 PM. I planned to grab a small snack from the deli, go upstairs to clean up a bit, and get to bed. Just as I walked inside the store, Mrs. Wolfson picked up a broom and walked toward me.

"Oh, dear! Good thing you're back!" she shrieked, pacing about the aisle with her hands on her head. "I was waiting for you to come and clean the refrigerators! The milk spilled all over the place and Paco left at five! Oy gevalt!"

Yuck! Is she for real? I dreaded the idea of drenching my hands in cold water and sponging up smelly, sour milk. I would have loved to help them with anything but this, especially after a long day of work. There was no way I could agree to this. *Why didn't she ask Mendy or the cashier to help clean?* I had no part in this mess anyway!

"I would love to help you," I replied in my goody-two-shoes voice and a polite smile. "But I'm wondering, why can't this wait until tomorrow morning when Paco is back? I'm so sorry, but I just got back from work and I'm too tired to do anything right now. I want to clean the apartment upstairs and get some rest."

"What do you mean, later? I need you to do it now. How dare you respond to me with such disrespect!" Mrs. Wolfson clenched her teeth.

Just ignore, breathe, let it go. I stepped outside for fresh air and saw Ms. Rachel Susner, a Rabbi's daughter, and Mrs. Blumenstein chatting at the street corner. I greeted them both and was friendly with Rachel. She, like me, was a rebel, and resisted her parents' matchmaking efforts. But Mrs. Blumenstein was her opposite— a traditional Orthodox, Austrian woman who never wavered from the Boro's rules, norms, and traditions. *How are they friends? I have no idea.*

They invited me into their conversation. Mrs. Blumenstein's eyes squinted as she gawked up at my head. I wondered what she was looking at, so I looked all around me for a second, but saw nothing.

"Where did you buy your sheitel (wig)? "The one you are wearing now has a gorgeous style, so shiny and thick!" She remarked, still in deep examination.

Ha! I wasn't even wearing one! By this point, I had become so fed-up that I refused to abide by Orthodox rules both inside and outside the home. The more I played this game of lies and deception, the more I disrespected myself. I hated who I was becoming.

"Thank you so much! It's my real hair!" I replied with a curtsy, twirling the strands around my face.

"Nein, nein! It cannot be!" Mrs. Blumenstein backed away in disbelief.

I stroked my fingers through my hair and gave it a pull to prove my point. "I promise you it's real, would you like to touch it?" I asked coming closer to her. She was stoic, still as a board out of shock. Rachel on the other hand, took me up on the offer. She was on the verge of a laughing attack, as was I.

"Wow, you have amazing hair!" She came close to me and tugged at my hair, "Good for you for not covering it anymore!" We both burst out chuckling. Rachel understood this restrictive, unforgiving culture. Mrs. Blumenstein sighed and gazed left, avoiding eye contact.

"I was having headaches wearing the wigs and hats, I couldn't do it anymore," I confessed.

Mrs. Blumenstein finally moved. She extended her hand over my shoulder, grabbed a chunk of my thick black hair, and yanked on it. "Shanda, Shanda! (shame, shame!)," she exclaimed. "What does Mr. Wolfson say about this!?" I committed a crime!

"Well, what can he say? It's her choice, isn't it?" Rachel turned toward Mrs. Blumenstein, defending me, "Why shanda, shanda?"

"I am going to tell you mother-in-law about this!" Mrs. Blumenstein declared. She shook her head and marched toward the Wolfson Deli. Rachel and I broke out in laughter again, mocking Mrs. Blumenstein as she drifted away.

"Be prepared for the gossip wire tomorrow, but just ignore them." Rachel warned.

"Yep! I don't have a worry in the world! I don't care what the Wolfsons think! I don't care what anyone thinks!" I remarked proudly, "I can't even imagine! This will certainly add some zest to the community drama. Let's get some rest before the storm tomorrow!" *Two strikes against me in one night! What a scandal!*

10

Dare to Dream,
Dignity into the Bloodstream

T he next morning was like any other: Get up, make coffee, and take the train to Ramaz. I went downstairs to grab some pastries from the deli and say goodbye to Mendy for the day. An older woman was chatting with Mendy's mother.

"Shanda, shanda!" She turned to me wide eyed, "You only cause problems around here. We have no peace from you and your dirty tricks!" Then she prompted to Mr. Wolfson, "This is your daughter-in-law! Shame on her!" He began scolding me as I picked up a box of rugelach. *Just tune it out.* Of course, people were upset. *What was I thinking last night? What did I expect? Think before you act, right?* I responded without thinking once again.

"Maybe you are the problem, not me!" I put a five-dollar bill on the counter and hurried out of the store before creating more commotion. *Oh no. What have I done?* There was only more trouble to come.

Upon returning from work that evening, I went straight upstairs to avoid everyone around me. Mendy was reading the Jerusalem Post on the sofa. He lifted his angry eyes and mumbled, "You know, your mom will be here soon." Then he burst, "Oy vey! The milk, the wig, you just cause trouble! I can't believe you!"

I flapped my wrists in dismissal and walked into the bedroom. He got up and followed me in search of a reaction. I wasn't in the mood to argue. Within seconds, the intercom rang. It was Mr. Wolfson.

"Mendy, come downstairs. We need to talk."

I was relieved that Mendy left, but why was my mom here? I suspected that the Wolfsons would gang up on me through my mom. They would often call her to complain about me, and I was never there to defend myself. It was as if I was back in elementary school, when my mother was called to the principal's office over my trouble making. At 21, I was still being treated like a kid!

I was right: Instead of discussing these issues with me or in my presence, the Wolfsons organized a secret meeting with my mom and Mendy. Quite the power play indeed: My mother hates confrontation. She was overly diplomatic and always appeased those who faced her. She had been molded, like other women raised in such confining cultures, to listen to men no matter what. Keep the peace.

I couldn't even think of what she would say to the Wolfsons, just as she played nice with my teachers behind closed doors while in awe of my rebelliousness. I plopped on the sofa and pondered my options: I could sit and wait for the news or go downstairs and disrupt the meeting only to insist that I should be included. Interrupting would create more unneeded commotion. This was not my purpose. It would be better to watch a movie and get my mind off things. I grabbed the remote and turned on the TV, munching anxiously on carrots and cucumbers.

174

Mama Bear: Protect, Defend, and Support

At around 9:45 PM, there was a knock at the door. My mother came in and sat next to me on the sofa. She told me about the meeting. I naively asked what this meeting was about although I already knew. These secret meetings with the Wolfsons were a regular affair, and my mother often told me, "Just zip your big mouth" or "have babies and Mendy will feel closer to you." I already presumed what she would say— a reflection of her old-fashioned paradigms echoing at me which I refused to prescribe to. I'd often challenge her and ask, "How would babies make my life better? Isn't that more of a burden? That would just bind me to Mendy further, wouldn't it?" These blunt and direct conversations with my mom caused rifts in our relationship. All I had to do was follow my principles toward self-respect and plan to regain my freedom. But this time was different— so different!

"I told them that you're not their maid and told them to hire someone to clean! They want you to clean something you didn't spill?! That's ridiculous!" She paused, and I was speechless. "I also told them that the sheitels give you migraines, and that wearing your wig in synagogue is more than enough. Your health is more important, don't worry about those women! This is crazy!"

Did my mother just stand up for me in defiance of these hypocritical rules? Did she just stand up to my husband's parents? My jaw dropped. But wow, I was so proud of her! And so grateful! I wondered what had changed for her to take such a strong stance on my behalf. Perhaps she realized that my destiny would mirror hers if I remained submissive.

"Mom, you are my savior, thank you! I really can't live like this anymore. His dad mixes into our marriage, and his mother always scolds me. His sister-in-law, Gita, always throws daggers at me. I love him but he never stands up for me. His parents are awful! I'm thinking of div—"

Before I could finish my sentence, Mendy barged in charging straight at me. I stuck my arms out and backed into the corner defenseless.

In a calm tone I begged him, "Mendy, please, we need to move from here, your parents are making our life together miserable."

He attacked back with fury. His hands grasped my shoulders, and he began to shake me, and then threw me against the wall. "No! It's you! You are a disgrace!"

Get away from me!" I pushed him and yelled, "You stay here! I'm leaving! You look refined! You look prestigious! But you and your family— look at you! You're a sick man with a sick family! I hate you and I'm sick of you all!"

He pulled me up, yanked my wrists, and thrust me across the room with full force. My mother was weeping in the corner.

"Mendy, Mendy, Mendy, please stop. Please stop," she stuttered, wiping her face. I was wailing too, amplifying my cries to relieve my physical and emotional pain. After minutes of silence filled with heavy breathing, my mom approached the inflamed man on the opposite side of the room.

"How can you treat her like this, Mendy? I love you and I see you as my son." Her palms rested on her head in distress.

"I cannot do this with her and my family. They're always fighting, and I do not know what to do. I trust you Zippy, please, tell her she needs to change."

My mother waddled towards me and planted a gentle kiss on my forehead. "Come on honey, pack your things, we're going home. Sleep with me tonight," she whispered in Juhuri. She turned to a distraught Mendy and switched to Russian. "It's for the best, let her come home tonight."

"No, please," he begged from his knees, "tell her to stay. Will you allow it, Zipa?"

No way! How could he ask for my mother's approval, over mine, to stay the night?! I was right there! I walked to the bedroom briskly and threw some essentials in a suitcase that would last me a few days.

It was already past 11:15 PM. My mom did not drive, so we had to walk home— a twenty block trek. I threw on my long black shrilling coat and headed towards the door where my mom was waiting. Mendy sank into the sofa with his hands over his head. I closed the door behind me gently, drained but with some renewed hope.

"Everything will be ok, don't worry," my mother repeated three times. She linked arms with me, and I clasped my elbow around hers with every ounce of strength left in me. We found serenity in just holding one another, walking silently through the windy dark night knowing that our experiences were shared. Deeply engraved with indelible scars, I felt bruised but stronger with my mother's solidarity. Her support towards accepting separation, and perhaps accepting my ultimate breach of taboo invigorated me: Dreams of divorce painted a far better reality. The serenity silence of night and shining stars relaxed until, over a sudden, an engine roared behind us.

"Zippy, please let Luda come home. I'm so sorry, I lost my temper." It was Mendy shouting from the car window.

"It's ok, my son, we all make mistakes, it is best if you both take a break," she replied compassionately. Fury was brewing inside of me: *Why wasn't he asking me? What about what I think?* He was negotiating with my mother as if I was a piece of property! For our marriage to work, he would need to speak and negotiate with **me**, not anybody else. My decisions were not my parents or up to his. My thoughts could no longer be contained.

"Why are you not apologizing to me? Why are you asking my mother?! No! I am not going back with you. I am done with you and your family treating me like a five-year-old!" I began to rant and couldn't stop.

"Shh! Please please keep it down, people are sleeping," my mother demanded.

I couldn't contain my frustration. "Mendy, go home! We're walking. I am not going back to the house until you and your family treat me with respect. If you love me, we need to get out of Boro Park. These are my terms!" My voice only got louder, and my mom tried to calm me down. She stared at me with her eyebrows raised and shook her head.

"Go home Mendy, Luda needs a bit of a break."

Mendy insisted on driving us home. We agreed only because my mother could hardly make it to the next block. I peered out of the glass as the moon glowed over us. Driving into the night, I sealed my commitment to freedom: Hope for the best and plan for the worst.

Challenging Norms to Break Barriers

After three days of staying at home, my mother convinced me to return to Mendy. He was calling her daily. Yet again, she attempted to help our marriage by encouraging me to have kids with him.

"It will make your marriage better. It will bring Mendy closer to you."

I strongly disagreed, "Mom, for the last time, stop giving me bad advice! Did having kids make your marriage better? Look at you and dad!

Having kids is only a burden!" My anger was full steam, but I regretted lashing out at her. My mother was innocent and knew no better.

"I don't regret having you guys. You are my life and joy. That's all I have in my life, you!" she sniffled. My sympathy was lacking.

"That's the problem, mom! All you have is us. You live for us, not for yourself. Is that what life is about?" I put my foot down. "Mama, don't you understand? We constantly fight and cannot resolve any of our problems. If we add kids to the mix, our problems will multiply. So, every time we have an issue, we need a conference with the parents to discuss our issues? I don't want to be tied to Mendy and his family more than I am now. I don't want to be responsible for raising kids either! No, no, and no!"

My mother always had good intentions and she understood my gripes. However, her advice served her personality and culture, especially in the Boro which affirmed her way of life. The Orthodox and Tat Jewish cultures were similar in some respects. A woman's role is to reproduce and raise children. The purpose of marriage is to build a family, and a family's purpose is to create children and continue the bloodline. This is the Jewish tradition of dor le dor, from generation to generation.

I pondered, *how can I sacrifice my existence, growth, and happiness to serve others?* I was struggling to find the balance to realizing self-fulfillment in a community where family, marriage, and community were privileged. But unlike my mother, I had options and some handle on my free will. I knew better. I knew that just outside of the Boro's borders were vast arenas of freedom: Arenas where hard-working, single women worked alongside men wearing pantsuits. Arenas where women and men could look each other in the eye if unmarried. Arenas where I was free to shape my identity around my experiences— not around some man and his family. Arenas where I could determine my own future and pave my own legacy. I was uncertain as to how I'd create this liberating life for myself, yet confident that I required some personal transformation to do so.

While mired in paradigms that confined women, my parents also prized financial independence, hard work, and persistence. To reconcile the differences, I'd remove the gendered norms around these values to accept and infuse those that promote personal growth. I eliminated others that were inhibiting my development and progress. Determining which values of my past to accept, reject, and change enabled me to discover the principles I'd ultimately live by.

Plan Prescription

Amidst our heated conversation, my mother brought up another barrier to my freedom. "What are people going to say if you don't have children with Mendy? And if you leave him!? What about preserving our family's honor and pride? This would be such a shame! What are you going to do?"

Claiming infertility would tarnish my reputation in the community. An infertile woman is not one of value. By this point, I could care less about what the community would say; the 'infertile woman' label would not bother me. Having kids with Mendy would be far worse, and I was not willing to bear the consequences.

"Is the community making me happy? If not, why should I care what they think? Why should their opinion of me matter more than my own experience?" I reasoned with my mom.

"Honey, you don't understand. Mendy and his family will wonder why you aren't having children," she warned, "this will be a big problem."

"Let them wonder, I don't care. I just need your help. I need you to call your Russian OBGYN and get me birth control pills. You know what I mean, right?"

"But you're not allowed to take contraceptives, how are you going to do it?"

"Don't worry. We just need to have an appointment and get the doctor to prescribe the pills," I assured, "leave the rest up to me."

My mom agreed to facilitate the appointment and put it under her name. If my in-laws ever asked, I'd simply reply, "we're working on it." Yet another little secret.

In a Fight? An Opportunity to Negotiate

Mendy kept calling my mother for me to return. My condition was simple: "I will return if he agrees to move out from his parent's brownstone." It was time to leverage each fight negotiating new terms and conditions. Mendy wouldn't budge.

"My parents really need me to help them in the store. Staying with my parents will help us. It makes my life easier. We also can save money for a bigger house. Besides, I'm the youngest son. If I don't help my parents, who will? They're getting old," he said.

I found this selfish. None of his concerns addressed our issues. But looking back, a primary reason I found Mendy so selfish was because I was overly exhausted and desperate to get out of the Boro. While grappling with the belief that he was giving up on me, it was I who already had. To cope with despair, I'd leverage reversals of power, just as I'd do here. Now it was I who was trying to change Mendy's ways, reframing his beliefs to fit my terms and save our marriage in a way I deemed fit.

"Mendy, come on, it's not always the youngest son's responsibility to take care of their parents. You have the entire family there to help them," I asserted. "And what about us? What about the infighting? How much longer will we continue the bickering? Mendy— every reason you give me is for your family's benefit and yourself. What about me? How would this help me? Our marriage? Tell me why this would be good for us." Resentment rushed through me like lava. It was spewing out. "Mendy. Listen to me! My condition is clear," I raised my voice, "You promise me that we will move out. Then, I'll return. I'll even look for the place. This is what I want! No compromises."

"Ok, ok, we will figure it out." He surrendered although I had little confidence that he would follow through.

"When you make that decision, I will return. I also want you to make that promise and my mother will be a witness."

"Ok. When I pick you up, we can talk with your mother, and we will find a plan to move away." By now, he knew that I was serious.

A couple of hours after our phone call, Mendy came upstairs with a basket of goodies— rugelach, kugel, candy gems, and chocolates. I missed him, however, remained unwilling to compromise. My mother was making chai and preparing a tray of desserts to bring to the living room. Mendy was following her around like a dog.

"You know how she is. She is stubborn, she won't let go," I overheard my mother tell Mendy from the kitchen, "You just need to agree with her to move out and build your life together." She understood Mendy's perspective as she too lived with her in-laws for a few years where there was constant infighting.

"Yes, I know her, she is stubborn like her father," said Mendy, who I could see nodding from the corner of my eye. "I love her, but she drives me crazy. She doesn't understand that my parents are old and need my help. I need to be there for them, but yes, maybe it would be better for everyone if we moved out of the house. Ok. We need to look for a house or an apartment. Where should we go?"

Mendy entered the living room, helping my mother bring out our spread of snacks and tea. She invited him to sit on the sofa next to me. As we began to chat, my anger levels dissipated, and relief streamed through my body. My clenched fists opened, ready to receive Mendy back into my life as he was willing to compromise. Even though we would potentially lose free rent and free food, we would be independent of his controlling parents, sister in-law, and the rest of the community.

For days following Mendy's negotiation, I felt like a queen with a shining crown of victory. But it was all fake: I had only won the argument. We failed to resolve our underlying issues and devise a battle plan to combat conflicts as a unit: Explosions had to happen first. Mendy and I were both young and lacked maturity. We did not know how to manage outside pressures, and more importantly, lacked the skills to manage ourselves. We lacked the skills to express our wants and needs with love and compassion. The blame-game took over.

"It's all YOUR fault! It's all YOUR parents' fault!"

We also played the guessing game, "You should know better. Don't you know what I need? You should know how to treat me better!" Void of respectful and assertive communication, I was stripped of my crown of victory and soon defeated.

11

Escaping Problems Doesn't Fix Them

My suggestion to move to Ocean parkway was well taken. We found a beautiful apartment on Ocean parkway and Avenue M with two bedrooms. The architecture of the neighborhood and community were far more contemporary than the Boro: Modern Orthodox Jews filled the streets and shop names were in English and Hebrew, with minimal Yiddish. Some women even wore pants and short sleeves. Our new flat was also close to the Sephardic community and Kings Highway, a large Israeli community.

I barely spoke with Mendy's parents and tried to avoid them as much as possible until we moved out. We still did not get along. It became apparent to me that perhaps, Mendy regretted submitting to my terms because he felt torn between his parents and me. His anxiety and my agitation led our conversations to blow up. Any negative comment or perceived criticism of his parents flared up into character assassination, verbal attacks, and even physical fights. "Your dad is…Your family is…You are …" would conclude with "I'm done with you. Done! I am going to stay with my parents for a few days. You are unbearable!"

This vicious fight-flight cycle engendered mental and physical abuse that drained our emotions and passion toward each other. Over time, dispassion fostered aversion. This unrelenting power-struggle— competitions for attention and control— eroded the mutual affection we once shared. Love was dying, slowly. Back then, I failed to understand why such remarks caused such heated arguments with violent reactions. I later realized that each unresolved conflict was another layer piled on a shaky foundation waiting to crumble.

It's Never Just One Person

Moving away from Mendy's parents did not improve our situation. We continued to ignore minor issues, which were in fact significant ones. Over the next couple of months, the severity and frequency of our fights exacerbated. They became increasingly physical. When a chain of issues occurred at high intensity and frequency, they turned into major altercations with violent attacks on unresolved past matters: "Remember what you did! You also did.... You always do this!" We fired endless missiles at each other until our tanks were exhausted. Then came silence and stonewalling. It was a constant waiting game for who would relent first and lift the white flag of surrender. When finally on speaking terms again, neither of us broached prior conflicts fearing that one of us would utter a statement to ignite the next cycle. We had normalized dysfunctional behavior. This could not be sustained, however, my emotions conquered me, and I knew no better. Conflicts were dealt with this way in my family growing up, too. It seemed as if most families in this community handled issues similarly. Reversing this fight-flight pattern to build a functional relationship would begin with a functional method to solve problems— something I had yet to discover.

Since we were living closer to my parents' home, and there were no 'terms' upon which my family could visit, I started seeing them more often. The comforting social-emotional outlet relieved me. Divorce became a prevalent topic of conversation. My parents, totally against divorce, used to blame "my big mouth" for every fight. Since I expressed tremendous suffering, it seemed as if my parents realized that I was no longer the cause of our issues. Now, blaming me and my strong character transformed into excuses for a troubled Mendy.

My mom would say, "Just be patient, he will come around, just wait a bit," as my dad claimed, "Mendy is in a difficult situation and his parents are difficult people."

They were both wrong: Mendy may have been in a tough situation, but we were both at fault.

Part III Life in the Boro

12

The Contingency Plan

I reminded myself of the time when I quit my post at the linen shop: I had found a new job first, at Ramaz, and kept others as back-ups. Options to choose from gave me the comfort and freedom I needed. A contingency plan.

Divorce started to seem like a reality within the next couple of years. *How will I survive on a 23,000-dollar salary?* That was barely enough to pay rent and monthly expenses. Before divorcing Mendy (and my financial security) I'd need the means to live on my own first. His family had money, but I had no right to their wealth. My father raised me to never take anything that I did not work for. I'd leave the marriage with what I brought.

In one conversation with my mother, along with librarians Esther and Nancy, I expressed a desire to continue my college education and obtain some technical degree. "If I can find some degree or job to become financially independent that would be ideal, I just do not know what it would be." Details and results were up in the air, but I was certain that with my strong will there would be a way.

Persistently Seek and You Will Eventually Find

I arrived home from work to the phone ringing. Mendy still wasn't back. I grabbed the handle quickly. It was my mom.

"Luda, how are you? I have good news. My friend Galina just got a job with a 35,000-dollar starting salary at City Hanover. This would be perfect for you!"

"What is perfect, mom?" I asked, without a clue of what she was implying.

"Remember my friend Galina? Well, she's been taking computer programming classes at Big Man Five, a six-month program that helps you find a job. You should sign up! It's an expedited track. If Galina got a job, you will too. Programmers are in high demand!" Her voice rang with enthusiasm.

Computer programming? Me? No way. Sitting behind a screen for eight to ten hours a day would be torturous. But dreams of freedom conquered my doubts.

"Ok mom, I'll look into it. Thank you."

The next morning, I spoke with Galina, and then called the school. They had night classes, from 7:00 PM to 10:00 PM. Mendy did not come home before 10:00 PM anyways, so I could keep my whereabouts discrete. I rearranged my schedule to integrate these classes into my routine. In the mornings, I'd be up by 6:00 AM to ride the hour train ride for work at Ramaz in Manhattan. I had an hour break for lunch. At 5:30 PM, I'd rush to the nearest metro station and catch the train back to Brooklyn for class. It was 11:00 PM by the time I dragged my tired legs back home and into bed. *Push through. Short-term pain for long-term gain.*

While a stellar student and a lively networker, coding was no love of mine. It was incredibly isolating for a girl like me with a gregarious personality and unquenched appetite to socialize. I knew that there were no shortcuts to achieving my goal— earning enough money to support myself and build a professional career. I'd make the best out of each day with a smile on my face, exploring how this logical discipline applied to my thought process and personal skills. This helped pique some interest.

To expand my social network, I'd stay after class to connect with new friends and exchange phone numbers. Most of my classmates, teachers, and the school staff were Russian. I befriended one of the owners, Greta, who invited me to come on Sundays for additional practice on the coding modules. I just needed to adapt and remain optimistic in the face of obstacles.

Reflecting upon what I did not like about coding actually helped me learn more not just about coding, but about myself. Knowledge of any sort is always power. Even if you fail to find meaning in the activity itself, you can always gain insight about your likes and dislikes, wants and needs, strengths and weaknesses.

Part III Life in the Boro

13

"Leah's Late Nights:" Gossip Sparks More Fights

All the gossip of "Leah's late nights" angered Mendy. Perhaps giving him a breather to spend with his parents would make him happy. Cool-off periods usually worked, but people were spreading rumors and lies about me. Mendy's picture-perfect portrait was stained. His wife was causing a scandal.

"I cannot deal with hearing people talk about you coming back late at night. It's so disrespectful! What is a married woman doing coming back so late at night anyway? I trust— trusted you! Stop going to school! I can't trust you anymore!"

I rejected his request, "Again, you're asking me to live my life for this community. You're not giving me any independence. These people gossip with empty heads! All they're busy with is collecting garbage on others and spreading it! Now you're using their lies to stop me from going to school?! No, no, and no!" I fired again, "You can close your ears. I will continue going to school whether you, your parents, or these people like it or not. They can find something else to be busy with."

I expected him to be upset, but his pale, sunken face showed deep pain. "Why can't you understand that everything you're doing is hurting my family and my reputation? I told you that you'd have to change your ways, and you haven't been since the start. It's shameful for a married woman to come back late at night without her husband on her side." Mendy wiped his face.

His words brought memories of my dad fighting with my mom over witch-hunt gossipers. My mom often surrendered and accepted my dad's demands, but I would continue standing up for my freedom. I tried to be rational.

"Ok, Mendy. Let's make a deal. You do what you need to do for yourself, and I will do what I need. I cannot be consumed by what people say about me. Those people are irrelevant to my goals. Are they going to come and fix our marriage? Are they helping me or you grow as a person? Obviously not. So, I will not be listening to anything they say!" My hostile tone opened the door to another shouting match. Neither one of us could contain our emotions. Violence erupted. Mendy grabbed an apple from the table and threw it at me— and another, another, and another until the bowl was empty. It was like playing dodge ball against the big and scary boys back in Israel!

"You are just insane! Out of control! You pretend to be such a gentleman, well-mannered, soft spoken, but you're an animal!" My voice intensified with raging anger. I snatched my car keys and bag from the counter, slammed the door behind me and bolted down the stairs to what would be another sleepless night. *Sleeping in my car is better than staying here.*

I contemplated going to my parent's house, but it was after midnight. Mendy would usually leave at 5:30 AM to open the store anyway, so I could go back home then. That would give me a good hour to get ready for work too.

I locked myself in my white Lincoln Town Car parked a few blocks away. As I flattened the seat into a bed position, I broke out in tears. *Tomorrow will be better. Everything will be ok. The nightmare will be over soon.* Talking to myself helped keep light flickering within me during dark moments. Somehow, I eventually fell asleep.

My eyes jolted open at the sound of a truck honking. It was already 5:00 AM. I opened the door to move around and stretch a bit until it was a bit past 5:30. I drove by the apartment building and saw Mendy's car still parked outside. Dunkin Donuts was a few blocks down, so I stopped by and sipped on my cappuccino to kill time. I circled back around twenty minutes later to check if his car was still there. It was not. Safety, finally.

Our unit was all tidied up. Before tumbling into bed for a powernap, I took a warm shower. Negative thoughts spiraled: *People are awful, my marriage is awful, I failed my family, I failed myself— I am nothing.* Any sense of comfort was found in the warm water washing away my tears. My heart felt frozen in this moment of grief, but I knew that self-pity would bog me down. *Think about your future. Keep your head held high. You are worth it.*

I woke up an hour later and boarded the train headed to Ramaz, my eyes hardly open. Students and staff greeted me at the library, the boost of energy I needed. Being surrounded by smiling faces put a smile on mine. The day passed quickly in Esther and Nancy's company who filled hours with stimulating conversations that affirmed my dreams for a better life: A life where people are open-minded, are willing to be challenged, and accept differences to learn from one another.

Time for class. I could no longer think about computer codes after a full day of work at Ramaz, let alone think straight after last night's debacle. *Come on Luda, just a few more hours. Focus.* School had reached its hardest point at that time: Endless technical terminologies were over my head, and I couldn't remember each detail of the computer commands to write programs. Missing a comma or column would cost me the entire code. With much mentorship and practice, I'd become a proficient programmer beyond the computer platform. I'd come to apply such detailed-oriented methods to decode my insecurities and reprogram my paradigms.

Dora ended class early and assigned a task for Monday. I arrived home at around 10:15 PM. Mendy was not home. I found a short note on the kitchen table that read 'I'm going to spend Shabbat with my parents.' A light from the phone was flashing. There were messages. *I'll deal with everything tomorrow.* I took a shower and jumped into bed.

Quantifying the Relationship: The Ratio of Good Days to Bad Days

A clear path towards separation was being paved. After any heated fight, Mendy would either lock me out of the apartment or flee to his parents without resolving the issue. Worst of all, he'd leave me alone on the holidays when I insisted on celebrating with my family. Sometimes, I'd chase him out of fear to be alone; some nights, I'd sleep in my car. This cycle felt like second nature by now: We'd argue, one of us would leave the house for a few days, and then we'd come back pretending like nothing happened. Only until the next time.

Although we had normalized this dysfunctional dynamic, I sensed that our relationship no longer made sense. I began tallying the good days versus the bad ones: We'd fight five out of the seven days a week— about

196

an 80% bad to 20% good ratio! The bad days were also so intense that they lasted for five or more. I needed to reverse the odds to have at least five good days and accept two to three bad days.

The better measure would be a monthly one. Twenty-five good days and with five to ten bad days seemed ideal. I expected to reduce the intensity of our fights over time, limited to verbal exchanges or disagreements. Physical altercations, throwing things, and destroying the house were unacceptable.

Evaluating the ratio of good days to bad days would become my measuring stick to quantify the quality of relationships. Such an evaluation evolved from integrating computer programming, commands, and structures into an understanding of myself and interactions with others. This mental measuring stick would later develop into a method I created called the IIIIF Model. It is based on an algorithm that assesses the severity and frequency of adverse situations in a relationship with the acronym standing for each pillar being evaluated: Intent, Intimacy, Injury, Impact, and Frequency.

Our fights only became more severe and more frequent. However, the divorce decision would require me to try and eliminate every possible solution to saving our marriage. I needed to know that I gave 110% to restitch our relationship. *Think before you act, so you have no regrets*. I suggested that we seek couples counseling to resolve our issues because for some odd reason, I still wanted things between us to work out. Perhaps it was because he was my first love, and I thought that I was his too.

"You're the one who needs help! You just need to do what I tell you!" Mendy refused adamantly. His resistance perpetuated our arguments and led me to throw "divorce" around casually. More fuel to the fire.

"You'll never leave me! Your parents will never let you!" He shouted.

I attacked back: "Your days are numbered, Mr. Wolfson! You married me, not your parents! For the last time, let's go see Mrs. Pinsky, she can help us fix this! Obviously, if you don't want to, you don't want me. You're always leaving me to go stay with your parents anyway! And for the last time, if you ever leave me on the holidays again, I will shame you!"

Lava was spewing out of me— again— sizzling anger out of control. Mendy leaped across the room, clenched my shoulders, and began shaking me. He wouldn't let go. I wrestled away from him. He was stronger. I kicked him as hard as I could. Game over. Before I knew it, he grabbed my waist, lifted me up, and threw me down on the couch. Ouch! I let out a scream. I recovered laying there curled up in a ball crying hysterically. Powerless. Hopeless.

Mendy left. I rushed to the bathroom with tears still streaming down my face. I bowed into the sink; my eyes fixated on the droplets of my marriage draining into despair. *Why have I tolerated this abuse for so long? Who am I? What am I living for?* I pulled away and looked at the mirror, staring at the shattered woman in agony. I hardly recognized myself: weak, humiliated, miserable. *What am I missing? I'm pretty, I'm smart, I'm friendly... why am I going through life this way?*

Until now, everyone— from my family to Mendy's— had tried to give me advice. *No one understands me.* My type-A personality and obstinate character made living in this community even more of a struggle. The wild horse had become a domesticated mare— a slave—

tamed under suffocating rules and norms. My own shame was trapping me, draining me, and killing me slowly. *I'll be stuck forever if I don't change things.* This scared me more than anything. And indeed, nothing changes if you change nothing.

I'd take matters into my own hands to regain every thread of dignity shed over the past three years. In my favorite philosopher, Joan Didion's essay, 'On Self-Respect,' she writes, "Character— the willingness to accept responsibility for one's own life, is the source from which self-respect springs." [7] Responsibility for my own life would mandate a paradigm shift into a thought-process that weighed options by their worst outcomes. *Ending up alone?* Not too bad. I would not drown in this toxic whirlpool of dysfunction and despair.

Liberating oneself from the expectations of others is integral to self-restoration. To glue the pieces of the shattered woman in the mirror back together, I had to revisit my true self— my values and principles. I realized that while my principles had stuck with me, my identity was lost in the storm. *Who am I? A Tat Jew, an Israeli, or an Orthodox Jew?* From this point on, I was committed to discovering tools for growth through self-awareness. Foreseeable challenges lay ahead, but everything worth having comes at a cost. My freedom, my identity, and my integrity were worth any price.

Reprogramming My Life:
Output Depends on Your Input

The programming certification exam was in two weeks. "You will be given six hours to complete it. You will be assigned to a computer

---

[7] Extracted from the following source: Didion, Joan. 1961. On Self-Respect.

program that calculates some scenarios based on various situations. You must produce a report to reflect the numbers accurately. It should include paging logic," Mrs. Dora announced to the class.

During a group study session that evening, my computer code logic output indicated repeated errors. The nested commands, if not properly sequenced, would display deadlock results. My fingers banged on the keyboard in frustration. *How come others got their output without errors? Why can't I?* The if-else commands were easy, but when the program required multiple if and else conditions, I was lost. It was too complicated. Too complex. I felt incompetent and discouraged. *Maybe it's because I don't have a college degree. Everyone else here is smarter than me.* Most of the students were Russian academics with PhDs. Wearing hats and long dresses, I felt like a buoy in a sea of intellectuals in suits.

"I'm going to fail. This is too hard. Why can't I get it?"

"Luda, practice makes perfect. Focus on your goals." Mrs. Dora stopped my ranting to help me refocus, "You're almost there. Let me look at your work and on Sunday I will help guide you." Her warm smile filled me with hope.

On Sunday, Mrs. Dora looked at my code: "See here, you have the same repeated errors. So, to debug your errors, you must fix one command at the time. If you try to fix all the errors at once, you won't isolate the infected code."

"Right. Thank you." I nodded my head, frazzled. I couldn't even think about the code. Her advice hit a nerve; it reflected my relationship. We had too many issues and it would be impossible to fix all of them at once. Isolate the infection and eliminate it. One error at a time.

Mrs. Dora adjusted her dainty glasses and puckered her dry lips in search of words to say. She could tell that I was missing something.

"Luda, look. You must understand that it's just like in life, when you miss a comma or a period— a small detail— it can mess up your entire program. The computer is not forgiving when you make a mistake, but you have tools to debug and fix your errors. Just be patient. It's a process for problem solving."

Beyond the technical tools of computer programming, Mrs. Dora was equipping me with life skills to understand the task at hand and gears of my psychology. The analogy between computer science and real life simplified the process for me: Examine your errors, isolate them, reprogram, test, and check your output. If incorrect, debug the code, and test it until it's accurate. This paradigm was new to me, evident as Eastern European Russians like Mrs. Dora held wildly different mindsets than people from Southern Russia, and of course, the antithesis of those in Orthodox communities. Then something clicked: I would live life as if there was no tomorrow. I would live life for me. This was my new code, and I had to debug the flaws in my paradigms to actualize a better life. In this frame, the individual is the highest priority while the latter focuses on prioritizing the community even if that means leaving infections unattended. To meaningfully contribute to any community, I had to be fulfilled with myself first.

Mrs. Dora interrupted my wandering mind. "I have a few good jobs for you. They are looking for intermediate level programmers with starting salaries between 32,000 to 36,000 dollars. Once you pass the certification exam, we will prepare your resume, and do some practice interview questions."

"B-b-but I don't have experience yet," my jaw dropped, "What am

I going to do if I get stuck?"

"You are ready!" She encouraged, "We are here to help once you get the job! Remember, one error at a time, and we will be here to help you solve and learn from each one."

Every day after work, I would go to school and spend hours on programming, testing, and debugging until I eliminated every error in my code. My personal transformation process would soon mimic this discipline. While there is no computer program to highlight our errors in life, there are clues revealed to us. Undesired outcomes and negative feelings were the signals I had erred, indicating disparities and conflictive beliefs between me and the world outside. Such errors would trigger self-examination, or debugging, to reprogram my beliefs and test them until I achieved desired outcomes toward progress.

I finally obtained my computer programming certification, and after a lengthy interview process, my position at Long Island Savings Bank was secure. I'd be making an annual salary of 33,000 dollars. With this flow of income, paying for rent, insurance, gas, and food among other expenses would be easy! My enthusiasm to start this new, busy, and independent life could not be contained, however, I was anxious with minimal proficiency as a coder.

The first six months on the job were nerve-wracking. *What if they fire me? What if I miss the deadline? What if they realize that I'm not good enough?* Imposter syndrome throttled my dedication to work hard, constantly improve, and build credibility. Days between work and study felt endless but knowing that supporting myself would forge a path of freedom instilled unrelenting motivation.

On weekdays, I'd arrive at the office as early as 7:00 AM and leave around 7:00 PM. After work, I'd rush to meet with one of the senior programmers to help me complete my work projects; Mrs. Dora and Dr. Gregor had assigned programmers to help beginners like me. It was about 10:00 PM by the time I'd get home, or even later. Mendy and I had very little time to interact. He was free to spend as much time on his family affairs with no demands from me. There was nothing I asked of him so long as I had the freedom to work and see my family.

14

Seek Support but Seek No Approval

D ivorce was inching closer. Although my initial salary was modest relative to the lavish life and material extravaganza afforded by the Wolfsons, there was no price for freedom, liberty, and self-respect. I was ready to make my final move, but to gain confidence in my final decision, I had to ensure that an annual income of 33,000 dollars was sustainable. I plugged every expense into a simple table with low and high ranges for rent, car insurance, gas, food, dining, clothes, gifts, and accessories among other things. Then I thought about my move-out: *How much do I need for starting rent? How much to set up my new place?* An additional 5,000-dollars minimum. Thankfully, my calculations sufficiently covered the new lifestyle I was plunging into. All I needed was six months to stabilize my job and save up a bit.

I decided that sharing the good, bad, and ugly news to my parents all at once would prepare them for my exit plan. If Mendy still refused to seek outside help, I was done. He had six months as his last chance.

Breaking News: The Good, the Bad, and the Ugly

Small talk and all good things: The prelude to difficult conversations. I sought to infuse confidence in my parents about my independence and financial stability prior to breaking the bad news.

"Mazal Tov! Bless God!" My dad congratulated me.

"Let's go celebrate. We are so proud of you," my mother rejoiced and pulled me into her arms. Lifted spirits were my green light to change the subject.

"Um…I also have some other news for you. You— you may not really approve of it… but you know that my marriage is in shambles…" I paused thinking of what to say next. *Prepare for a lecture about divorce.* I armed-up with counter arguments. "I know I will be undesired for a decent man. I know I will be treated as second-good merchandise. And I may even end up alone for the rest of my life…b-but I have a job and I can support myself. I will be OK alone. And if I can't find a decent man, I will be OK on my own!" Word vomit. I couldn't stop venting. My eyes swelled. My face heated. "I will not be stuck in this abusive marriage. I can't live in these artificial norms, taboos, traditions, and boundaries. Whatever you want to call it…I don't care. This will not be my life!" I broke out in tears.

"Luda, do what is best for you. It has been over three years. You are like cats and dogs who fight non-stop. You need some counseling—" Before my mother could finish her sentence, my dad interrupted, "You need to finish this drama one way or another. They are mean people. I told you that nothing good would come out of this."

What? Did my parents just say that they'd accept my divorce? For the first time, they didn't blame me for the failed marriage, accusing me with, 'it's your fault…it's your big mouth…just do what he says.' This was the first time that they didn't pity Mendy's troubled situation. Now, they shifted to directing me toward taking responsibility over my life, exhausted by the constant drama over the past three years. Although my parents were truly worried about my status and uncertain future, the "I told you that nothing good will come out of this" meant 'I know that it might get ugly and nasty.'

There was no one to blame, no one to shame, and there would be no more dirty games. The frame would shift from **you** to **I** as I spread my wings beyond the Boro's boundaries. Knowing that I did my best with what I could at the time freed me from feelings of guilt and shame. Knowing that I tried every possibility or solution comforted me and encouraged me to move forward despite some discomfort with my diminishing status. It was the final chance before the point of no return: *Would Mendy try counseling? Doubt it.* A man in need of emotional help, a man desperate for a remedy to rescue his sinking relationship— absurd! The burden of a weak image overpowered necessity.

15

Holiday Season

Fall came around. It was the Jewish New Year, Rosh Hashanah, marking the High Holiday season. I barely attended Shabbat dinners and special occasions in efforts to avoid Mendy's family and the community. On the rare occasions that I did attend, there were always criticisms contrived about me. Everything I did guaranteed a smack in the face no matter how hard I tried. My in-laws would constantly flaunt Mendy's brother's wife, Gita, in front of me: "You see, she works so hard! She cooks, cleans, she takes care of the kids! Look at how well dressed she is and how beautiful her boys are!"

I'd glare at Mrs. Wolfson in contempt of these preposterous comparisons. Their disrespect discouraged me from trying to please them anymore. Now, more than ever, I was ready to throw their disrespect towards me right back at them.

It was Sunday morning. Mendy and I were munching on toasted bagels and lox. "What are we doing for Rosh Hashanah? It's next week."

I asked, curious about his plans.

"I'm going to my parent's place. They are organizing a dinner with some friends after services. Why don't you join me?" He responded with a shrug.

"Thank you, but I'd prefer to go to my family or stay home. I haven't celebrated the holidays with them in a long time. We always go to your parents, and every time I go, there's something that I do wrong. I do not want to put myself in that situation. It's not good for our relationship." I wiped the cream cheese around my mouth, and asked casually, "What are you doing today? Do you want to spend time together?" I hoped he would say yes so that we could have a constructive conversation about our steps as a couple moving forward.

"No, I can't. My parents need me to go to the wholesaler to pick up merchandise for the deli. You know, my dad is getting old, and he can't carry heavy stuff anymore." There were no big incentives for him to change his routine. His parents were a priority. No time for me.

"Alright then. I'll go shopping for the holidays. Do you need anything?" I offered gently, masking my disappointment. I wanted his attention. I liked him. But his priorities were clear. *Don't push it. Just focus on you.* So, I got ready: I pulled on a pair of tight black jeans topped by a white collared shirt underneath a black V-neck sweater.

"You look good. Just don't walk into Boro Park like that. If you plan to shop there, please change your clothes into something appropriate." Mendy looked me up and down. I rolled my eyes, bit my tongue, and said nothing. My priorities were clear too.

The dawn of the Jewish new year calls for several symbolic rituals: For instance, it is traditional to wear white and buy new clothes to represent purity. Gift-giving blesses one with sweetness and prosperity. If not with family, many youngsters in the Boro make fun day outings out of Rosh Hashanah shopping. I had no friends besides Ziona, who had left for Israel; since Sunday is a working day in the Boro, my parents were busy. I'd go myself— I was used to it by now. I shopped all day long.

Around this time of year, and especially after Shabbat, Boro Park was jam-packed with double-parked cars all along 13th avenue. Families were restocking for the week and preparing for the high holidays. Women were shopping for dresses, shoes, hats, wigs, Judaic artifacts, and food. Men were racing the streets buying suits, shtreimels, shoes, and prayer books.

I stopped by my parent's place that evening. My mother's famous mejadra and meat stew permeated the home— great timing on my part! She was glowing with a holiday smile.

"Oh! Luda, so good to see you! What are you doing for the new year?"

"Uh— I think I am going to come here. Here, to your house," I tried to replicate her happy expression.

"Well, what about Mendy? Is he coming?" She asked, concerned.

"He wants to celebrate with his parents and wants me to go with him. You know how it goes…"

My mom interrupted, "Go to his family. Just go, don't make a big deal out of it." Her line of conversation was predictable: Go with your husband. Do not cause any conflicts, you will be fine, and so on and so forth. The last thing I wanted was to get into this discussion. I kept my mouth shut and refrained from making any definitive decisions.

We finished up dinner and concluded our discussion over doing the dishes. I grabbed my bag and headed back home at around 9:00 PM. Mendy still wasn't home. I put the gifts in the closet and placed their matching cards aside so I could write them before the holiday. After a warm shower, my tired body crawled into bed. I was out like a light.

I woke up feeling Mendy's body puzzled into mine. He wanted to cuddle. I peeked at the big clock on the wall: 5:45 AM. Late for me. I pulled away gently, trying not to wake him, and tiptoed around the closet to get dressed. *Why is he still in bed?* He was usually at the store before 6:00.

"When are you coming back? Tonight?" His raspy voice caught me just before exiting the apartment.

"Why does it matter?"

"Just wondering. Nothing special," he replied yawning, and turned to his side. I hoped that he would ask to spend time with me. Of course, he didn't. I swung my purse over my shoulder and headed to work.

I arrived home anxious to know what we were doing for the holidays. Ignoring issues was our forte: Avoid the elephant in the room and pretend that nothing's wrong. Sometimes, ignorance was bliss because the alternative— a big and ugly fight— was worse. But I had to ask. Tomorrow was the big day, and we had no cemented plans. *Just stay calm.*

"Mendy, what are we doing tomorrow?" I brought up casually.

"If you want to come over to my parent's place, you are welcome to. My sister, brother, and their families will be there for sure. It's up to you. Do whatever you want." He seemed completely indifferent.

"Are we a family or not? What is the sense of staying together? Who are you married to— your parents?!" My barrage of questions turned into uncontainable rants. Emotions, once again, took over. I failed to stay calm. I defeated my purpose.

"It is your choice. You can come with me, or you can stay here or go to your mother," Mendy kept repeating. I was fuming.

"If you leave me for the holidays ever again! I'm warning you, it won't be pretty! I am done with you and your parents and your stupid priorities!" My anger burned through the roof with each of his nonchalant responses. Mendy walked into the bedroom and pulled a suitcase out of the closet. He started packing.

"I'm going to my parents now and will stay there for the holidays. You do you, and I'll do what's good for me. You will never leave me. You cannot do anything. All you do is be angry!" He grabbed his suitcase aggressively and slammed the door behind him.

No tears were left to cry. My pain was transforming into an urge for revenge. *I'll teach him a lesson. I'll teach them all! Let's get even.* While well warned, Mr. Mendy Wolfson had no idea what awaited him.

Embattled, Emboldened, and Emancipated

Happy new year. I was supposed to wear all white that night. *Ha!* I slid into my tightest black jeans and pulled on a low-cut black top. Black booted heels to go along. I aggressively pressed on the gas and my engine roared as I drove raging with my windows open into the Boro...

My unlawful presence at the back of the hall had not yet been noticed. Each person in that room was entranced in celestial harmony. There wasn't even an inch to move, but people were still bowing and rocking to chants of Avinu Malkenu, a melodic prayer that recognizes God as king of the universe with blessings for love, compassion, and longevity. The aura of holiness was disrupted as I barged into the men's section of the synagogue wearing my all-black scandalous skinny jeans and a V-neck looking for Mendy. He was lost in a sea of shtreimels, black hats, and prayer shawls. I tapped one of the men on the shoulder.

He turned to me and whispered aggressively, "You can't be here! What are you doing here?! Get out of here!" His eyes fixated down at my lower body. He abruptly turned away, then back around again. Of course, he couldn't help but gawk at the obscenity before him!

I got closer and shouted into his ear, "I am Mendy Wolfson's wife and I need you to find him for me now!"

"Oy vey! Something happened?" He jumped backward and his sacred siddur (prayer book) fell out of his hands and onto the floor. What a sin! People were staring. He picked it up and kissed it. God would forgive him.

"Yes, something bad happened. Go call Mendy," I told him firmly. He weaved through the loud crowd towards the bimah.

I waited outside, across the street by the Wolfson deli. Mendy came out of the synagogue breathing heavily. I waved with a sarcastic smile.

"Are you MAD?!?" he yelled and marched toward me.

"Yes, I'm mad! That's what you get for leaving me alone again! This is the end!" I pointed at him aggressively, marched toward my car, and drove away. The exhaust fumed with steam as if I had huffed and puffed every ounce of anger into it. I peered out the window to observe the mess I made. People exiting services had seen the whole thing unravel— from my scandalous entrance to shaming Mendy at his family's corner brownstone. They witnessed the scandal that would fill tomorrow's newspapers and one that would leave enough gossip for months to come. How dare she enter the men's section of the synagogue in jeans? How dare she drive on the holidays? Was that really Mr. Wolfson's wife? She's crazy!

The infamous drive out of the Boro that night marked my point of no return. At twenty-three and four years of this toxic relationship later, I'd had enough. It was a new year— a signal toward new beginnings and forgiveness toward me, Mendy, and his family. This relationship brought out the worst in me, so it was my duty to cut off the destruction it spewed. It was in everyone's best interest for me to end things once and for all.

My blasphemous Rosh Hashanah revenge affair actually made me feel bad. I wondered why. *Didn't I achieve my goal to hurt them as they were hurting me?* Maybe in the moment I felt powerful with leverage over Mendy's image. However, reflecting on what had transpired made me realize that all I wanted was my husband's attention, respect, and admiration. I wanted him to want to spend time with me. I wanted him to attend to my needs as he did to his parents. *Where was reason in all of this? Where was my ethical character? Where was my commitment to purpose? And love?* Collateral damage. A heart-broken girl who achieved nothing. Everything I believed in had vanished in that moment. A shattered woman indeed.

Mendy stayed with his parents even after the holidays concluded. Over the following weeks I called him frequently, but he didn't respond. The end was near.

I decided to give him one last chance. I wrote him a long and unapologetic letter that concluded with a simple if-else condition:

If you want to save the marriage, then we shall seek help; else, I am moving out by the end of this month and filing for divorce.

~ Luda

No response from Mendy. None. The message was clear.

16

Moving Out: Ask for Help!

"om, I need your help. Ask your boss if he knows anyone who has an apartment for rent."

"Are you sure this is the end?"

"Yes, it's time to get out of here. I'm ready."

"Ok." My mother assured me that Violetta, her Greek next-door neighbor, was renting-out her apartment. "Come and see her place, I'm sure she would love to give you a tour."

The building was small, and so was my unit. 550 square-feet including a bedroom, a bathroom, a kitchenette, a round table and four chairs. That's all I needed.

"When can I move in?" I asked Violetta.

"Next Sunday, will that work for you? I will send you the lease so you can sign it. We also need a 1,400-dollar deposit and one month's rent one month in advance."

It was a good deal. The apartment was newly renovated. All that was missing were final furnishings, electronics, some linens, and bath accessories. I shopped for my new place every day after work. On Friday,

I packed my stuff in preparation for Sunday's move. A month had passed with no response from Mendy, and I had no choice but to break the news. He didn't pick up. I left him a message: "Hi, Mendy. On Sunday, I am moving out. You can come back to the apartment. It's all yours."

That Sunday morning, my brothers rented a truck to help load everything up. My sister, Marina came along too. There was not much to move, but it was nice to have my siblings' support. On the short, rickety drives back and forth, I had sporadic thoughts about my marriage. *Is there anything more I could have done? Is this really the right choice?* No turning back now. No regrets.

At around 10:30 AM, Mendy finally walked into the Ocean Parkway apartment after a month of zero communication between us. I passed the final box to my sister and turned abruptly.

"Hi, are you ok?" I hesitated, barely looking at him.

"Yes, I am fine, I will contact you to proceed with the Get (Jewish divorce papers)." He was pacing around the unit without a word about me or our marriage. I feared an unpredictable reaction but felt safe since my brothers and sister were with me.

"Here are the keys. Take care, Mendy." I placed them on the kitchen table and walked toward the door, like shackles around my wrists released.

"Don't let the door hit you on the way out," he said stoically. Just as I was about to reply, my sister put her hand on my elbow.

"Let's go. Ignore him. It's not worth it. It's a closed chapter now," she said. As she pulled me out the door, I turned my head back. I glared at him.

"You'll be back," Mendy smirked. Those were his exact last words to me, and I will never forget them.

PART • IV

Out of the Boro

A Transition Period

1

Know Thyself to Love Thyself

It was my first time living alone. From Dagestan and Israel to the Boro, I had always been surrounded by people. I reminisced about overcoming that hunch of isolation in my transition to America, and I could do it again. But this time was different: Love was a part of the equation. Love came and left. I felt love's package of cozy comfort and belonging once, and after it left, I felt more alone in my marriage than ever before— a stranger to the world I was living in and a stranger to love. A stranger to myself. Maybe living alone would give me the opportunity to make a new friend: Me. Perhaps I'd feel less alone than before.

I wasn't all alone. I had the pleasant view of a public high school overlooking a diverse crowd of teenagers— White, Black, Chinese, Jewish— together and lively. My new apartment was only three houses away from my parent's. Fragments of love that had dispersed coalesced with each of my family members' support. Marina helped me unpack my clothes, and my brothers built a custom black lacquer queen bed for me.

Over the moving days, I saw each moving piece coming into my apartment as pieces of a new life merging for the better. So I wasn't alone. However, there was something missing. Some void. I still felt lonely.

During my marriage, I had become entirely dependent on Mendy's circle. I failed to keep in contact with my old friends, most importantly Ziona, someone who always had my back no matter what. This was a grave mistake. Now, I had no one to confide in besides my brothers, sister, and parents. Although they loved me, accepted my divorce, and supported me through it, my stained status brought shame upon them.

Separated and no longer a virgin: Second-hand merchandise. In my culture, any divorced woman was impure, scarred and disowned by a man. "Decent men don't fall for second-hand women," my father would say. His belief system conflicted with my goals in this new world: *Who will want me? Where will my identity place me? Who do I want to be?* Who I wanted to be is what I needed to discover. Forging ahead was my only solution. I'd never think twice about going back to Mendy even with the prospect of never marrying again. Never.

Loving and being loved are innate human needs. To fulfill these needs, a person must start with oneself. I was distressed by my past relationship, but still had an urge to spread my love in the future. However, for me to give love, I'd need to learn to love myself first. Self-love comes with self-acceptance, and self-acceptance comes with forgiveness. I had to forgive myself by understanding the impact of my behavior on myself and others. I had to get to know me first. *How would I know that I don't know myself? What are the signals that indicate lack of self-knowledge?* It was just like the errors in my computer programs— failed attempts, unexpected outcomes, inaccurate reports, negative feelings, and deceptive details. All these signs demanded a self-examination of values, paradigms, and beliefs.

A riptide of negative feelings was pulling me further and further away from my goals. I was in an internal battle with myself. This battle was not so much about lacking motivation or knowledge about **what** to do next, but the absence of tools as to **how** to forge ahead. That affirmation got me back on track. This was my first indicator that I'd have to investigate my own behaviors, and emotions in different situations.

Emotions aside, I was doing well with a stable job, a roof over my head, food on the table, and my family just doors down. I enjoyed my time at work and kept my days full, chatting with colleagues during breaks or after our shifts. All that was missing was my identity— probably the most important thing. Reshaping it would require an array of social outlets. Hence, the commitment to 'know thyself' through others and my experiences, where I'd analyze the beliefs driving my reactions, likes, and dislikes. This would ally me closer to my values and help me manage situations based on fresh paradigms. Mastering myself was key to moving forward and liberating myself toward not only full independence, but confidence. And confidence, indeed, is the currency of freedom.

PART IV Out of the Boro

2

The Jewel on My Crown

A t Long Island Savings Bank, I befriended a special girl named Jewel. She was the administrative assistant to the CEO. We connected like magnets— polar opposites attracting to a degree of inseparable, everlasting friendship. Her mindset and lifestyle were the antitheses of mine, a target at the traditional tenets ingrained in me. While initially baffled by her beliefs, the confidence she carried inspired me to transform my philosophies.

Jewel is that one friend with an effervescent, electric spark of positivity. She transmits it by osmosis. Petite and slender with sleek blond hair, she'd scurry around the bank jumping on task after task with a smile. She never hesitated to confront men working alongside her. She never hesitated when choosing to reveal parts of herself to others.

A few months after meeting her, I noticed her belly bulging little by little each day. "What's up with your stomach? Too many Reese's Pieces?" I joked.

"Don't be silly," she laughed, "a little Jewel is on the way!" She began talking about her family. I was shocked to learn that Jewel was pregnant but never married. Her boyfriend, who she had dated for a few years, broke up with her. Now, she was on to the next. "I slept with both of them, and honestly, I don't even know who the baby belongs to!"

This blew my mind. Through Jewel, I saw that there was a different world out there— that I could transform my beliefs and become anyone I wanted. Self-acceptance and self-liberation are ingredients to reigning one's life with confidence. Over the past several years, I had been wearing a crown of duty to please others or in tribute to tradition. Directing my life toward my true throne would involve throwing this crown away.

"Wake up missy! You're gorgeous! Why do you need a man to have kids? We aren't living in the 16th century!" Jewel would say. Her words shook me to my core. She made me realize that the source of my shock was rooted in envy. I envied her free spirit and how she held her head high regardless of others' opinions about her. Rather than taking offense to perceived derogatory comments, she defended her crown with pride in her being. Jewel inspired me to do the same: To spark an internal revolution to gain confidence within.

Embrace and Appreciate Differences Confidently

As we grew closer, Jewel became my confidant. On our lunch breaks, we would run to the nearest vending machine, praying that Reese's Pieces Peanut Butter Cups were still up for grabs. With our coffees in hand from the café across the street, we settled at the outside tables and dipped our cherished chocolates into creamy liquid gold. (Coffee and chocolate are still half of my diet!). Over our guilty pleasure, we'd converse about our relationships and how they've driven us through

226

life. I gave her an insight into my heritage so she could understand the inner conflict I was wrestling with.

"You only need to find one guy to share your life with, one man to make you happy. Who cares what other people think, he will be your man, no one else's," Jewel assured me, "There is a sea of men out there, and if you create ample opportunities, you'll find one."

My friendship with Jewel opened new horizons. She introduced me to her boyfriend and his team from LISB. While Long Island housed a large Jewish population, Jewel's circle included mostly Catholics, Italians, and Irish. We all shared a love for basketball, and before I knew it, I was shooting hoops with new friends a couple of times a week after work. Afterward, she'd would invite us to her house for the best recovery meal— homemade pasta, pizza, and salad— paired with beer for the guys, of course. We'd sit butt-to-butt on the couch and talk about life as it was, plain and simple. No masking our struggles, no concern for image, no blaming, no shaming. We'd crack jokes about each other; all her friends would ridicule my accent, meanwhile genuinely curious about me. Through sharing my story with them, I learned to find beauty in the range of cultures I've lived in. This was certainly a different crowd than I was used to. I loved anything different.

Jewel came up to my desk on a Monday morning following a fun night her place. "Hey Missy! We were talking about you last night! Roger is all over you, and he can't wait to see you. Can't you take a hint?!"

"Jewel!" I threw my pen aside with a smile, "For the millionth time, I'm not ready to date until I'm, I guess, stable? I just need to get myself in order. Plus, I'm not a virgin anymore. No 'decent' man will marry me anyway."

"Oh, stop it! Common, give it a try!" she flapped her skinny wrist against my shoulder, "You live for you. Never compromise yourself! Never compromise yourself for some norms. Own your sh*t, missy!"

I was still trapped in my old-fashioned bubble. Jewel would give me the strength to poke it, and eventually pop it. I took her advice to heart because she was a living example of it. If she was not, my instinct would let her words go through one ear and out the other. While struggling as to how I'd apply her advice, I began with an easy change— beginning to wear elegant short skirts that revealed my pair of lean muscular legs. Not football player legs. *They are mine, and they are beautiful.* This was the first time in years that I dressed to suit my physique as I deemed fit. Dress to please yourself, no one else.

The impacts of coloring myself with this foreign fashion of freedom sparked some mental changes. My disposition and body language translated into my personality. I began to express my thoughts freely, delving deep into my curiosities and questioning everything as I had done before. Jewel was right. Once I returned to aligning my values with my actions, people became attracted to me! And I wasn't even trying to be noticed! Imagine if I did...

When Priorities Shift, Friendships Need Not Drift

I found a routine that kept me busy and fulfilled during the week. I was working, meeting new people, and playing ball with tons of guys. My fresh, flirtatious attitude renewed my self-esteem, pushing me to crawl out of my cocoon a little bit more each day. On weekends, I devoted time to my family, whether it was having Shabbat dinner or shopping with my mom. I'd go out with my brothers in the evenings and sometimes, Jewel would tag along. She became a part of our clan. A sister to me.

Our dynamic changed when Jewel gave birth to a beautiful baby girl. We couldn't go out as much, but we found pockets of time to spend together. When she needed space or family time, I'd go back to my apartment. Although motherhood became Jewel's priority, our connection was maintained through strong through phone calls and stopping by her place after work. We'd keep in touch no matter the distance.

We all need Jewels in our lives— people who provide a balance of unconditional support and room to breathe when needed. Jewel blessed this shaky period of my life by embracing me for who I was, recognizing my struggles, and encouraging me to shift my mindset to emerge stronger from them. Her motto, "Never compromise yourself," became mine, which would evolve into 'own your story with pride and confidence.' It only takes one person, a few words, or a single event to startle a realization and start a revolution. Jewelster, I thank you for starting mine.

PART IV Out of the Boro

3

Loosen Up and Learn from Lazuli

My mother had connected me with a few of her friends to ease my transition into living alone. She worked at a small grocery store nestled in a community of Syrian and Moroccan Jews. Lazuli, a young Moroccan girl, was a routine customer. We hit it off after a brief introduction over coffee. We began to tour New York City's hottest spots, where she'd enter each as if she was a model with her confident strut. Her lanky legs carried her gyrating hips from side to side with every step— and oh, that smile never dimmed! There was something asymmetrical about her face. Her dark features and light skin made it even more noticeable. She wasn't very pretty, but in her head, Lazuli was that model which she walked like, and it showed: Confidence. A catch indeed. Gregarious, authentic, and profound, Lazuli's company was exactly the remedy I needed.

Listening to Lazuli's fresh perspectives on love and life rejuvenated me. I confided in her with my story just as she did with hers. At 36, she was still single and looking for someone to date. She reserved some relationships for sex only. While Lazuli kept her promiscuous side on the down-low, like Jewel, she shared every element of herself with pride. I had yet to pick up such an enriching tool to uphold my self-esteem regardless of troubles.

Some members of the Brooklyn community who saw me hanging out with Lazuli warned my parents. Clearly, Lazuli's wish to keep her sex life low-key didn't work out.

"Luda! You can't be hanging around with Lazuli anymore! She's a bad influence on you!" My father burst, "The neighbors told us that she has sex with multiple men!"

"Remember the saying, tell me who your friends are, and I'll tell you who you are," my mother added. Her didactic tone agitated me. I could understand my parents' concerns, especially now that I was the stained woman and talk of the town, but I refused to follow their advice blindly.

Integral to 'knowing thyself' is becoming one with your values and drawing the lines necessary to remaining confident. Mere differences in philosophies and values should never determine the state of a friendship unless they pose harm. I questioned if and how Lazuli's scandalous activities were impacting me: They weren't at all! She wasn't influencing me to join her in her sexual adventures; I couldn't even fathom having sex just for fun. Hanging around Lazuli enriched me regardless of what she did with her life. Befriending people like her, with unique approaches and paths, fosters opportunity to reflect on one's own. At this moment, I learned to separate my friendship with someone from their independent choices. In Hebrew, there's a saying that goes, 'you can learn from everyone and become smart.' As for Lazuli, she gave me the key to unlock a door of myself I had yet to explore.

During one regular shopping day in Manhattan with Lazuli, she asked me if I had any sexual desires. I replied, "I don't want to contaminate my body with someone I'm not sure about. I'm not ready yet."

"Well, do you masturbate?" she prompted casually. *Wow! I've never talked about this before!* It was always forbidden. I never had sex-education. *Ok Lea, let go of your old self and be honest with yourself. Speak freely.*

"No, I don't. I don't know how to do it. Do you?"

"You don't know how? Really? When I was a teenager, I used to do it so I could get to know my body, it's the best way!" Lazuli said casually as we crossed the street. I smirked trying to withhold my giggles. *This girl is insane!*

Sensing my discomfort, Lazuli bumped her shoulder against mine and chuckled, "Luda…you're a special girl, and maybe you need some special toys…you know, there's a store next block that sells vibrators." She stopped walking, got closer to me, and whispered, "You can just put them up there or stick your little fingers in there and roll them around to find your sweet spot! It's easy! Hey, and if you want to do it more cleanly, use the showerhead and play around with the different settings!" She cackled and snorted, witch-like. I was giggling like a five-year-old girl. Now two crazy girls were collapsing in laughter on Madison Avenue!

"Come on, Lazuli, let's grab coffee, enough of this nonsense!"

My body's pleasures were still a mystery to me at the age of twenty-four. Inhibited both mentally and physically, the idea of touching myself was incomprehensible— it seemed totally wrong. The only sex talk I ever listened to was 'find a husband, marry, make love, and have many many children.'

After Mendy, I didn't know when I'd be ready to have sex again. In my eyes, sex was commitment. *But how can I ever date, or even find someone, if I refuse to have sex?* Noticing more Americanized single women like Lazuli— seductive, flaunty, and confident— triggered me to contain my sexuality but explore it with me and for me. Besides, this aligned with my mission to master myself. *What's mastering yourself without knowing your body?* Body, mind, soul: Each piece is essential.

Holistic self-awareness is the recipe to a nourishing life. Digesting knowledge of oneself nurtures a person's inner trust. Then, following visceral feelings in sticky situations and managing relationships becomes second nature. Lazuli's instinctive actions and reactions— derived from experimentation and self-knowledge— illustrated her confidence. Lazuli completed the piece of the puzzle I was missing to embark on this adventure, transferring my emotions and mentality to my physicality. She'd soon become my teacher, I just had to be willing to learn.

4

Alone, Not Lonely

My brothers indulged in their single life, packing weekends with outings at New York's electrifying clubs and speakeasies. "Luda! Come to the disco with us! You'll love it!"

With nothing to lose, I gave it a shot. But let's just say that this scene wasn't for me. Sweat sprayed everywhere, spritzing like musical fountains; moist, blubbery skin rubbed on mine. That pervasive smell— not only of sweat but of crusty hair gel, cigarettes, and alcohol! Yuck! And the music was so loud that I couldn't hear anything besides BOOM BOOM BOOM. Youngsters tried to overpower the sound, rambling vulgar nonsense as they escaped into a world of ecstasy. Not my vibe. I decided to hang out with my sister, Betty, or make my own plans.

One Saturday evening, Betty and I planned to see a movie at the Sheepshead Bay theater. I pulled on the latest additions to my wardrobe: blue boot-cut jeans topped by a white silken collared shirt. As I was about to lock the door on my way out, my phone rang.

"I can't make it. I can't leave the house, Luda." Betty was crying hysterically. She had a big fight with her husband again. Their marriage was on the brink of collapse.

"Ok, good luck." I hung up the phone, disappointed.

My sister and her husband had been married for over twenty years. Twenty years that reminded me of my situation not too long ago. The 80-20 rule applied to them: They fought 80% of the time and enjoyed one another the other 20%. Such a poor ratio could not yield a happy life, but she was scared to get divorced as she needed her husband's financial support. She also needed my parent's approval to get divorced and could not disentangle herself from such taboos twenty years later. Without a contingency plan, her exit seemed worse-off.

I wasn't upset with Betty but felt self-pity more than anything. *Now I have no one to go out with.* Instead of recognizing her agony, I hung up the phone and began to weep tears of my own misery. My reaction was unlike me— emotions had conquered my character once again. Not once did I ask her if she was ok or if she needed help. This was a selfish move that, in a moment of darkness, would spark a light toward a personal change.

Fifteen minutes of sulking rekindled some strength. I wondered why I depended on others for my outings. My happiness is contingent on me, myself, and I **only**. *If I want to go to the movies, I should go regardless of anybody accompanying me.* Although the experience is slightly altered, my incentive or mood toward the activity should not change. The gears in my mind were churning. *Just go, don't hesitate.* I washed my face, sprayed some perfume, and grabbed my car keys determined to go to the movies alone. This was a big deal.

Headed southbound, a negative thought bubble returned: *Everyone will be staring at me. What are they going to say?* I thought that people would perceive me as a lonely and bored weary woman. A weary woman— no, not again! *Nobody goes to the movies alone!* My legs began to shake as I drove across the bridge and over the bay. I'm scared of heights; the anxiety wasn't helping. *Don't think. Just drive.* Identify your needs, focus on your purpose, and go get it. *Don't compromise yourself.* Uttering Jewel's motto to myself relaxed me, both literally and figuratively. My foot pressed firmly on the gas as I breezed back onto the main road. *The needs and decisions of others should not influence mine. All I want to do was see a movie, and whether I go with someone or not makes no difference.* I repeated this several times to myself in my head. Part of knowing oneself is finding comfort in being alone. Enjoy your own company.

I parked a block away from the cinema complex. Seas of people walked in toward the ticket booth— couples linking arms tightly and groups of friends crowding together. *And here I am, all alone. Don't back out.* Getting through this would push me to do other things on my own. Finding comfort in discomfort expands boundaries with the potential of unexpected rewards.

"One-one for, um, Sleeping with the Enemy." I mumbled. I couldn't even look up. I slipped the ticket into my pocket and made my way inside. To remain inconspicuous, I crept up to the left back corner. The movie had already started.

'Sleeping with the Enemy' is about a woman struggling in an abusive marriage who chooses to leave her husband in the end. I had been looking forward to watching a film I could relate to but could hardly focus. *People are staring. What are they thinking?* My foot was tapping on the seat in front of me incessantly. I couldn't control it. *I'm probably disturbing them.* I got up and walked out of the theater embroiled in disappointment with myself. Stewing in the imaginary thoughts of others burned me to the bone. My lack of courage broke me. On the way to my car, I saw a large shopping center across the street and decided to wander around there for a bit. *Something is wrong here.*

Embarking on this outing was intended for me to overcome my fears and expand my boundaries, not fall into them. I committed to try again the following weekend with a promise to sit through the entire movie— from previews to credits. From now on, I'd spend an hour with myself once a week doing things I enjoyed. Alone, but not lonely.

Next Saturday came. I arrived at the theater a bit early and chose the side seat in the middle section as opposed to the back. As early as the previews, I caught myself staring at groups of friends and couples taking their seats around me. *Embrace your discomfort. Own it. This will make you stronger.* I sat back, took a deep breath, and pinned my eyes on the screen straight ahead.

The movie passed by in a flash. I wanted to flee before anyone saw me leaving alone. Walk out with everyone else. No escaping. Face reality. When the credits ended, I emerged from my seat and strode towards my white Lincoln with pride. Couples exited the theater swarming around me, yet I no longer felt sorry for myself. I smiled at them and waved. *I did it!* I was eager to memorialize this event as the path of walking alone but no longer feeling lonely. This success was a milestone of building confidence with the courage of expanding beyond societal confines to satisfy my needs.

The notebook Yafa gifted me in the fifth grade eternally remained by my bedside. It became my diary where I wrote down puzzling thoughts, transformative experiences, and advice to myself. I wrote in bullet points:

- Focus on your needs
- Get comfortable being alone
- Enjoy doing things for yourself. Even if you're BY YOURSELF ALWAYS THINK: What's the harm in trying?
- How can I learn or benefit from this situation?

What does it mean to "think before you act, so you don't have regrets?" Value-based decisions are made by measuring outcomes by their best and worst-case scenarios. One must assess potential losses versus gain, risks versus rewards, blunders or benefits, and pain versus pleasure. *If I choose decision X, what price I am willing to pay for my potential pleasures, gains, rewards, or benefits?*

Another epiphany of mine emerged from acknowledging good and bad feelings equally: Positive feelings are evoked with excitement, confidence, and passion that motivates further action. Negative feelings cause aversions but should be treated as signals toward self-discovery. I now understood that I could only be happy for others when I'd be content with myself. This applied to how I reacted to my sister on the phone and to how I felt in the theater alone the week prior.

PART IV Out of the Boro

5

Transform Regret to Beget Greatness

Weeks passed by and I still had not heard from Mendy. Distance cooled my heart and let me fledge my independent life with a free mind. I grew accustomed to living alone, making new friends, playing basketball, and working long hours. Nonetheless, conflicts surrounding my failed marriage still hit a nerve and I was not yet ready to dissect them. Despite growing pains and challenges, I'd come around to this through my transformation. For the time being, I focused on expanding my world with fresh energy and motivation.

Jewel approached me just as I was about to leave work one evening. "Wanna come over tonight? Tom and I invited some friends last minute."

"It's a Jewish holiday, Simchat Torah, I'm going to have dinner with my family. Next week for sure!" We hugged her and I waved goodbye.

I arrived at my parents' home at about 7:00 PM. The house was full. My sister and her family, my brothers, and their friends, among families from the Persian and Greek communities were clustered around the abundant trays of mezze stationed around the house. The chatter, laughter, abundance of food, and high spirits of the holiday brought a rejuvenating warmth to the room.

After everyone left, I stayed to help clean up. My mom lifted her head while scrubbing a plate. "You know what happened today? Mendy came to talk to dad." Her tone was solemn.

"What does he want? Did he bring the divorce papers?" I dropped the fork I was cleaning and looked back at her.

"No. He wants you back."

"What?! Really?! After all of this, he wants me back? For what reason?" I was shocked. My mother wiped her hands and placed one on my shoulder.

"He regrets the way he has been treating you. He is willing to go to therapy. He wants to give it another try. He asked us to facilitate a meeting with you and he is willing to make changes."

There was no going back. "Why do we need this vicious cycle to compromise every time? There's no need to negotiate new terms. No need to compromise. He took me for granted, and I'm at a different stage of my life now. I'm trying to heal, regain my inner strength, and gain independence. The only thing I need from him is to sign the Get and the divorce papers." I took a towel and began to dry the dishes. "There's no point discussing this any longer. Onwards and forwards, I am done." I shut down the conversation. I was done. My mom was not.

"You know, Luda, one more thing," my mom said, "when he was trying to talk to your dad, you know your papa, he told him to get the f*ck out of here and kicked him out the house!" It was really no surprise that my dad would do that. I glanced at my father who was lounging on the sofa eavesdropping on our conversation.

242

"Dubbina (idiot), he ruined your life and now he wants you back," He exclaimed, "Poshtel k chertu (go to hell)!" My dad's fuse was short, and his anger was reflected in a barrage of Russian curse words: "Balvan (fool), pidaras (a*shole), poshel nahui (go f*ck yourself)."

While bursting with laughter, I acknowledged and was proud that I possessed his tenacity and grit. Our decisions were firm decisions— no turning back. I made my way to the sofa and kneeled next to him.

"It is over, papa. I will start a new page with better opportunities. Do not worry, all will fall into place within time." I kissed him on his forehead and hugged my mom. As my dad continued to curse Mendy, I packed up my things. "Lailah Tov, Good night." I gave my goodbyes, went downstairs, and closed the door behind me.

The air was cold yet refreshing. I was at peace and vindicated knowing that Mendy was willing to cave in to all my terms. *How pathetic! Did it take him three years to acknowledge me? He really still wanted me!* Sometimes, we need to lose people to appreciate them.

I wondered why I would want his loss to serve as his motive to respect my wishes. Definitely not. While Mendy brightened my world in dark moments, he also stripped me of dignity that disintegrated my being into ashes. This wasn't only his fault— it was mine too. I allowed it to happen. But it was too late to turn back time. Too late for regrets. Now, I'd leverage toward future objectives.

Over the next eighteen months, Mendy would pay frequent visits to my parents asking about me. He'd persistently negotiate with my mother in efforts to mend our marriage. Again, he was asking my mother and not me!

"Mendy, your train has passed, and remember, when you build a life for yourself, my son, never take your partner for granted," my mother admonished lovingly. My family knew well that, for me, it was over. I was laser-focused on transforming obstacles to opportunities, learning about myself through forging new connections and building my career. There was no better place than New York to launch my mission, and it would be up to me to pursue it. *Me, on Wall Street?* Absolutely.

6

My Oath of Allegiance: Leah Becomes Lea

Life didn't change, but I was buried in boredom. That's precisely why: Change is fun for me— it's my fuel to keep pushing and exceling. Working at LISB no longer provided me adequate intellectual stimulation; constantly hanging out with the same crowds was dull. In search of something different, I had yet to discern how I'd venture out.

I got lucky. A recruiting company called me with a prime opportunity to work as a programmer for Dean Witter's trading systems. I couldn't resist but accept the job interview, which happened to be on the same day as my naturalization ceremony. I was eager to obtain papers for myself and start the citizenship process for my parents. With papers, I could finally push for my Get which Mendy was refusing to grant me.

City Hall was teeming with hundreds of colorful faces soon to beam beneath the American flag. Embodying a new identity and fulfilling my role as an official US citizen sent chills down my spine. Like other immigrants, my family found opportunities here they couldn't have elsewhere. The American dream: A dream I could have never imagined, a dream I had yet to conquer.

"Ludmila Leah Wolfson." My name pierced through the room.

I jumped, awoken from my silent prayer of gratitude. I proceeded toward the table to receive my certificate.

"Are there any errors or changes you'd like to make to the documents?" The officer handed me a pen. I looked down at my certificate, the pen wavering between my jittery fingers above.

"Can-can I change my name?"

"Certainly. It's a good time to do it." He smiled at me sincerely. But I couldn't decide on a new name to take on. There were endless possibilities to reconfigure myself: *Who do I want to be? How could I merge my scattered pieces under a single name?* Choose something bold, something versatile, something that stays true to my roots but still feels like liberty. Finally, it came to me:

"Can you remove Ludmila completely, slash the letter 'h' from 'Leah,' and change my last name from Wolfson to Wolf? Please." I looked at the officer deeply in the eyes, begging. Begging for freedom.

"Easy enough." He nodded his head, scribbled away, and stamped my certificate. Freedom was sealed. Streams of euphoria ran through me as if I had the post-work out glow. It was like I had been sprinting on a treadmill all this time— three years of running from problems, people, and myself. The torture was over. I was elated, ready to recover from my identity crisis and come back into the world stronger as me: Lea Wolf. No more Luda challudah or weary and tired Leah Wolfson. I was not Gulçimen— a fine, dainty, beautiful flower. I was not a reflection of the iconic Russian actress, Ludmila. I recited my new name to myself again, again, and again: *Lea (LEE-AH), Lea Wolf.* I fell in love with the sound of it. Music to my ears. It made me feel like a princess with the heart of a warrior.

Jewel was the first person I called after the ceremony: "I changed my name to Lea! Princess Lea!" My voice rang through the wind and over honking cars.

"Let's celebrate over the weekend, I am so proud of you, love!"

I informed her that I was rushing to the World Trade Center for an interview with Dean Witter. "I'll probably be leaving the bank."

"Are you serious, missy? You didn't tell me about that!" she exclaimed. Usual Jewel— she wanted to know it all.

"I have to run, but I'll tell you this weekend! I promise!" A tear fell on my cheek. "I love you, Jewelster."

Within three weeks, Lea Wolf would be working on Wall Street. Not quite the 'Wolf on Wall Street,' but a woman who would chase intensity and constantly crave more. Another cultural extreme awaited.

Talk the Talk, Walk the Walk

I no longer needed to drive 120 miles each way to Long Island Savings Bank. My daily trip involved one train ride on the F line, reaching downtown Manhattan within half an hour. The subway had its own culture to itself as if a pot, simmering with a rainbow of ingredients made pungent by a medley of spices. Diverse ages, intriguing faces, unique clothing, foreign scents, and conversations over topics I'd never heard of. No boarders here. Spurts of energy revived me each time I ascended the subway steps from the underground and camouflaged into the city's bustling life. Vibrant colors flooded the streets as people hustled to and from work in top-of-the-line suits with briefcases in hand. Through the avenues I twirled and through the shops I explored, the dance of this city never bored me.

I gazed up at the peaks of the twin towers; their sheer power overwhelmed me. I took a deep breath and marched inside tower two as confident as my body allowed. Up sixty-seven floors, I'd land at Dean Witter. Older White men surrounded me in the elevator talking business with direct mannerisms. I had yet to learn how to engage with such characters in an environment that they dominated.

Upon securing my new position as a software engineer, I was given exactly two weeks to familiarize myself with a portfolio management module including 120,000 lines of code. I had never heard of demand this high in a single corporation or seen teams of this size working on such a complex system. The entire LISB branch consisted of only 160 people; on my floor at DW, there were over 160 people working in IT alone! In my small group of twelve, three were women. This ratio applied to the entire technology department: 70% male, 30% female. Although the extreme gender gap was mind-boggling and somewhat intimidating, I saw golden opportunities ahead.

Plunging into the waters of the workplace forced me to wade through wavy challenges and many times, wacky people. I would grow to embrace this lifestyle, embodying its intensity and direct disposition. Wall Street was another dream come true for me. A dream come true for any single woman. The stories will soon be told...

7

What I Unveiled at Chippendale

I met Maggie Asteria at the Dean Witter cafeteria during lunch. She looked a bit like me and was Greek. Although our ethnicities were different, we shared similar culture and energies. During one Friday lunch break, Maggie invited me to join her for dinner with some friends.

"Yeah! I'd love to! Where are we going?" I asked eagerly. The other girls at the table made sharp eye-contact and chuckled but gave no answer.

"You'll love it, trust me," Maggie giggled looking at the girls. "Let's meet at Il Molino. Tomorrow, seven o'clock."

After a whole day and a half of waiting, Maggie finally picked me up. She reserved any hints of this mysterious location until we arrived at the intersection of 61st street and first avenue. Straight ahead was a lean building flashing in neon pink and red lights. A line of women snaked around the corner awaiting entry in form-fitting dresses and stilettos. *A disco? A nightclub? Stop guessing.* We entered to smoke blowing into our faces and electronic music blasting. Acid lime strobe lights blinded me.

"What's this!?" I shouted into Maggie's ear. Before I could even move, she grabbed my wrist and dragged me into the mosh pit crowding the stage.

"C'mon now! Let's get rowdy!"

I caught a glimpse of five men dressed in sleeveless shirts and skin-tight boxers gyrating their hips erotically. "Yeah, more! More!" the women howled, riveted in a sexual trance. Some were drooling and touching themselves to the beat of the music. Chippendale was not my thing.

Maggie and her friends joined in with the others. There was no way I could. This was a public display far too seductive for a conservative girl like me. While open to new experiences in the New York City scene, this was over the top. These muscular men wearing skimpy underwear were supposed to turn women-on, but it had just the opposite effect on me. Maybe Lazuli would have enjoyed it. I could only imagine how my parents or even members of the Boro would react to this! Shanda, shanda!

After a long forty-five minutes, the performers came off the stage and into the smoky mist. Women huddled around them and began shoving dollar bills in the men's speedos. *Yuck!* Maggie and her friends rushed into the mosh pit to take pictures sitting on the guys' laps. I wanted to run away. Not so sexy.

"Excuse me, sorry, excuse me." I weaved through the sea of people toward the exit. Instead of expressing my discomfort to Maggie and her friends, I decided to wait outside until the show was over. I wanted to leave, but my discomfort reflected me, not them. They had been kind enough to invite me, and I didn't want to ruin their evening. Having consideration for our friends' wants, needs, and pleasures, so long as they aren't harmful, demonstrates your respect for them. We all have different palettes. To each their own.

I finally found my way out and leaned against the wall in relief. My eyes flickered and aimed at the ground in search of peace. I looked up. OH MY GOODNESS! One of the dancers was towering over me with his palms planted above my head. I was trapped underneath him, pressed into the wall. He wanted to eat me alive.

"You look mighty lovely tonight, my darling," he goaded. He started to rub against me.

"No, please no. Stop! Please," I protested, trying to slither out sideways.

"Why not?" His tongue flickered. "Aren't you here for some fun, sweetheart?" He was salivating. The rubbing intensified.

"Get off!" I exclaimed, pushing with all my might. He backed off. I think he got the message. This wasn't a joke; and no, I wasn't playing 'hard to get.'

I was sweating profusely. More than the physical challenge of escaping this man, my body was swept by anxiety. *Why me? Why did he chase me all the way out?* There were hundreds of beautiful girls in that room begging for a moment like that. I never even made eye contact with him! And yet, here's this macho who wanted a piece of me. Gross! I waited until the girls came out. They couldn't stop giggling.

"Wow! That was amazing! Ooooo that one guy…. he was smokinnn hot!" Maggie said, twirling her luscious locks. I said nothing, just smiled. We walked to the subway station as a group and parted ways for the evening.

I crawled into bed that night unable to resist writing down what happened in my diary. After skimming through my other entries and documenting this one, I noticed a pattern: There was something about me

251

that attracted men. I fell asleep pondering what my magnetic touch was...A pure coincidence? My body? My demeanor? If only I could leverage my sexuality. If only I knew myself a bit deeper.

After my crazy experience at Chippendale, I couldn't stop thinking about my dear friend Lazuli. *What would she have done? Probably play along and enjoy the game!* Through my whirlwind of thoughts, Lazuli's words echoed in my mind: "Masturbation is the key to your sexuality, the key to your liberation." Maybe this tool would unlock my pandora's box and help me understand why I was averse to manly seduction, something all girls wanted.

Although initially reluctant, I resolved to explore myself in the cleanest way possible. There was nothing to lose by trying, only something to gain. The very next morning, I headed to the hardware store bright and early to buy a new shower head with a mixed bag of settings at various strengths. I called my brother to help me install it: "Just need a replacement, that's all."

The only way to fully know oneself is to be in touch with all our senses. Embracing emotional, mental, and even some physical discomfort infuses us with confidence. Although not an easy process, it is eternally liberating and propels us to improve. Becoming masters of our own domain makes life easier regardless of the outcomes because we discover how to manage our actions and reactions in future situations.

As for me, getting to know myself wouldn't get any easier. Intimate relationships induce deeper connections with insights still mysterious to me. It was up to me to continue my introspective journey so I could analyze my behaviors and understand others.

PART • V

The NYC Single Scenes

1991-1996

1

Select, Don't Be Selected

My job offered financial stability. Plus, I got perks like fully paid college tuition. This was a great opportunity to obtain my college degree, meet like-minded people, expand my network, and broaden my perspectives. The recipe of productivity, new people, and fresh skills always enriches my life.

I found my study sanctuary at New York's 42nd street library, a serene setting overflowing with resources and reminders of American history. Red sofas spread across each floor popped against the plain white walls and big windows overlooking Bryant Park. My hub on the upper level was a bit different: Long, brown wooden desks that stretched across the entirety of the floor with bookcases surrounding. I settled down in the middle spot facing the window, clueless that an ordinary study session on a Saturday afternoon would culminate into a life-changing experience.

At first, I did not notice him. All I could see was his blond hair; his nose was in a book. It was only until his legs touched mine that I did. Maybe it was an accident. He was entranced in thought, jotting down beautiful cursive notes in a notebook overflowing with annotations. I pulled away to create more space between us, yet gentle touches against my legs continued. The width of these antique wooden tables gave us **plenty** of room. No accident.

For some reason, this young man piqued my interest. I peered up to investigate this cause of distraction. *Wow.* He was handsome— beyond handsome— with some unexplainable force of attraction and energy. I couldn't focus. I couldn't help but make subtle, intermittent glances at a flawless face featured by bone structure so defined that each slight tilt revealed another inch of his beauty. I looked downward, examining veiny arms which swelled by the mere grip on his pencil. It was as if this man had been sketched in my imagination. Now he was appearing, as if a painting, before me.

His lips pursed upward, and his oceanic eyes peered left, mesmerized in deep thought. My knitted V-neck seemed to interrupt his line of sight back to his text: He'd fixate on it for a few seconds, and then continue downward. I couldn't grasp what he was reading, but it wasn't hard to read him— clearly distracted, as was I. This new case study of mine posed a total deviation from my dissection of the First Amendment. I was learning about freedom of speech. *Can I speak to him?* My breathing paused. Something was stopping me. *What was that other one?* Yes, that's it— freedom of expression!

Oddly, the sporadic moments of contact between our legs induced unexplainable heat and energy within me. I'd pull my feet away and my hands would dampen in desire. Just as I was wiping my clammy hands on my black skirt beneath the desk, our feet would find each other's again. *Oh no.* Flashes of heat struck like lightning fermenting chaos inside of me. *Why was my body reacting this way?* My thighs pressed together in defense. *Restrain yourself.* I tried to hide my crimson cheeks by using my book as a shield. Embarrassed. Confused.

As the weak light from brass lamps dimmed, a mutual gaze finally connected us. My curiosity grew as our game of footsies continued underneath the mahogany table. There was not a single exchange of spoken word. All this time, totaling about two hours, I had been interested in this man with a visceral urge to ask him just one question. *His name, his phone number, the book he was reading.* That's not the conduct of courtship: He's the man. He should be approaching me. *Just wait.*

It was almost five. The library would close in fifteen minutes. I looked aimlessly out the window wrestling with my emotions and inhibitions. *What was holding me back? Would either of us gain the courage to speak?* At 4:55, I packed my bag and headed towards the door. He followed a few steps behind. I prayed that some miracle would happen, and he'd just happen to bump into me, drop something, or trip so I could interject. However, the path was clear, his satchel was sturdy on his shoulder, and he had nothing in hand. Both library doors were open, too. No gentleman-like gesture could occur. One last time, I tried to conjure the courage to speak. I could not.

We split at the fork of the road, slithering south of each other. I trekked toward the subway tackled by regret, my body and soul in disconnect. What had anchored me to let this man off the hook? Now, he was back swimming with the rest of the fish in the sea, and he was the catch that I craved.

Riding the F train back home, I couldn't stop pondering what happened. The interest was clear between us. Pure body language flushed my body with heat like never before. Usually, I was unbridled. *What*

restrained my wild nature? Why was I so inhibited from acting on my emotions? The paradox was unsolvable.

I lay in bed journaling that night in search of answers. *Why were men that I **wasn't** interested in swirling around me while I couldn't get those I **was** interested in to approach me?* It took me a couple of hours of writing until I realized— AH-HA! My inhibition to approach this mystery man stemmed from my upbringing. A man should court a woman; it is more respectable if a man initiates the conversation. My dad's commands echoed in my mind.

No wonder that most of the men swirling around me were those who initiated conversations with me. These men had selected me, I did not select them. Since they liked me, they initiated, so I found it easy to connect. I had relented my power to these men, ingrained with the belief that the man **had** to select me. Men with the courage had the power. The only way to gain such power was by unchaining myself from old fashioned paradigms. I needed 'a man's' courage.

It later became clear that my belief-oriented behavior applied to every relationship. I felt confident rebelling against norms with my parents, teachers, or friends, but intimate relationships were different. The rules changed based on my emotions and feelings toward a man. To avoid another lost chance or future relationship mishaps, I committed to understand the principles impacting my emotions, speech, and actions. So, if I was interested or curious about a man, and he didn't know me, there was no way I could spark his interest if I didn't initiate. *What did I expect?!* The only solution: Be assertive.

Courage was the magical ingredient I was missing. However, just gaining courage would not be the magic pill: I wondered how I'd go about starting a conversation— what I would say and how I would say it.

How do I act without an introduction? They'll think I'm awkward, desperate, and needy! How embarrassing.

Fear could have contributed to my inhibition. It is a source of hindrance for many, but it was not my culprit. For me, the shame of improper womanhood and lacking tools to directly assert my curiosity toward a man reigned. However, fear and shame are malleable emotions mired in perspective and perception. I learned that many American women initiate, so I could do it too! To reprogram my perceptions, I needed to rewire my beliefs and devise a plan that would make it easier to test the waters. *Would I look awkward? How would he perceive me? What if he rejected me?* Then again, why would his perception of me matter anyway? I didn't even know him! The more I practiced, the better I'd become. To free my mind from this cycle, I wrote and boxed in my diary:

- Short term pain for long term gain. Nothing is disrespectful about a woman courting a man! This is a cultural gap!
- YOU must SELECT, don't be SELECTED!

I analyzed my situation from another angle. Connecting with others and developing a network of people who are aligned with my interests, values, and needs contribute to my growth. I had no problem reaching out to and connecting to new girlfriends, so *why couldn't I just treat a guy just like them or my work friends?* Of course I could! Just brace the hormones! Act like you just met a new colleague or random person along your daily adventure.

Changing my beliefs wasn't the hard part— channeling them into actions was. I planned to initiate random conversations with one new man each day whether it be on the subway, in the elevator, or during any outing. Some starters would include asking a situationally dependent question, like what they were reading, writing about, or studying. I could compliment on something unique about them, say that they reminded me of someone, or pretend that I may know them. And the easiest one: I could innocently ask for help or directions. *Common, Lea, it's not that hard! Start tomorrow, no ifs, ands, or buts.* I had prepared myself for rejection, awkwardness, or any unexpected feelings. So long as I selected to satisfy my curiosity, there would be no regrets.

Although Mr. Mystery Man would forever remain a mystery, he helped me question my preconceived notions and take action to debunk them. By the time I'd come across my prince charming, prompting conversations would be my sixth sense. My new principle— to pick, persuade, and persist until my curiosity is satisfied— would be religiously followed. Fears of shame or rejection would never again interfere between me and my confidence. These fears would become my greatest strengths.

Forging self-discovery and self-acceptance through meeting new people has fostered great progress toward my goals. Results were not initially perfect, but improvement was achieved only by testing clear communication— assertive and respectful speech paired with confident body language. Today, I can claim that of this craft, I have become a master.

2

Ari Tests My Self-Respect:
Be Direct and Project

Every Saturday morning, I called my sister, Marina, who was still living in Israel. "Hey, sissy! How you doin'?"

Her voice cracked with excitement, "I have great news for you! My boss, Ari, will be in New York for a couple of weeks. He is a highly desired bachelor in Israel and is looking for someone. I've already shown him pictures of you, he is very much interested!" I thanked her for thinking of me and assured her that I'd love to meet him. She gave me his number.

On a Thursday morning a couple of weeks later, my phone rang: "Shalom Lea, this is Ari. Your sister works with me and says that we should meet. I'm staying in Manhattan. I'm happy to meet you anywhere. What's your schedule?" He spoke quickly without wasting words. Direct and to the point, classic Israeli! I paged through my calendar. My dating marathon would last through Saturday evening!

"How about Sunday brunch?" I proposed. We planned on

Serendipity at eleven o'clock sharp.

I drove my little red Mazda into the city in a flurry-black skirt and flats. The tantalizing aroma of roasted espresso and toasted waffles lured me into the café. At a booth in the back was a redhead with green eyes and freckles reading the paper. He recognized me instantly.

"Shalom Lea, what's up? Nice to meet you." He walked towards me and gestured with a handshake, "Coffee? What would you like?"

"Just a latte, please, thank you."

At first, I was not attracted to this well-built and stocky man with shaggy, ginger hair. I was often drawn to clean-cut and leaner athletic men with a light complexion. Perhaps other qualities of his could foster some sort of attraction. We bit into a bright introduction over an assortment of truffles dunked into frothy cappuccinos.

"Which paper were you reading?" I asked. He pulled out the New York Times, leaning over the small booth to show me.

"You know," he began, setting the paper down, "I read four to five newspapers in an hour. I have photographic memory."

"Really? That's so impressive!" I decided to put him up for a challenge. "Can you tell me about this article?" I pointed to a random piece in the opinions section.

"Yes, of course!" he nodded with certainty, seeming to appreciate my daring spark. Indeed, he impressed me. Within five minutes, he was blabbering all about five different American economic policy strategies with terms I'd never heard of before! Amazing!

Ari proceeded to ask me questions about my background and life's journey. My identity as a Tat-Jew and Israeli infused into an American woman fascinated him. I returned with similar questions about his upbringing and work in Israel. Before we knew it, three hours had passed.

"I would love to continue our conversation at dinner tonight if you can." He wanted to keep going. I already had plans to see Lazuli and besides, this was enough for one day.

"How about tomorrow after work?"

"Perfect."

We met on the Upper West Side for a stroll around Central Park. He delved into his aspirations and what he was looking for in the future. Our dialogue transitioned into a conversation over Israeli and American politics followed by an exchange on the differences between American and Israeli cultures. We discussed everything, from politics and religion to gender and our dating scenes. No formalities, no filters, no taboos.

Ari also made me realize how aggressive, masochist, and blunt Israeli men are. They have chutzpah, shameless audacity. "Israelis are New Yorkers on steroids! Big egos, big balls!" I joked.

Ari and I enjoyed each other's humor and passion as we got closer. I could sense that he wanted to take things a step further, but I could not engage with him physically. He did not ignite the same spark in me like Mr. Mystery Man did. The attraction was purely cultural— a comfort of shared Israeli identity, Jewish traditions, values, work ethic, and intellectual stimulation. We also shared Alpha, go-getter personalities.

Our relationship grew complex. Ari held certain misconceptions about me. I realized that I projected my feelings with words, and not actions. I spoke like a liberated American woman working on Wall Street, but my attitudes toward sexuality were mired in insecurity. My inhibited body language and coded communication about intimacy lacked integrity. I was just as confused as he was, if not more. Ultimately, it was Ari himself who detected this gap.

My father's reminders were reverberating within. Although my heart yearned to break away from my conservative roots, I was unable to apply change or convey my dilemma to Ari. He would say, "Lea, you are an enigma, I can't figure you out." It was I who couldn't figure myself out. No wonder I couldn't communicate my feelings!

When Ari was back in Israel, I relished in the freedom to see more of my friends. Over the next few months, he would fly back and forth with every excuse to visit New York. Within a month of seeing each other every couple of weeks or so, Ari would openly share that he was meeting with other women. I didn't appreciate that, but his confidence to communicate honestly appealed to me. Since we never made our relationship official or exclusive, I figured that nothing was wrong with having multiple dates at once. And even though I didn't feel so good about it, I held it in.

As our unofficial status freed him from commitment to me, I should have felt the same. Competition is OK! It allows a person to make quality decisions by evaluating a diversity of options. However, at the time, bitter jealousy blocked me from recognizing that his honesty was doing me a favor. Ari's blunt yet respectful style shows strength, trust, and maturity in a relationship. I wished to have these traits: The true portrait of a liberated woman!

I could eventually decipher why Ari was seeing other women. I was yearning for his loyalty and devotion without sex, which he could not possibly provide. Furthermore, the disconnect between my confident talk and cowardly actions was a red flag. Our relationship would be built on a façade of who I thought I was— a burden for him. The woman I was at the time was not what Ari was looking for: He sought a woman who knew herself, respected herself, and projected authentic confidence.

He Should Know Better!
Don't Expect Others to be Mind Readers

My expectations from Ari and my inability to communicate with him sent me spiraling. Rather than expressing my interest in him directly, I felt that he should have been the better person to explain himself. Resentment and anger took over as I focused solely on his relationships with other women. I felt betrayed. I kept my distance, sulking in my own envy. When he tried to touch me, I pulled away, and his eyes would roll in frustration. I answered his calls less frequently, too. When we would talk, I'd make remarks like, "What do you like about other women? Why don't you make time for me?"

"You seem a little jealous, Miss Lea…what are you going to do?" He was playing.

"I don't care, do whatever you want." Obviously, I cared! I hated his game! *He should know better.* But I couldn't tell him how I felt or what I wanted. *I'll just show him.* The warm waters between us were cooling.

Ari and I took an evening stroll around Times Square one evening. We took a coffee break at an Italian café. He pulled a chair for me, "Here, sit down," and gestured. Within minutes of sipping on steamy cappuccinos, he began, "I want a woman to put me in my place when I disrespect her. She will be my partner for life."

What? That's so random! Why is he saying this? I had no idea how to respond. I neither knew what he meant in practical terms, nor did I dare to ask him what disrespect meant to him. This passive-aggressive game of ours would soon freeze our relationship. It was just a matter of time until Ari's dagger would strike hard.

The Nail on the Coffin

Ari invited me to dinner with his close friends at Il Mulino, a fine Italian Restaurant in downtown Manhattan. A husband and wife, both successful Israeli entrepreneurs from Tel Aviv, among a couple other friends, were already there. We joined them at the bar where we warmed up with some wine (I ordered my fancy seltzer) and soon moved to a dim-lit round table. The conversation debuted with casual small talk, and of course, transitioned to politics and cultural gaps.

Then jokes started. Ari was all into his friends' humor. Emboldened by their amusement, he began to tickle me brazenly. I pushed his hands away trying not to cause a scene. He wouldn't stop. The tickling intensified, and he kept rambling on as if completely drunk. He wasn't. One glass of wine never did it for him.

"This girl, Lea, yea… You keep digging a hole for yourself!" He cackled, "I want a woman who stands up for herself when she is being disrespected. I wouldn't mind if she slapped me across the face! Come on, Lea! Do it! Why don't you, huh?"

Everyone at the table egged him on. I felt like a bird tethered back to the Boro's cage, feathers of my dignity being plucked one by one. I really did feel like slapping him across the face. I wanted to punch him. But it wasn't in me. *How could a woman slapping a man be 'respectful?'* This totally contradicted how I was raised or how I wanted a man to treat me in return. My Caesar salad remained untouched. I was disgusted but continued enduring this mortifying humiliation until the dinner concluded.

Ari opened the door for me on the way out. Cabs were already lined up at the entrance of the restaurant, and I hopped into one right away without a word.

"Good night, Lea, sleep well, I'll see you soon," he said, smirking. He hadn't even acknowledged what he did. I feigned a friendly wave.

I peered out the window wondering how I could have allowed someone to treat me that way. *Why did I just wallow in my own weakness?* No clue. My confusion was a signal to reflect and redeem myself. It became apparent to me that I fell into the same pit as in my prior relationships. Again, I was confident in speaking up to my teachers, friends, and authorities, but not to men with whom I had relationships. Men seemed even more superior than authority figures to me. This had to change.

My mother harbored this belief too. I observed her as a silent victim of humiliation by my dad all her life. She never fought back; she didn't utter a single word in degrading moments. Years later, I asked her why she remained silent. Sullenly she said, "It will only get worse, I don't want to embarrass him in front of people and then suffer consequences in the community and at home. It would take weeks to shut him up."

Silence was my mother's way of de-escalating reactions to maintain peace. It did just the opposite. It was just normalized. These reflections prompted me to consider effective ways to respond respectfully without diminishing the energy in social settings. I had yet to possess these skills in my twenties but would master them by my thirties. Amuse to diffuse, challenge and gain knowledge, equalize to neutralize, among a few other tools were those I needed to better understand my relationships and most importantly, myself. Any man that needed to put me through tests did not deserve me. Certainly, I was not strong enough to stop his tribulations. We were right for each other for a period, but no more. This incident put a nail on the coffin.

I Failed the Test

Ari's trips to New York became infrequent. Our relationship was rusting and was not ending smoothly. "You dug a hole for yourself, and you fell deep into it, Lea." His know-it-all show host voice vexed me. Ew.

I still couldn't wrap my head around what he meant. I couldn't figure it out for many months. However, I knew that despite my irritation, his message held some meaning with an important lesson for me. My first initiative was to write him a long letter to comprehend how I was digging this hole and how deep I had gone under. Scribbling these thoughts on paper helped me realize the roots of my repeated mistakes and how my actions countered my desired outcomes. My actions were once again stripping me of self-respect and contradicting tenets of respect altogether.

Respect is not a one-way street. A man **is not** superior when he makes a woman feel inferior. A real man is superior and strong when he empowers her. A real man helps a woman close-in on her weaknesses. If a man preys on her weaknesses, he is a predator— not a superior, respectful, or virtuous man. There are predators out there, and there always will be, but it was my responsibility to develop tools to fend off narcissistic, masochistic men. This goes without saying: I would never seek a man who preyed on my insecurities in my future relationships. I wanted one who would leverage them to build strengths. But there it was:

"I want a woman to put me in her place when I disrespect her." The jigsaw was coming together.

My search for answers motivated me to visit Ari in Israel a few months after our relationship dissolved. "Lea, you didn't get it?! I was testing you!" All that time, he was hinting that to be respected, I had to respect myself first. I had been eroding my own dignity this whole time by letting him disrespect me! I should have told him how I felt instead of expecting him to know. My inability to pick up on this signaled that my wisdom was lacking on other fronts as well.

Patterns for Predictability and Stability

A gentleman I recently met at a dinner among friends said that "wisdom is pattern recognition." Through Ari, I was able to gain some insight about clear patterns in my relationships thus far. The first pattern I noticed was that when a man is interested, in love, and has the resources, he will travel thousands of miles to see you and be there for you. I sought verbal confirmation from Ari to rest assured of his love for me despite him coming from Israel almost monthly just for me! When he stopped coming, Ari conjured up thousands of excuses as to why not. I sat there pondering the real reason instead of asking directly until he called me many months later with a clear explanation. Luckily, Ari was blunt, direct, and honest. Most men are not. In years to come, I would understand that a person's actions may speak louder than their words, or the opposite (as I was acting). It's best to use both words and actions to show care, however, it is always up to the individual to recognize patterns of behavior to best conduct relationships.

The problem with patterns is that they become overly routine. We become so secure in our predictions that they lead us to eliminate any unexpected possibilities. Sometimes, like when learning vocabulary, we repeat the pattern of letters until we memorize it. But what if within that standard definition is a hidden meaning, something unknown to us but standard to someone else? This is a very important reality. Each person is their own dictionary and possesses their own definitions of words, ideas, and concepts.

Let's take the word 'respect.' Respect in my world was at the polar end of Ari's. Pleasing Ari with polite complicity while I allowed him to demean me was disrespectful in his eyes. I saw this as normative for a respectable woman. Therefore patterns, although representing repetition, are also an archetype for anomalies. One **can be** wise through pattern recognition, but when one becomes perceptive of a pattern's twists and turns, that person becomes brilliant. As patterns of human behavior are not always reliable, to recognize their components and understand their movements is essential to navigating relationships confidently. So, for me, next steps were developing friendships rather than expecting commitment from the onset. Once I felt secure enough by noticing patterns of healthy behavior, I would assert my feelings, wants, and needs.

At the beginning of my single life, men swarmed around me, and the ones who selected me were undesirable to me. I now knew that men like to hunt, but will only chase after women who are attractive, exciting, and consistent. There was something I was projecting onto others that hindered me from maintaining anything sustainable. "Lea, you're an enigma" was Ari's artful way of saying, 'Lea, you're confusing me.' This wasn't the first time (or the last!) I would hear this from a man. As an "enigma," I represented agitation, discomfort, and distrust not only to a man, but to myself.

Ari was right: I dug my own hole and fell into the pit by allowing him to disrespect me. My passive behavior demonstrated me disrespecting myself. Respecting oneself is necessary to building relationships upon principles, boundaries, and values. I resolved to communicate openly and provide each person I mingled with a lens into my world. Sharing the perspectives from my world with pride would make me feel more confident in it, no matter the outcome of the relationship. I'd learn to find liberty in every situation, and yes, even in rejection.

Part V The Single Scenes

3

Bill Miller:
Finding Liberty in Rejection

"Where are you walking so fast?" A voice called from behind. Sardining between New York City's masses in my swift red coat and long black boots, I turned to the sight of a lean suited guy with circular glasses. We were stopped between blocks.

"Hello," I gave a gentle grin, "I just love walking fast and I'm heading uptown to see a friend." We traversed the crosswalk in sync.

"May I join you for a walk— that is— to wherever you're headed?" He asked. *Why not?* Talking to strangers in New York City is commonplace, its streets home to endless streams of intriguing people. *You don't know what you don't know.* So long as I felt safe, I was more than happy to engage.

"Of course! But only if you can keep up, I'm not slowing down!" Beaming confidence lengthened my stride. Within minutes he was huffing and puffing, determined to maintain my pace.

"Where are you from? Israel?" he speculated. I stopped for a moment to grant him a few breaths.

"Yes," I nodded, "I'm from Israel, but I wasn't born there." We continued our walk with the guessing game.

"Yemen? Iran? Morocco?" My clues brought him close, but not on target.

"Dagestan, a province in southern Russia," I finally confessed, then returned the favor. "Where are you from?"

My intrigue grew after he shared that his family had immigrated to New York from Russia and that he was Jewish. "I settled on the Lower East Side, went to Ramaz for school, and now I'm the Chief Editor of the Pacific Post." His tone rang with sophistication like he expected some sort of 'wow, I'm so impressed!' reaction. I was clueless about the publication, its political affiliation, and the prestige of his profession. By the time I could ask, we had already arrived at my destination.

"We never formally introduced ourselves." He extended his arm. "I'm Bill. And you are?"

I couldn't help but flirt back, "I'm Lea, but I like to be called Princess Lea!" Giggles escaped me.

"Alright Princess Lea, well, may I have your number? I'd love to see you again."

"Sure." I curtsied and handed him a slip of paper with my contact information.

As my friend stepped out the front door, I introduced the two: "Michelle, this is Bill. Bill, meet Michelle." I thought that they would make a nice couple: Both were highly professional, intellectual, and shared a non-athletic, small-framed look. They nodded at each other briefly, feigning interest. Bill turned back at me, adjusting the round glasses sitting on the tip of his pointy nose.

"I'll follow up with you, Lea." He winked with certainty.

Safety Bounds on Unfamiliar Grounds

It was well past midnight when I arrived home. A message from Bill awaited my call back. He wanted to get together on Saturday evening and offered to cook dinner for me at his apartment. Nice gesture. But I preferred to have my first dates at a public venue since I didn't really know the guy. Safety boundaries were clear. I called him and suggested that we dine at Carmines, my go-to for scrumptious Italian food.

My dates with Bill reminded me of the ones I had with Mendy or Ari, highly stimulating with unabated conversation. Although I was not physically attracted to Bill, I was attracted to his intellect. He was gifted with genius, had a way with words, and was ambitious.

"My next step is getting into politics, I'm trying to establish my campaign," he stated, tightening his light gray tie. "What about you?"

"I'm not sure. I like my job at Dean Witter but I'm just exploring myself and what I want to do by connecting with others one day at a time."

It was exciting for me to leap into another microcosm of New York society: The intellectual elite. I was fascinated by his worldliness, prestige, and sophisticated nature— a contrast from my previous relationships. Since I wasn't looking to commit seriously, our differences were immaterial to me. He didn't have a problem with them either. For now, at least.

Bill and I had busy schedules, so we'd only see each other once or twice a week. Despite our infrequent outings, I grew comfortable in his company and agreed to dine at his apartment. Even after long days at work, where Bill was immersed in researching, writing, and discussing all-things politics, he'd still ramble on about American government and international affairs while stir-frying vegetables. My knowledge of these topics was slim. Worse yet, my command of the English language was unsophisticated in these advanced areas. He would always ask for my opinions on his articles, but I couldn't contribute critically. Reading Bill's work was like a scavenger hunt; I'd have to pull out the dictionary as my key to his linguistic code. Feelings of incompetence trickled in.

Recognizing Misalignments

Bill invited me to countless social gatherings with his friends, mostly men. It was always political talk. I listened avidly, however felt ignorant, nonetheless. Their interactions were so fluid that any question I'd ask seemed to interrupt the conversation. Limited involvement made me bored, so I shifted my attention toward what I could learn, enjoy, and do in the meantime. Pretending to know what they were talking about with empty comments would have made me feel like I fit-in, but pretending is not for me.

While making the best out of these situations, the more time I spent in Bill's circle, the more my excitement over him dissipated. The thrill in my body from that day at the library was still tender. *Would I ever feel that again?* While smarts were important to me, his intellect wasn't enough to turn on sexual attraction toward him. I appreciated Bill's gentleness, genius, and of course, his Jewishness, but had yet to discover what was missing.

Each time Bill asked to have sex, I refused. I kept clear boundaries.

Hugs, holding hands, and gentle affection were acceptable; I engaged in these actions to test my feelings, desires, and limits. He sensed my boundaries, but he'd attempt to climb the fence in a gentle manner. It was two-sense by this point: I'd put my guard up before he started.

Sex was beyond a physical act for me: My attraction toward Bill would have to surpass the qualities I appreciated in him. Personality or looks might be the foundation of attraction but it's the bare minimum of an intimate relationship. There were many other ingredients I needed. Plus, he was thirty-six and I was twenty-five! It was déjà-vu from my parent's relationship! Regardless, I valued the intimate and authentic bond we shared. I didn't feel obliged to break it. We carried on as usual until Bill, too, realized that we were far too many worlds away from each other to stay together.

Prepare for Rejection: It's Guaranteed.

Memorial Day weekend arrived. As usual, I planned to spend time on Long Island with Jewel. Right when I was about to leave, the phone rang.

"Hey, Lea...do you have time to talk?" It was Bill.

"Sure, I'm just about to leave for Long Island, but I have a few minutes. What's up?"

"Well," he cleared his throat, "I've been thinking, and um... I don't feel like our relationship is working out. I think we should reconsider our standing here...in my opinion, it should be over."

I wasn't shocked but was curious about his thoughts. "Can you explain? Tell me why."

"I just can't see us growing older together," he said plainly. That seemed shallow to me.

"Why? Why don't you think so? Did I do anything that I should be aware of?"

"No no. You didn't do anything wrong. I just want a partner to be able to have political discussions with, that's all," he finally fessed up.

I thanked him for his honesty. "I understand, thank you for telling me directly."

This all made sense to me. I would not feel insulted by his rejection; his rejection aroused relief as I, too, knew that we were incompatible. I felt liberated, no longer having to live up to his standard of sophistication. But I'd get to that standard either way. If I were to find another man with similar qualities to Bill, I would ensure that my inability to have "political discussions" wouldn't be the downfall of my next relationship.

Reflecting upon my break-up with Bill bolstered my self-esteem. I thought about how far I've come— from a quaint village in the Caucasus to the fledgling state of Israel, then to Brooklyn's Boro Park, and now New York City. Here stood a new American citizen, a twenty-five-year-old woman, working on Wall Street! I had only lived in the United States for seven years! Credit was overdue.

We all have our expertise in certain fields. Admitting that you're learning about one afresh can only bridge you to new ones. Although American politics were still foreign to me, I could rattle-off about Israeli politics while others could not. There's always an opportunity to learn more and explore beyond your boundaries. So, no, I am not totally incompetent. I am not stupid. I am not an inadequate partner. For Bill, I might have been, but least I had the audacity to ask why, to think for myself, and the courage to convert my habits. At this point of my life, I was committed to appreciating myself for the knowledge I gain and how I improve. Just acknowledging this increased my self-worth. Deeming rejection as liberty **from** someone while realizing and appreciating the knowledge, competence, and confidence gained from the experience shifted the painful moment to a positive one.

My relationship with Bill Miller and his honest rejection inspired me to expand my horizons. During my seven-mile treadmill runs in the mornings, I usually watched Knicks games on TV; now I'd be flipping through news channels. My first coffee upon waking would be paired with paging through a variety of newspapers and magazines. This has become a routine practice. Keeping up to date with current affairs has enriched my life through its constant circulation of information and diverse philosophical perspectives. There is no one I can thank more than Bill for that!

Cement Values and Purpose Before Taking Risks

I can understand people's frustration and passion for politics. It's like a game of chess with pawns that reveal psychologies behind human behavior. Alliances between politicians are a liaison of self-interest, just as relationships are tied by mutual benefits to both parties. A treaty between two states may kick off with such great enthusiasm that two leaders may deal all their cards into it. It's risky though.

During this all-in honeymoon stage, many couples have sex out of initial passion just as politicians who swear by their moral dogmas before stepping into an agreement. It's natural to be overly excited about new things, but it can be dangerous. When the luster wears off, we grow disappointed when expectations fail. We become distressed, resentful, and sometimes seek revenge. Then we regret the relationship in the first place.

We should never regret any relationship because it's about the experience and what we take away from it. Therefore, we must cement our values and purpose in each relationship before we act in a certain way. From my experience with Bill, I learned that I could explore any man or as many men, all the while remaining authentic, intimate, and genuine, absent of sexuality (for me, because this was my value system). My commitment to refrain from sex until I felt emotionally and mentally connected would leverage my control in relationships to follow.

4

My Makeover

With three to four dates weekly, my gregarious personality was a magnet for men. As men swarmed around me, 'select, don't be selected' became my mantra. I grew skillful at engaging anyone and everyone in small talk, having practiced with friends and guys I went out with. I initiated conversations and dressed differently than most women on Wall Street. Many of my suits were originals from Brooklyn's Russian boutiques like Le Monti, designs nowhere to be found at the classic Barneys or Jones's New York. While I felt like a queen-bee, my parents thought otherwise.

"Why do you dress so provocatively? Your clothes are so tight, your skirt is so short! You're inviting men! You're dishonoring the family!" My dad exclaimed from the couch when I came for dinner one evening. My mom looked me up and down in disdain. I could comprehend their difficulty accepting that I was transforming into a progressive, independent woman, but was sick of constant scrutiny. In need of some privacy, I moved a short three miles away.

Even though I projected much confidence, I was struggling to sew my new world values into an old-fashioned tapestry. My emotions and reactions in different situations would signal that something needed to be redefined. *What should I accept, reject, or change?* I'd use my dad's grit and resilience to branch out to uncharted territories beyond my comfort zone one step at a time. Each step I took was one toward better understanding myself.

I realized that my daily routine required a balance of physical, intellectual, social, and emotional activities to feel fulfilled, fit, and focused. My first step was signing up to the Sporting Club, a high-end gym on top of the Hilton in World Trade Center 1. It became home to my rigorous workout regimen— a sanctuary of stress-relief, the prime ingredient to a jitter-free day. From there, I'd head to Dean Witter for work, and I'd conclude my evenings with a class at Baruch or an outing with colleagues whether it was watching a show, playing basketball, or a new activity. I was meeting new friends, friends through friends, and potentially, friends with benefits!

5

Tom Manning:
Wet Dreams, Dry Promises

"What are you doing for Valentine's Day?" Cecilia, the receptionist at the Sporting Club asked me after an intense run.

"Nothing. I have no Valentine to take me out, just some admirers here and there!" I giggled with a wide smile, snatching a Hershey's Kiss from Cecilia's desk on my way to work. "Thanks for the chocolate! See you tomorrow, C!"

Upon arriving at my 67th-floor cubicle desk, I was surprised to see a big magenta box with a heart-shaped card on top. I wondered who left it for me. Bill and I had just broken up a few weeks ago. I opened the card: In immaculate cursive it read, 'Please Be Mine, Your Valentine. 1996,' signed with Tom's name. At the back of my mind was always the suspicion that this old married man had wet dreams about me. Maybe my answer would be inside the box. I peered around to make sure nobody was around and proceeded to peel the tape off the box quietly. OMG! A plush teddy bear holding a red heart with the words, 'Please Be Mine on

Valentine's' was now sitting on my desk, staring at me. I gently packaged the fluffy bear back into the box, only to find a red tray of chocolates underneath it. My favorite— dark chocolate covered marzipan! I munched on my third truffle of the day with my second cup of coffee. A match made in heaven. My cupid. The perfect valentine.

Caffeine kick-started my brain for the morning. These extra jolts of adrenaline got me thinking hard as to how I'd approach Tom. The dirty old man was relentless, but I still needed to thank him. I figured that it would be strange to call him from the office since everyone would hear the conversation. I resolved to express my gratitude the next time I saw him in person; there, I'd reiterate my boundaries.

Flashbacks: Meeting Tom Manning

My mind wandered to when I met Mr. Tom Manning through my friend, Maggie, at a happy hour a few years back. They both worked for DW's Merger and Acquisition Department. Tom was Maggie's boss.

The bar at Pier 23 was filled with handsome men in dark suits. Maggie waved as I weaved through the crowd. "Meet Tom! He is the head of my department!" After a few minutes of introduction, Maggie left us talking.

"Would you like a drink?" He asked in the most gentlemen-like tone, sliding into the seat next to me.

"Just seltzer, please, thank you," I replied.

"Really? Can I treat you to something a little more exotic?"

"Well, how about Arnold Palmer?" I suggested, smiling. He ordered my exotic elixir of iced-tea and lemonade along with a Vodka on the rocks for himself. As our discussion evolved, I found Tom a pleasant conversationalist, personable and engaging.

At the conclusion of the evening Tom said, "I'd love to continue our conversations, call me if you'd like to go for a walk or lunch. I am in the directory, Tom Manning." He closed out the tab.

"Sure, sounds good." I thought nothing of his friendly offer and went to reconnect with Maggie and her friends. It was almost midnight. Work tomorrow! We all headed toward the subway station— some were still chatting, some falling over after quite a few drinks.

I reflected on the conversation I had with Tom. He was so interesting, and I wanted to learn more from him. There really was a whole other world out there! My only regret was that I had only conversed with Tom that evening, all the while surrounded by a variety of handsome, younger men. At times, I still felt inhibited. I had yet to develop the art of leading and managing myself at events to interact with purpose and clarity.

Different Perspectives on Mr. Manning

The day after meeting Tom, I was excited to share my new experience with Jewel and Lazuli. Surprisingly, they each held totally different perspectives.

Jewel warned me, "Missy, be careful, these Wall Street guys are super sly, don't get yourself entangled with them, especially a married man."

When I told Lazuli while shopping with her later that evening, she burst excitedly, "Hey girly! You might have found yourself a sugar daddy! If you aren't interested, just pass him over to me!"

My friends' outlooks baffled me. I had no idea what my relationship with Tom meant or where it was headed. *Just go with the flow. Enjoy getting to know him as a friend.* Like with Bill, I just had to set my boundaries. I did not want anything to do with a married man, less so entangle myself in a messy relationship with an executive at work. My priority was maintaining my job and connecting with new people to gain clarity within rather than being swayed by the values and perspectives of others.

A nice weekend passed. Monday again. At around eleven, I was interrupted by my work phone.

"Hey Lea, it's Tom. Would you like to meet at Battery Park City today for lunch? Maybe we can take a stroll..."

"Sure, I'll see you there." I had no plans.

Tom opened me like a book with an insatiable thirst for my life story. While flattered and excited to share, I was curious about him too. I tried to divert the attention onto him.

"Tell me about you, your background, your family, your work..."

He shared easily, "I am married with three sons, one of which works for Lehman Brothers, one who's in college, and another who was just recently married. As for myself, I have been with DW for over twenty-five years, and I love traveling, meeting new people, and making deals." He paused, then asked, "Do you like your work?"

"I enjoy the creativity in designing systems but sitting behind my desk and coding for ten hours a day is no love of mine." I was honest.

"If you had a choice to do something else, what would you do?"

"Your job sounds really interesting, but I'm not sure. I'm new here, and I want to explore other opportunities before I settle in."

Our walk came to an end. Time to get back to work. We headed into the elevator standing quietly amongst black suits sputtered by touches of colorful dresses. Tom's landing was on the sixty-fifth floor.

"I enjoyed spending time with you, what about next Monday? Same time, same place?"

I nodded.

Monday lunchtime walks with Tom became routine so long as he was in town. We shared our weekend's adventures, work, the art of making a deal, and discussed cultural diversity. Tom was a devout Christian, prompting us to talk about differences and similarities in Judeo-Christian philosophies. Sometimes, we ran errands together or sat down to eat at the DW café to chat. We preferred walking and talking since I usually ate a light lunch at my desk— a cup of coffee with something sweet, a cup of soup, or a smoothie.

Tom became a fatherly figure to me with his mentoring spirit. I enjoyed his support, smarts, and strength. He was safe: A married man with a beautiful family, and biblical principles who projected proper mannerisms, elegance, status, and respect as a top executive. Because of Tom's age, experience, and insider status in the men's world, he became a sounding board for my inquiries about Wall Street culture and men in general. I would turn to him for insight on encounters where I had doubts or blind spots.

"Maybe You Should Smile More"

A few months into our friendship, I became comfortable talking about trivial girly stuff with Tom. He'd lightly touch my shoulder and make gentle, suggestive comments like, "I love what I see under that silky top of yours" or "Lazuli seems like a very spirited lady, you girls seem fun. I wish I could go out with you."

Initially, I thought nothing of his remarks, and instinctually brushed them off with humor. "Thank you! Maybe one of these days you can come out with us when your wife lets you!" I joked, giggling with a cute curtsy.

I recalled one Monday when I returned to work after a long weekend of clubbing with my friends in the city. Coding away that morning, my mind kept circling back to what had occurred just the night before. Lazuli, Michelle, and I entered a pool table room with huddles of guys socializing with pretty girls. Many of the men flirted with Michelle and Lazuli, but none dared to approach me. *I was right there, in front of them, and the men treated me as if I was invisible! I was just as pretty, if not more!* This was not the first time this had happened. I had an idea as to why but wanted to run this by Tom since he seemed interested in my girls' nights outs anyway.

Upon arriving at work that Monday, I called Tom to confirm our lunchtime meeting. "Good morning, how was your weekend? Are we on for today?"

He assured me that we'd meet at 12:00. At 11:55, I went to the bathroom to freshen up before heading downstairs. The elevator doors slid open to Tom already inside.

"Hey, it's so good to see you! How was your weekend?" I greeted him cheerfully.

"It was great. Thank you," he got closer to me, "You smell so sweet today."

This was a little weird, but I decided to play along. "Thanks, it's Paloma Picasso, Lazuli uses it and I decided to try it."

We reached the DW café on the forty-second floor and waited in the salad line. After some small-talk, I soon found the opportunity to bring up my weekend's event.

"Hey Tom, I want to ask you something and want your honest opinion." I shared what happened at the club. As my story progressed, his grin broadened. He had his answer already.

"It's quite simple, Lea. Look— most men are intimidated by attractive women. You're charming, beautiful, and confident. Especially when your demeanor is stern, your striking features make you a bit...hmm... intimidating. You project 'stay away from me.' Maybe you should, you know, try smiling more."

"Ok, I'll try." I took his proposition seriously: He was probably right. This conversation was pivotal in altering my demeanor in social settings. On display, I was friendly, blunt, and bold, but not yet boisterous toward men. To become a force of attraction while fortifying my freedom, I'd put Tom's advice to the test.

Misleading or Self-Confident?

Smiling. It's an incredible thing. It actually did increase my opportunities! It made me popular. Men were swirling around me. Now I really felt like a queen bee! I smiled at people who made eye contact with me during my runs at the Sporting Club and on my way to work. The more I smiled, the more involved I became, and the more I found myself accessible to new friends and guys. I was eager to tell Tom that his advice was successful. However, around him, my smiley-flirty self would indicate otherwise...

Another conversation I recalled was when Tom confronted me with his supposed doubts: "Lea, you know that you have a very charming, gregarious, and friendly personality... but it's confusing." He peered up at me sternly, "You send mixed messages. It's misleading."

"How so?" I asked. I wasn't even interested in any of them! I was dating men outside of work!

"Well, you are so delightful, always so warm, and inviting conversations. Flirtatious, if you will." He awaited my response.

"It comes naturally to me, it's my personality." I lit up after a brief pause, "Just because I'm friendly or flirtatious, it doesn't mean I'm flirting, right?"

"Good point," he humbly confessed.

I pondered Tom's remarks for a while. Although I challenged him and he agreed with me, I wondered how else to act to avoid being 'misleading.' I had been misunderstood before, in Israel. Journaling that night, I asked myself whether I should change my personality. *Maybe I can just change myself at work, and act as the gregarious Lea outside the office.* A storm was brewing inside of me. In moments of inner conflict, Jewel was my go-to-gal: I called her with the down-low on my conversation with Tom.

"Missy, are you kidding me? Don't you realize what these men are doing?"

"No." I was clueless.

"Oh, Lea! let me ask you a question: If you were three-hundred pounds and had a face full of acne, would they be interested? If you were timid and shy, would they be flirting with you? Men say that you're 'misleading them' to manipulate you! Don't you get it?!"

"Oh my! Yes, I do!" Finally, it clicked: Maybe Tom was giving me honest advice, but men like Tom are masterful in building a woman's confidence. All this time, he had been complimenting me, buying me gifts, and asking me about my career. I had to take his comments with a grain of salt. Floating in dreams promised by flattery is dangerous, especially for someone like me— young, naive, innocent, and new to America. *What if I had fallen for Tom?*

Despite my rebellious character, I was cautious to overstep my boundaries without knowing the risks. Assessing risks by accepting responsibility for potential negative outcomes became integral to my decision-making process.

Tom would increasingly ask me about my aspirations, especially when we were alone— never among fellow colleagues: "Let me know how I can help you accomplish your goals, Lea." He leaned forward, speaking into the steam rising from his Americano. I had to think about "my goals" for a minute, teleporting myself through my life's journey thus far. A proud smile beamed from within, but I was always eager to climb up the ladder.

"Hmm...I'm still exploring. An increase in pay would be great though!" I confessed smiling.

Tom's demeanor remained unchanged— serious, stoic, and professional— like the way he worked. "I have many connections at DW, I can put in a good word for you with IT."

His offer sounded great, but it was against my character to get anything without working for it. "Sure Tom, that's kind of you, thanks."

I wanted nothing from Tom other than our friendship and his insight. *What kind of a deal was this? Jewel could be right— maybe he is trying to manipulate me.* The stars were aligning into a constellation of his true intentions.

The Day After Valentine's: Shattering Wet Dreams

Downpour flooded NYC. What irony— the day after Valentine's! Tom called me with an invitation to afternoon tea.

"Just to warm up. Let me treat you, darling."

"Ok, uh, sure." I hesitated, wondering why he'd say that to me. I wondered what I'd say to him about his little 'be mine' surprise. But I went along: It was the perfect opportunity, and perhaps the only one, to thank him for his gift.

I entered in all black— pants, heeled boots, turtleneck, and all— topped by my long houndstooth coat and a smidgen of lip gloss. Tom was already sitting there.

"Hello, so nice to see you here." He looked me up and down, pulled my chair, and presented me with an ornamental box of tea. "Which would you like? A box of all of your favorites, so hard to choose..." He elongated his words, trying to tempt me.

I pointed to the classic Earl Grey. "With lemon and sugar, please."

"Same here," Tom nodded at the waiter. We began a casual conversation, and I slipped in a thank you for his gift box of chocolates.

"You know me well, thank you, the chocolate was delicious." I didn't mention the teddy bear— too weird.

"My pleasure," he said in his smooth, deep voice. "I also wanted to talk to you about a great opportunity in my department. It's double the pay of your current income and it's a position more, what should I say? Hmmm...befitting to your chaaaaarming personality," he leaned forward and explained, "M&A is about developing relationships and win-win negotiations. I believe that's something you may be interested in."

It seemed like a wonderful proposal but sounded as if he was trying to seduce me with a job. Doubt crossed my mind. *Is this a part of his Valentine's Day gift?* It came a day late. *What if things didn't work out? What were the risks? Did the risks weigh more than the rewards?* I couldn't give him a yes or no.

"That's a great opportunity," I admitted, "Really, I am so flattered, but I'll need to think about it first."

He stared at me for a moment, making me a bit uncomfortable. "That's something that any girl would dream of. What's your hesitation?" He paused, and placed his palms on the table, "On the subject of dreams, I want to tell you that I had a dream…"

What he dreamt is better left up to your imagination. Any response was adrift in disturbance. I took my first sip of tea— medicine for tranquility— ignored the dream and thanked him again for his generous offer. It became apparent that he had been dripping big promises as bait to lure me into his pool. Jumping in naked could have been disastrous.

I was still disoriented by Tom's wild dream on my ride back to Avenue M. The plush teddy bear's sparkling eyes were haunting me. *What did "be mine" mean for a married man?* Lazuli and Jewel seemed to be right. My focus had to remain on emotional and financial stability: I had to weigh the two. Although I wanted to increase my income, it was stable. My job, friendship with Tom, and emotional well-being couldn't be compromised. Working in a separate department from him would secure my boundaries, so I had to reject his offer because he was certainly sly.

The next time I saw Tom was for a usual lunchtime walk a few days later. Honesty was my impulse. "I thought about our conversation last week, and I feel a bit overwhelmed by your offer. I'm not sure that I am ready to make that leap to working for you...to see you all day, every day, and take orders from you. Hmmm, I'm just not sure about it. I like our friendship and I want it to stay that way. I can't give you power over me." I laughed to soften my brash comment. I left no room for misunderstanding but eliminated the prospect of being rude or offensive. The boundaries were well defined for me, and hopefully for him.

"Understood," he said, looking down at his Brooks Brothers loafers. But it didn't really seem like he understood. Slippery as an eel, he started to swerve around me seductively. This gave me the perfect opportunity to confront him about his strange fantasies, too. I needed a funny way to express that he needed to stay in the friendzone. Only in the friendzone.

"Tom, in my culture, we reserve sex for serious relationships. I'm not one to sexercise for fun," I said comically, and ridiculed some of my dad's slurs about purity.

He gently nudged my shoulder, "Lea, lighten up! I really do understand, I'm just playing!" We both laughed.

With an understanding of my conservative background, Tom's wet dreams soon dried out. They may have lingered in his fantasies, but our friendly strolls along Battery Park City were our only reality. He was happy to continue being my mentor, my sounding board, and simply a good friend. I achieved my goal of maintaining our friendship without compromising my job or values.

A young, divorced, traditional girl strolling weekly with an older, married man would be a scandal back in the Boro, even more so in my parent's culture. Imagining myself having a friendship with an older man before my personal transformation began was unthinkable!

My shift in my paradigms were clear through my actions, as I defined what a healthy relationship looked like to me by setting boundaries based on feelings and values. I could enjoy flattery and flirting knowing that nothing would come out of it. Flirting did not imply a sexual invitation either. *Why should I contain my charisma, a quality that people invest time and effort to develop?* I wouldn't. Changing myself for anyone would contradict every tenant of my character. It no longer mattered whether Tom was satisfied with our friendship or not; even what he thought of me didn't matter. This to itself was a radical transformation because I always cared about others' opinions of me.

I used to change my behaviors because I wanted to protect others and the relationship we shared. My experiences with Tom affirmed that I could still protect others' feelings so long as I was vocal about my intentions in the relationship. Protecting one's feelings means being honest with them, especially when you feel uncomfortable. Protecting one's feelings involves debunking their perceptions about misleading or being misled. These sincere conversations are integral to sustainable relationships between friends or couples because they free an individual from responsibility for the other person's decisions. With Tom, I clearly communicated my boundaries and values that differed from his desires. Our disparity in needs created some conflict, but my clear communication freed me from an obligation to fulfill his needs. The decision to maintain our friendship was up to him.

6

Daniel Schwartz:
Entangled in a Three-Year
Package Deal

I woke up one Friday morning and packed my gym bag and an extra change of clothes. After work, I ran a sweaty seven miles at the Sporting Club (yes, seven, no exaggeration!), took a quick shower, and headed to Midtown's hottest bar to meet Michelle and her friends. Bar scenes weren't my type of outing, so I preferred to arrive late and leave early. I took my time getting ready and jumped on the B train headed uptown.

"Lea! Over here!" Michelle shouted, waving at me. I squeezed through the congested entrance, music blasting and smoke puffing into my face.

"So good to see you!" We hugged. "Hey, guys! Meet my friend Lea, who works for Dean Witter!" Michelle introduced me to the group, and each person seemed to have a different cultural and professional demographic. They gave inviting, crooked smiles— probably on their second or third drink. I could barely understand or hear what they were saying. I just smiled back.

I ordered my seltzer at the bar as usual, where someone seemingly sober approached me. His eyes weren't flickering like the rest of them. He was polished with a light clean-shaven face and dark hair.

"Hello Lea, I'm Daniel, I grew up with Michelle on Long Island. She told me all about you and that you moved here from Israel. I thought it would be great for us to connect."

"Of course! I used to work at Long Island Savings Bank, and I have some friends out there too!"

We delved into our careers and backgrounds until the club raucous became far too chaotic for us to engage comfortably. I was enjoying Daniel's company, but my fuse was short.

"Daniel, it was so nice meeting you, maybe we can chat over coffee somewhere a little quieter." I jotted down my contact information on a note and handed it to him.

"Yes of course," he nodded. "Are you grabbing a cab to head home? Let me walk you out." As we walked towards the exit together, he prompted, "What are you doing tomorrow? Would you like to go out for a quiet dinner?" He followed me to the line of yellow cabs.

"Yes, sure. Where are you thinking?" He opened the taxi door, gestured for me to take a seat, and waited for me to sit down and look at him.

"Let's talk tomorrow. We can decide from there." His face sparkled with joy, as did mine.

"See you tomorrow." I leaned my head back on the seat. The cab took off, and with it, my feelings for Daniel. There was some spark there.

I arrived home at around 10:15 PM. *Shoot!* I forgot to say goodbye to Michelle and thank her for inviting me. But the night was still young at the club. Michelle was probably on another round of drinks and playing pool. I decided to wait and call her after my shower.

I tumbled into bed and journaled my initial impressions of Daniel: Gentlemanlike, pleasant, friendly, handsome, considerate…. Thoughts spun through my mind as if it were a hamster wheel, imagining scenarios and feeling emotions personifying love. *Shut it off!*

At midnight, I called Michelle hoping that she would be home— a valid distraction.

"Is all ok, Lea?" She was worried about me since I left two hours early.

"Yes, I didn't say bye to you or thank you for inviting me. I feel terrible..."

"Oh, Lea! Don't worry!" She changed the subject entirely, "I saw you talking to Daniel! He's a great catch, he comes from a very influential and loving family. I know them all very well. He's like my brother, we grew up together."

A smile crept on my lips as I dozed off, "Yes, I enjoyed his company. Thank you, Michelle."

My Brother and I Reminiscing

The next day on my run, I passed by my parents' house. My brother, Aidan, was outside repairing his Ford Thunderbird.

"What are you doing? Are you on drugs or something? It's 6:15 in the morning! Tell me your secrets so I can have your energy!" He blurted out and approached me for a hug. He lifted me up by the waist mid-run with his tattooed, muscular arms. "You're so light! Tiny Luda!"

"Yeah, tiny, but I can kick as*!" I laughed and gave him a knuckle bump.

"Yes, sis, you always could! Want to take a drive with me to pick up bagels after your run? I'll pick you up at seven!"

I sent him a quick thumbs up and finished my three miles back home.

"Sis! You are glowing! Seriously, what are you ON?" Aidan bombarded me as I hopped in the passenger seat.

"Nothing!" I laughed, "Just have a date later today with a new American Jewish guy, I guess I'm just excited!"

He gave me a baffled look and jested, "American guys are sissies, you could probably eat him up for breakfast! I know you— you want to keep the man on the leash! You have balls bigger than their head!" Aidan couldn't keep his mouth shut. Both our heads jerked back convulsing in laughter.

Of course, compared to Israeli and Middle Eastern men, American men are softies. But I was ready for some sissies, sick and tired of macho men who used 'manliness' to control women for their own desires. My mind trailed back to my childhood in Israel, where I did have bigger balls than the guys' heads.

"Remember Moishleh? He'd pick on me because the guys would make fun of him when I scored three-pointers and he couldn't! His friends would say "she dusted you again!" And then he would get upset and yell "why don't you find girls to play with? Go play with them!" I remember during one game he kept rambling sexist slurs, so I knocked him to the floor with my hip. Then he fell and began to cry! Everyone was calling him an idiot and his friend said, "You're a sissy, come on, get up, stop crying like a girl!" It was so funny! I remember kicking their butts! So, Aidan, what do you say? Maybe I do need a 'sissy' as a partner to balance my toughness and intensity!"

He slapped me on the shoulder, "You would kill any sissy man in a month...he wouldn't be able to stand you!"

We continued reminiscing over our childhood as we chomped into our bagels, faces smothered in cream cheese. I had forgotten how much fun my brother and I had together: Never-ending episodes of laughter from energies and memories that we drew from each other. Our personalities meshed, rough edges never smoothing out despite living in the States for seven years now. But of course, New Yorkers are tough too, similar in style to Israelis. Israelis are New Yorkers on steroids!

My brother made a sharp turn on avenue M to drop me back at my apartment. He parked and walked me to the door.

"Thanks, bro, I'll see you soon!"

He pointed at me and exclaimed, "Don't you forget me, sis! Come by and visit, Luda! And, have fun with your sissy tonight."

I waved goodbye and went inside. A message from Daniel was in my voicemail box. He suggested that we meet on Long Island or that he would be happy to drive to meet me in Brooklyn. I decided to visit Jewel on Long Island first and see Daniel afterward.

A Villager in the Castle

Daniel and I met for a 7:30 reservation at the fanciest Italian restaurant in the neighborhood. He sported a charcoal blazer with a pair of leather dockers.

"Good evening, Lea, how are you, so nice to see you again." He gently pulled the chair back and waited until I sat down. I felt out of place.

"Thank you, this is beautiful." The villager in me was disguised. I gently unfolded my meticulously folded napkin and placed it on my lap. Our discussion began over our mutual friend, Michelle, then transitioned to our backgrounds, personal lives, and careers.

"I work in D.C. for a pollster who my family is close to, but I'm at a crossroads right now. I may be returning here to finish my masters in the city, at NYU." Daniel shared openly, "I'm just not sure yet."

Michelle couldn't have been more right— he was a good catch, and his family certainly stood in the upper-echelons of New York society. I was swept by his status. *Could I ever be of the same caliber? Would I meet his standards?*

Daniel interrupted my train of self-doubt, "What about you? How long have you been working on Wall Street? Where were you before?"

I told him my story but left out my divorce. I didn't want him to be turned off by my second-good merchandise tag. He was someone that I wanted to keep close: smart, funny, good-looking, Jewish... And for some reason, I trusted him.

Daniel crossed his utensils over a paucity of unfinished pasta, "I'm flying back to D.C on Monday, but would you like to spend time with me on Sunday? There's a new exhibit at the Guggenheim, and I was looking forward to seeing it. I would love it if you joined me."

"Deal! I'd love to!" I graciously accepted his invitation, having yet to visit any museums in New York.

On Sunday, I slipped on light wash boot-cut jeans and a tight white shirt paired with my favorite black loafers. We met at Central Park and strolled towards the Guggenheim. "I've always had an appreciation for the arts, this display should be stunning." His excitement shined through his calm tone as we proceeded through the double doors. Daniel acquainted me with the various paintings, explaining their histories and the significance of their detailed brushstrokes. That feeling— trust coupled with comfort— ran through my body as he empathized in the beauty of each masterpiece with me. Butterflies.

"Lea, I would love to take you to performances at the Metropolitan Opera and Carnegie Hall," Daniel offered. "My family has annual subscriptions to a variety of artistic performances across the city."

"Thank you, that's very kind. That would be amazing." My eyes sparkled in delight. This would be my first-time experiencing NYC's delicacies. I couldn't wait to lavish and love in such elegant heights.

Night fell. Daniel placed a gentle kiss on my cheek, and we agreed to meet again when he returned from D.C in a couple of weeks. On my way home, butterflies were still flooding me with good feelings, but I grew a bit disappointed with myself. I was open with Daniel about everything and him with me, however, I couldn't reveal my deepest secret. I felt like one of the characters from Arthur Miller's stories or the Great Gatsby, living in deception.

I found my journal and a pen on my bedside table, where I had left it three days prior to my weekend's social marathon. Jotting down my thoughts about these past few hours with Daniel was easy. My writing slowed as I began reflecting upon why I couldn't tell him about my divorce. My stomach growled, hungry for the truth. *Why do I still feel like hiding? What are my fears and insecurities?* Some root belief was tying me down.

Rationalizing my emotions for Daniel clarified this concern to me. First off, I really cared for Daniel and wanted our relationship to evolve. This care, however, translated into an unhealthy fear of losing him. My father's words washed through me, 'no decent man will fall for a divorced woman.' No longer pure, I felt embarrassed and ashamed admitting that I was stained. Then something occurred to me. My pen dropped. *Wouldn't I feel more ashamed deceiving those around me and deceiving myself? Living a lie would strip me of self-respect even further!* Emotions were conquering my values of honesty and integrity. Feelings of insecurity had opened the doorway for fear to kick in, preventing me from expressing myself honestly. I felt miserable failing to be totally transparent with him. These feelings signaled that I needed to accept myself and gain confidence as a divorced woman. *Own your past with pride and move on.*

I flipped back to the page in my journal where my technique to measure outcomes was written: *What's the worst thing that can happen?* Rejection. *Am I willing to accept the risk of him rejecting me in exchange for building an honest and healthy relationship?* I didn't want to, but I was— for my sake and his. I could always move forward as I had done in previous relationships. Staying true to myself and others was the only way I'd remain confident.

Ok, so I met my first goal: I committed to tell him. *But how?* For sure, face-to-face when he returned from Washington. I crossed my fingers, praying that everything would magically fall into place.

Secret Revealed, Insecurity Relieved

Daniel was back in town two weeks later. He invited me to dinner at Boulay, a fine Spanish restaurant in the city. He gave me a warm welcome at the entrance as if time hadn't passed since our last date. A good sign. We situated at a cozy booth, where I sensed myself acting off— not as vivacious as usual. With every comment, I looked into his eyes for approval, then looked elsewhere trying to shield my vulnerability. Worrisome thoughts forced my head down at the menu. *How will he react to my little secret? Will he still accept me? Will his family accept me?* I was replaying the conversation in my head for the hundredth time. *Has Daniel been trying to talk to me this entire time?*

"Lea, you ok there? What would you like to drink? Any appetizers?" I finally acknowledged Daniel's voice. I lifted my head upright to the sight of a waiter in white silk gloves.

"Ummm I'll— I'll take seltzer. And to eat, just a vegetable paella is fine, thank you." My foot was still jittering under the table. My stomach was churning out of anticipation for Daniel's reaction.

I deemed the ideal moment for my reveal just after our dishes were served. The warm colors of vegetables on my plate and the inviting aroma of saffron comforted me. I looked up at Daniel once more before taking my first bite. The contrast between his refined etiquette and my raw mannerisms reminded me of class differences and cultural gaps from My Fair Lady. I wanted to be regarded like the character Eliza: "A tower of strength, a consort battleship." To emulate her, staying true to myself and others was an absolute must. *Ok, Lea, just be you. Tell him why it's important **to me** that he knows the truth.*

"Daniel, I have a small confession. At first, I wasn't sure why I hesitated to share this with you, but after you left, I had some time to reflect. My fears and insecurities were driving me, not my principles. Our friendship is important to me and being honest is one of the things I value the most." I couldn't make eye contact as he was. His hands clasped together atop the white tablecloth, his salmon dish steaming and waiting to be touched.

I was done holding it in: "I've been married before, and I'm divorced." I paused, still looking just past him.

"So, what's your secret?" he asked, trying to find my eyes.

I could hardly find the words to say it again, "That's it. That's my secret. I'm-I'm divorced, and I'm not sure if you'd be interested in someone like me, umm, divorced. I-I just don't know if your parents are ok with you being in a relationship with, you know, someone like me."

He giggled, "You are really silly. You have to meet my parents. They'll adore you. Trust me." He forked up a piece of flaky salmon.

I giggled back flirtatiously and shoveled up a mouthful of spinach, the anxiety trapped inside of me finally released. *What just happened? Am I dreaming?*

"Lea, if you are comfortable sharing your marriage and divorce, I am happy to listen. There is nothing you should be ashamed or embarrassed about. You're different from anyone I've ever met before, and I'd like to know everything about you as I will tell you everything about me."

I had surely heard this before, and I could understand why. Daniel was fascinated by the diverse worlds that I had lived in while his planet seemed stable and homogenous. He shared his close bond with his parents and siblings; he saw his father as a mentor, speaking highly of his intellect and influence in his personal and professional life.

"And my mom— well, she's a bit crazy but has an amazingly big heart."

We carried on conversing about our families, and I shared stories about my father's strict rules that contradicted the woman I wanted to be. Daniel's embracing attitude comforted me, but even if he hadn't accepted me, narrating my story in full infused me with pride. This ownership bolstered my self-esteem and gave Daniel the respect he deserved.

"Lea, you're a very strong woman. I am so delighted to have met and gotten to know you. I want to keep getting to know you and bringing you into my life. With that said, are you free tomorrow?" His puppy eyes always got to me.

"Thank you, Daniel. I love spending time with you too. Let's make plans in the morning," I said on the verge of yawning, exhausted by my tangent of mixed emotions.

"Ok, we better," he said softly. He kissed me— this time, not on the cheek but tenderly on the lips— and wished me good night.

I liked him. I liked what I saw, what I heard, and the way he was treating me. His touch evoked a sensation that this relationship would last. But this was just the honeymoon stage. Not a real honeymoon of course— just a novel phase where everything seems flowery, blossoming, and beautiful. However, all things that seem perfect eventually crack due to false perceptions that lead to disappointment. If I could predict eventual disappointments, I'd be a magician. No magic wand yet!

On the drive home, I hummed away to my favorite song, Don McLean's *Vincent: Starry, Starry Night,* fantasizing about a future life with Daniel. Although he was on the younger side and I wasn't drawn to him sexually, his charm and affection were luring me in. I was completely enchanted.

Managing Parents: Change Your Reactions, Don't Try to Change Them!

I woke up at 5:00 AM on Sunday for my morning run. Passing by my parent's apartment on my trail back, I saw light shining from their unit. I let myself in to check in on them.

"Ah, Gulçimen! Who threw you out of bed so early?" My mother was surprised to see me. It was barely 6:00 AM, and she had already whipped up breakfast. "Coffee?" she asked, serving my dad his meat mixed with scrambled eggs, potatoes, and a bread loaf on the side.

"Yeah sure, why not." I sat down to take my first sip of only to be bombarded with questions.

"How are your dates going? Have you found anyone yet? Why didn't you come for Shabbat last week?"

I put the mug down. "Mama, please. I'm not ready yet. I just want to make friends."

"Why have you been coming back so late? What are you doing out there so late at night? Who were you with? Your brother told me you had a date!" She couldn't help but expose me. *Alright, so I'd tell her about Daniel.* I shared his background and that he came from an affluent family, instilling confidence in her that he might be the right guy.

She placed both hands over her chest in prayer, "Ha-levay, ha-levay." (Ha-levay means 'I hope so' in Hebrew).

To manage my parents, I usually had to bear good news— tell them what they want to hear, infuse them with hope, and divert some subjects with a question. I had enough of this conversation.

"How are you, Papa?"

"Thank God! Thank God," he announced lifting his loaf of bread to the ceiling, "I have work and am making a respectful living. This is life, dear." He kissed the piece of bread and whispered a prayer under his breath, grateful to God for the opportunity to work and put food on the table.

Although we had been living in America for almost a decade now, my dad remained a devout simple man and my mom remained inhibited by old-fashioned norms. Living in the Boro and its proximity to me in time and space certainly did not present a window for personal liberation. I had to make it. And sometimes, in those moments where the goal seems impossible, the opportunity becomes even greater.

I jogged back to my apartment and took a shower. Daniel called me, suggesting that we meet in the city around noon to grab lunch and visit the Metropolitan Museum. We sat down to eat at a quaint, boutique restaurant. Daniel told me about his brothers: Both had completed their academic careers, and now, one of them was a reputable bankruptcy lawyer and the other, a successful trader for Lehman Brothers.

"I've decided to move back to New York. I want to continue my education like Jake and Mark did. I want to get my master's degree," he said.

I sensed that Daniel was living in the shadows of two successful siblings, striving for their level of prestige. This concerned me because I hadn't completed my education. However, when Daniel insisted on introducing me to his parents, I knew that to him, my being was more important than my credentials. I happily agreed to meet the following Saturday for dinner. While excited that our relationship was evolving, no sexual attraction had aroused. Perhaps I just needed more time.

Trust Fall, With a Boundary Line.

Daniel and I spoke on the phone daily during the week. We planned to go out with Michelle and her friends on Friday night in the city, then drive up to Long Island on Saturday for dinner with his parents.

"You can stay over the weekend. We'd love to have you. We have empty rooms, you can stay in my brother's room," he offered. I knew that he was well-intended, but I felt like it was too early in our relationship for me to spend the night.

I declined kindly, "Thank you. I just don't feel comfortable quite yet."

"I understand, no worries at all," he sympathized.

After Friday's outing with Michelle and her friends, Daniel suggested that we spend the night at my place and drive to Long Island early the next morning. I was still a bit hesitant. I never had a man stay at my apartment before. *What would my parents say?* But I really didn't want to drive through the unknown windy roads through Kings Point alone. I caved in. Upon returning to my place, I suggested that Daniel sleep on the sofa.

"Can we share your bed? I promise we won't do anything you don't like." Puppy eyes again. Harmless.

"Sure." I crawled nervously into bed wondering how far this would go. *Set your boundaries, Lea. Say no if you need to.* Daniel indeed kept his promise, refraining from anything beyond a warm, gentle touch.

I woke up the next morning at 5:00 ready to run. Daniel was not an early riser, so I left him sound asleep until I came back. At 9:00 AM, Daniel was still in bed. I decided to make breakfast, shower, and journal while waiting for him. He was finally ready at 11:00 AM.

Freedom from Expectations Eliminates Disappointments

Daniel held my hand as he navigated me through the windy roads of Kings Point Estates. *What will his parents be like? Will they approve of me? Stop right there.* I reminded myself of what I had written in my journal that morning: *Free yourself from expectations, don't make assumptions about unknown situations or people. Let it play as it comes.*

Grand properties surrounded by luscious greenery welcomed us to the neighborhood. Daniel instructed me to park directly behind a red Volvo at the foothills of the long driveway. *Wow, Michelle was right: He does come from a well-to-do family.* I unbuckled my seatbelt and took a deep breath. We began to walk toward a house behind ornamental gates, like the ones in the fairytale stories read to me as a kid. A small round fountain greeted us in the front. Trees and floral gardens of all sorts led us to vine-wrapped arches at the entrance. I peered upward, intimidated by the breadth and beauty of this magnificent home with light gray pointed roofs, embellished by touches of white brick. My shoulders stiffened.

"Don't worry, they're going to love you," Daniel whispered. He kissed me lightly on the cheek and caressed my neck.

We entered through the kitchen to the sight of a man munching on kosher dill pickles while reading the newspaper. "It's so pleasant to meet you, I'm Brennon. Brennon Schwartz. We've heard so much about you." His father greeted me with a hug.

Brennon's towering height overwhelmed me although he was soft-spoken like his son. I noticed a pencil-thin blond lady sitting at the counter slurping on diet coke, meticulously cataloging some index cards.

"Hello Lea!" she said in a cheery voice, her blue eyes piercing with joy. That was Daniel's mom, Sara. "Come sit, want a coke?" She pulled me a chair.

Soon enough, we were all closely gathered around the small round table as if we were family. His parents pleasantly inquired about my family, career, and interests. They were fascinated by my cultural background and roots as a Tat Jew, which they had slim knowledge of. His dad and I bonded over shared experiences on Wall Street. Daniel mostly kept quiet as he witnessed the instant connection between me and his parents.

Sara gestured with her lanky arms, "I made reservations for 7:00 PM at Osteria Antonio, is that good for you?"

I looked to Daniel for approval and nodded my head. He confirmed, "Yes mom, we'll be back by six."

I was amazed by how welcoming Daniel's family was, a total contrast from my debut at the Wolfson household. There was something different about them— affluent with influence yet authentic and humble. They prized not the image or status of people but the substance behind them. What's behind the portrait— one's values, experiences, and actions— mattered more than the figure painted on the canvas itself.

During dinner, Brennon was intrigued by my family's culture and how I saw the world. Over a sudden, he got up, wrapped his hands around my shoulders, and said, "I want you to know that we love you just the way you are, and no matter what. Welcome to the family." This imbued a warmth and comfort in me that eliminated self-doubt. These simple words of kindness and compassion fostered my sense of security and confidence in the Schwartz family.

Another Perspective on Jewish Life:
From Orthodox to Conservative Judaism

Within three or four months, Daniel would settle with me in my apartment. We continued our weekend road trips to his parent's home in Long Island. I was invited to join the family's weekly Sunday pinochle tournament and pizza dinner. Over the next few months, I would have amassed many new experiences going to Broadway shows and performances at Carnegie Hall, the Metropolitan Opera, and a variety of gastronomic eateries where Daniel or his family paid for everything. I was like their little princess.

While a new world opened for me, I had little time for anything or anyone else. On the Jewish holidays, I split my time between my family and Daniel's. On Rosh Hashanah, I joined Daniel and his parents for services at their local synagogue.

"Women don't sit separately?" I asked, shocked to see no mechitza (separator) between men and women.

"No, we sit together," Daniel remarked casually. This was unlike the Orthodox setup. It was my first time in a conservative synagogue. I enjoyed the secular twist on the sermons and felt embraced by this community of Jews. The Rabbi's speeches preached adhering to principles delineated in the Torah by working on yourself first to contribute to the community and repair the world at large. The principle of Tikkun Olam came alive in a free lifestyle rather than an imposing one such as that in Boro Park.

Although rituals in the Boro were beautiful, unifying, and unique, their restrictive elements subject one's entire faith to the hands of God. Although Orthodox Jews dissected verses of the bible, they never questioned God and His identity. In conservative Judaism, anything and everything is up for debate; religion takes on a practical role, a philosophy to life. I was thankful to have found Jewish values consistent with my principles in a liberating light, executed by like-minded people.

My First Thanksgiving

I spent my first-ever Thanksgiving with Daniel's family. Holding space for expressions of gratitude is a concept I was blown away by and is one that I treasure until this day.

"I'm thankful for having been embraced by you all and being here with such wonderful, kind, and loving people," I shared out.

Each guest at the Schwartz Thanksgiving table was intelligent, willing, and capable of engaging in hearty, moderated discussions. This contrasted any holiday celebration I had experienced before. In my family, it was impossible to speak over our passionate, loud bunch; in Mendy's home, many subjects were taboo. Here, all questions were welcome— none were inappropriate, none were stupid, and none went unanswered. Just listening-in and contributing to the conversation was good enough. 'Good enough is good enough' was a foreign concept to me; it's a paradigm that Daniel's father would ingrain in me.

Is Good Enough Just Good Enough?

I noticed my relationship with Daniel strengthen due to my strong bond with his parents. Sara was always kind to me, but I especially enjoyed my interactions with Brennon. He provoked me with stimulating questions that made me think and reflect. Over time, it seemed as if my friendship with him was tying me into my relationship with Daniel. A package deal indeed.

I woke up early one Friday morning at the Schwartz home. Everyone was asleep besides Brennon with his morning brew in hand, skimming both the New York Times and Wall Street Journal.

"Good morning, Lea, help yourself to something, please."

"Good morning, I'm ok thank you." I was eager to go for a walk and grab a coffee but refrained from touching anything because Daniel's mom had severe OCD. I filled up a glass of water and sat at the table next to Brennon. The articles he was reading were a bit too sophisticated for my level of English, so I opted for the New York Post instead.

After a good hour of filling our brains, Brennon and I took a stroll through the hidden trails of Kings Point Estates. This turned into a weekly ritual. We stepped on the crispy autumn leaves in pure satisfaction and chatted away about his childhood, philosophies to life, and my future.

"Lea, you're so charming, like honey to a bee," Brennon encouraged, "You can do so many things, you have so much potential, I'm telling you. I know that you don't like sitting behind the screen and coding for ten hours a day. Would you consider doing something else?"

"I would," I knew that Brennon truly wanted to help guide me but was reluctant. "I'm just not sure since I don't have many other skills. I don't have other credentials or licenses besides developing codes for portfolio management and trading systems. I wouldn't know which direction to turn."

Brennon insisted, "Your charm and warmth are so personable. You know how to develop relationships. That is an extremely valuable skill! It can present so many opportunities."

While I understood his point, I was perplexed as to their practical application. "How can I make money using those skills?"

"Lea, seriously." Brennon stopped walking and looked me in the eyes. "You have foundational skills, some that even formal education cannot provide. You're a critical and diverse thinker, you're extremely wise. You can acquire any technical skills easily, and I can help you." He laid out an array of ideas, and proposed, "You can build a wealth management firm that serves the Israeli and Jewish community. Your first step would be to submit a request to DW to get series-7 training and other required licenses."

Through this conversation, I realized that Brennon was planting seeds for me to apply my soft skills to foster my independence and a high income with other benefits. He envisioned me polishing my rawness to manifest the potential he saw in me.

Brennon committed to guiding me as if I was his daughter, equipping me with the tools I needed to succeed. He used his intellect and compassion— a different style of guidance than I experienced at home. I found solace in his acceptance and respect for me. At one point, I even started calling Brennon 'dad!'

Growing up, my father often felt that no matter how hard I tried to achieve something, I had to do better. It's not that he didn't love me or believe that I could not succeed; he simply lacked the tools and resources to help me excel. Pushing me to reach an unattainable bar was his love language. He also considered my stubborn, rebellious personality a hindrance from achieving my full potential. "You're like a wild horse," he would tell me, "Look at your sister, she obeys and is so dedicated to her studies." He idolized Marina as the role model for me.

I later realized that the cultural, skill, and resource gaps explained the differences between my father's and Brennon's guidance. Brennon was more comforting because acceptance was the central element of his philosophy. All the while, it was my cultural background and family values— especially my father's— that endowed me with the soft skills that Brennon praised. Combining Brennan's expertise and resources with my technical skills, character traits, and cultural ethics would build my confidence as I worked toward any goal. So long as I put my best efforts forward, there was progress, and I felt fulfilled, the outcomes didn't need to meet some unattainable, subjective standard of perfection. Sometimes goals involve some standard to be met but building something new takes time. Through the process, each obstacle gives way for more opportunities to expand knowledge and forge new connections.

Brennan's message, "Good enough is good enough, not everything needs to be perfect," resonated over time. My perspective shifted entirely. I was gaining confidence in my perceived weaknesses by refraining from comparing myself to others. *Look at how far you've come from where you started!* I didn't have a college degree, only two years of technical certification. *Is this good enough? Yes!* I was going to college, earning a living respectfully, and working in a high-demand profession. *So long as I work hard, do so ethically, and feel good, the outcomes are good enough for now.*

Self-deprecation is rooted in comparisons to others— people, societal norms, or standards— that compose our own definition of perfection. Perfection is an abstract of reality, merely a man-made illusion created to fuel our progress. Perfection is a good motivator, but it's important to credit oneself when making even the smallest steps toward the objective. Small steps are what individuals should be striving for because they remove the pressure of reaching a high bar with no thought-out steps in between.

As for me, I decided to continue my schooling with one or two classes a semester to obtain my degree. *It might take me ten years to complete, but that's ok!* The saying goes, 'shoot for the moon, but if you miss, you'll land among the stars.' Most often, the stars are just good enough, and sometimes even better, because they shine light upon areas for improvement or new opportunities that one could not have seen from the moon. I gave my daughter a bookmark with this quote years later.

While Daniel and I spent Friday nights and Saturday mornings with my family, we spent almost every Saturday night and Sunday with his parents. I looked forward to the social outings that Daniel's mom organized with fellow neighbors and friends; I relished my long morning coffee walks with Brennon. On Monday mornings, Brennon and I would drive into the city for work before the sun would rise. As months passed, I felt my close friendship with him compensating for Daniel's shortcomings. I adored Daniel, but sex was dull. I let this go, willing to sacrifice three hours a week for constant respect, care, and compassion. Power struggles were absent, my comfort was made a priority, and I simply loved being around them all. At this juncture of my life, the package deal won me the lottery.

Can Informality be Justified with Morality?

The Schwartz family was invited to a wedding in Los Angeles. Of course, I would accompany as Daniel's date. This would be my first time traveling within the United States, my first time in California! My airline ticket, hotel room, and meals were covered in full. We would be staying at the Beverly Hills Four Seasons, where the celebration would be held.

I had never seen a venue so glamorous. Upon arrival, we sat down to have lunch together on the outside patio overlooking the colorful garden below. We ordered a platter with fine deli meats and olives, which I helped myself to with my fingers.

"You're like an unpolished diamond, Lea," Brennon would jest whenever I picked at food with my hands. It another way of telling me that I was a gem that just needed some refinement. We laughed as Daniel and his mother inserted their thin forks into slices of beef carpaccio. They didn't seem to mind.

The wedding celebration was later that night. We arrived at cocktail hour greeted by bow-tied waiters and waitresses circulating trays of hors d'oeuvres. Cubes of truffle-infused aged gouda made their way toward Daniel and me. I delicately picked up a cube with my fingertips. Daniel's face turned red.

"Really, Lea!? With your hands!?" he scoffed into my ear, "That's just embarrassing!"

"Oops." I said unapologetically, nibbling. He had never criticized me before. *And besides, what's so bad about picking up a single cube of cheese with my fingers?* I wasn't hurting anyone, nor were we seated at a formal dinner table. His remarks infused such discomfort that I no longer wanted to be at the event. I walked outside in a fit.

"Where do you think you're going?" Daniel shouted, chasing after me. I ignored him and kept walking towards the elevator, high heels in hand and my long black dress sweeping the marble floor.

"Leave me alone! I am going to the room!"

He grabbed my wrist and yelled, "Stop! Stop reacting! Why do you eat with your hands? Can't you see that this is a white glove wedding?

No one touches food with their hands!"

I lashed back, "So what? It's MY food, not anyone else's!" I was furious. Even when we sat down at a fine dining restaurant, I ate with my hands, and he said nothing.

"Lea! You have bad etiquette! You act like a total savage!" He continued to shame me as I pulled away from him. *Ignore.* I was already in the elevator. Doors closed.

That night only spiraled downwards as we failed to mend our differences. The blame game took over and escalated the conflict— my fault, in part, for reverting to my old habits instead of focusing on the event's purpose. It really wouldn't have mattered if I simply apologized with "I'm sorry, I won't do it again." Afterall, we were there to celebrate the joy of the occasion and spend time together. But I didn't care. I selfishly held my belief that fingerpicking at small foods was an acceptable personal preference, and that it would never change because it neither harmed anyone nor directly affected anyone but me.

I sought revenge over Daniel, holding my moral premise over his trivial manners. *How can I get back at him?* I ripped my dress off and tumbled into bed. *Maybe I won't go to tomorrow's brunch.* I fell asleep soaking in resentment, failing to see Daniel's perspective, respect the formal environment, and the higher purpose of the event.

I awoke the next morning with Daniel beside me, still in his seventh dream. I decided to go for a jog and explore the property. My morning runs were often used as reflection time: There was some wonky feeling in my stomach. *Was I wrong? Should I have responded differently? Who lost in the end?* Yep, it was me. All me. In trying to punish Daniel— seeking to equalize the pain— I punished myself. I also impacted the bride and groom since Daniel wasn't there to fully participate in their jubilant celebration. This was a bad habit inherited from home and my marriage in the Boro: A tooth for a tooth, an eye for an eye. I remembered the tension only escalating when my mother used this tactic against my father: "You go, I'm not coming," she'd say. We all hated it. Nobody wins.

Sometimes though, a tooth for a tooth, an eye of an eye, is needed to get a message across. At twenty-six, I had yet to decipher when retaliation was worth it. I had to think about my purpose in a particular situation and act accordingly. At the wedding, I surely overreacted. I was adamant that my ethics and principles compensated for my lack of proper etiquette. But the two were unrelated.

Justifying my informalities with morality was a fallacy I had yet to realize in the future. In certain situations, both morality and formalities are necessary. When trying to do the right thing, a person must present oneself with the same degree of poise as the intended actions. One won't be trusted unless the message is conveyed with mannerisms tailored to the environment and target audience.

I grabbed a cup of coffee and sat down to journal after my run. I wrote: 'Protesting by disengaging hurts me and others around me.' I wondered, *how should have I reacted?* Maintaining my composure and brushing off Daniel's snarky remarks with sarcasm would have worked. I could have replied, "Oh my goodness, I'm so sorry I contaminated the platter by touching the cheese! Forgive me for my sins!" or calmly with, "I understand, this may be perceived as improper at an event like this, I'm sorry."

Since it's always been difficult for me to contain my emotions, I resolved that from now on, I'd diffuse the source of my temper and wait until after the event to discuss it. And I **would** go to the wedding brunch; I would brush off my anger and pretend as if nothing happened. I would act extra proper and exaggerate a sophisticated use of utensils in front of Daniel. Unfortunately, we never ended up discussing our differences as I had wanted. None of us ever brought it up.

I soon recognized that this whole fiasco was less about Daniel and good morals, but more about me and my behavior. We failed to understand differences in our behaviors, rooted in our dissimilar upbringings. I considered Daniel and his family to have a pristine set of morals, yet we still had seas of cultural gaps to bridge. This was just one incident that revealed it.

A Major Turn-Off

A week after the wedding, we were back in New York and conflict-free. We were staying at the Schwartz home in Long Island that weekend. One Saturday morning, I came into Daniel's room. It was already 11:00 AM. As usual, he was still snoozing.

"Are you getting up?"

He yawned, "Soon, Lea, soon." He tumbled out of bed lazily, and his pillow toppled over. OMG! Hundred-dollar bills were flying across the floor.

"Daniel!? Where did that come from!?" I was astonished, wondering why that kind of money wasn't in a safe or in his wallet. He scurried to his knees and began picking up the money anxiously.

"Uh, my mom gave it to me. She gives me spending-money," he said. No comment.

I exited the room at a loss for words and went downstairs. It dawned on me that while Daniel was going to school, he was not working. His parents were paying all his bills. This totally turned me off. It gave me the ick. Although a nice gesture for his mother to provide him with money, this was hard for me to digest. He wasn't making any money of his own! *Maybe it's just a cultural difference.*

I worked my way up the ladder since I was fifteen. In my family, what you earn is what you get. I always hesitated taking money from my parents and never wanted to take money from anyone else. While Daniel was still young— only twenty-five— I believed that a grown man (anyone for that matter) should work for his living and be independent of his parents. Financial independence was important to me, but the unconditional kindness, respect, and generosity Daniel and his family provided overrode any criticisms I wanted to make. Still, no comment.

I had yet to realize how Daniel's financial dependence would impact our relationship. A pitted approach to resolving problems paired with Daniel's financial dependence led to our demise.

With Me, It's All or Nothing

I stopped by my parent's house on the way back from my run as usual. My brother, Aidan, was in the kitchen prepping breakfast. "Hey, sis! I was just about to call you!" He was mid-munch on a cheese-filled toasted pita bread.

"What can I do for you?" I asked.

"Well, there's this watch I want to buy. I just need to borrow like 6,000 dollars. I promise I'll pay you back, just give me a few months."

Since I was making good money at the time, I was more than willing to help him.

"I'll do my best to get you the money by the end of the day." I also knew that if I needed anything, he'd always have my back.

"Thank you, sis. You're the best." He hugged me in gratitude.

I headed back to my apartment, where I was surprised to see Daniel wide awake and studying on his computer by 7:00 AM.

"Good morning, well you're up early," I placed a light kiss on his cheek. "I need to stop at the bank on our way to Long Island this afternoon if you don't mind."

"Why?" He spun around abruptly. I explained the situation and emphasized that my brother would repay me within a few months, as he always followed up on his promises. "6,000! On a watch? Why does he need it? He shouldn't be using OUR money to buy himself a watch. That's ridiculous!"

I tried to diffuse his anger by keeping my cool. "I'm not the judge of my brother nor is it my place to tell him how to spend it. Daniel please do not worry. I trust him, he will return the money." He needed to understand that my brothers and I had a special relationship. I reasoned, "When I moved here, they did everything for me. They put my entire apartment together and built me a custom bed." Additionally, money came secondary in my family; unconditional support was the priority. Daniel's priorities lay elsewhere.

"It's a luxury item. Why does he need to borrow money for something so... frivolous?"

"Daniel, this is my money and I can loan it to whomever I choose. This conversation is over!"

"No, Lea! We're about to get married. It's OUR money!" He flared up again.

"You have to stop! I am SO SORRY, but I was the one who worked hard to save that money and I will give it to whoever I want!" I opened my desk drawer and snatched the checkbook. Daniel grabbed it from me. I tried to grab it back and he pushed me onto the couch. *He's insane!* I had never asked him or his family for a penny. *This man wants to control my money and we aren't even married!*

The doorbell rang. It was Aidan. I ran downstairs, opened the door, and handed him the check. My face was flushed.

"Is everything ok?" He asked.

I nodded my head yes and told him not to worry. "Just take the check." I closed the door quickly and stayed downstairs for a long 15 minutes to cool off. As I made my way up, Daniel was coming down with his suitcase.

"I'm going home," he declared, and pushed me onto the staircase. I fell backward and tumbled down the first couple of steps and sat there simmering. I rushed outside to confront Daniel while he was loading his car.

"If you leave now," my finger pointed at his face, "I am packing all your stuff and taking it to your parents!"

He said nothing. He just spit at me, shoved me against the fence, and drove away.

As the fumes from the exhaust faded, my anger faded too— into despair. I felt hopeless, disrespected, and humiliated once again by a man using his force to hurt and "put a woman in her place." This brought memories of the arguments I used to have with Mendy, physically aggressive and void of constructive conversations. Neither of us understood the importance of letting things go during a flare-up. Neither of us were able to de-escalate heated situations.

How could a mere gap in our values yield such a big fight? In retrospect, I realize how the differences between Daniel and me disrupted our harmony. Once harmony is disrupted, small issues can accumulate and infuse toxicity in what was once a healthy relationship, especially when both partners lack the skills to confront conflicts collaboratively. Conflicts are inevitable, and I had yet to discover these constructive methods. *Will I continue running to Brennon when Daniel and I fight?* I could not see my relationship with Daniel functioning as a standalone without his family. I particularly enjoyed the fatherly figure Brennon engulfed me with, along with the comfort and support of his family. But in a partner, I sought someone who understood my value-set and could agree to disagree.

Unpacking the Package Deal

I walked upstairs slowly and soon gained the strength to pack all of Daniel's belongings. I called my younger brother, Emilio: "Are you home? I need your help." I told him what had just happened. He arrived at my place minutes later.

Together, we loaded my dad's station wagon and drove to Long Island. *How would I break the news to Daniel's parents? What should I say? This is so awkward!* We had been planning our wedding, looking at venues, table arrangements, and caterers. *I considered this an informal divorce. How will I break out of this mess?*

Upon our arrival in Kings Point, I planned to run inside, quickly inform his parents of the situation, and drop off Daniel's things. My brother waited outside. "Good luck sis. Just say how you feel, you got it," he encouraged. I gave him a hug and walked up the driveway toward

326

the house lugging a large duffel bag.

 I rang the doorbell, and Brennon welcomed me inside. "Lea! How are you!? Good to see you!"

"I'm so sorry," I said, and told them what had happened. "This just isn't working out…. I love Daniel, and I love you all, but it's just not working." I sniffled, about to cry. He brought me to the quaint kitchen table where we had met for the first time.

"Lea, I know you're upset," He placed his hand atop mine and looked into my teary eyes. "Take your time. But know that you always have a place here no matter what. We love you too, we love you so much, and we always will."

Brennon's words never failed to touch me. I knew that I'd miss our morning strolls and our heartfelt conversations that filled my world with laughter and love. The package deal became all or nothing, and I had to choose nothing. Through unpacking the package deal, I realized that my relationship had to be sustained on its own, independent of the man's parents or any external factors that enriched it.

Unpacking Once Again:
The Aftermath of the Breakup

I felt relief in Daniel's absence, going about my same socially-intellectually-physically balanced routine. A few days later, my mom handed me a 1,000-dollar check, a portion of the money my brother owed me. I wasn't worried about the rest for now. I was financially stable with the means to treat myself to whatever my heart desired. I was truly content, well-aware that I had come a long way on this quest to know myself. But there was much more to learn. I'd continue exploring every avenue along this journey.

Daniel called me a few weeks after our breakup: "I know that things are over between us, but I just want to let you know that I'm leaving back to Washington, D.C. for work. If you'd like to reconsider our relationship, let me know."

If he was hoping to remand, why did he decide to move? Something still felt off between us, apparent by our inability to have an open and honest conversation about our situation. I would not reconsider. "I really wish you the best of luck. Let's stay friends. You have shown me the world and opened my heart, eyes, and mind. Thank you, Daniel, truly I wish you the best."

He hung up.

As time passed, Daniel and I were able to restore our friendship through frequent phone calls and casual outings when he visited New York. I much appreciated our ability to reconnect as friends and set our differences aside.

Several years later, before my wedding, he took me out for coffee and told me that I was the best thing that ever happened to him. "Lea, you were the love of my life, and I will love you forever no matter what." His eyes no longer had the same sparkle. Those words built my self-esteem in the moment, but he remained in pain.

"I have learned a great deal from you and your family, thank you for everything, really." I paused to take the final sip of my latte and concluded the conversation, "Let's go?"

Daniel nodded looking down with pursed lips. We hugged goodbye, sensing that this would be probably the last time we would see each other. And it was.

Sporty and Spunky

My treadmill station was magnetic. I'd maintain a solid pace for two hours, flipping between news channels, the stock market, and basketball games.

"I get tired of watching you run! You're like an energizer bunny!" People would say, huddled around me. Sometimes, they'd join in to watch the Knicks's last play. I felt like a celebrity.

"Running is my drug! I love it! What's your name? It's so nice to meet you!" I'd reply, smiling, and of course, still running.

While monthly fees at the Sporting Club were steep relative to my income, I remembered what Brennon used to tell me: "If you use something daily and enjoy it, and it's not breaking the bank, spend the money and create opportunities for yourself with like-minded people." So, I did, and it paid off. My queen-bee status was elevated: Swarming around me were fan clubs of high-producing stock traders and executives soon turned workout buddies! I must admit that I certainly did have a cute smile and striking features that lured people in. Besides, ranging from speed seven to nine on the treadmill, I couldn't be ignored— great training for my boys' club at the basketball court anyway!

My new project manager's name was Chen. He became a close friend. A single Asian man in his thirties, Chen was reserved and quiet, the opposite of me. All the while, we shared a mutual love for basketball and pick-up games at Battery Park City.

"Do you want to join some Morgan Stanley and DW guys and me

for a game after work on Thursday at 5:00?" Chen invited me one day after work.

"Yes! I'd love to!" I couldn't have been more excited.

Shortly before work ended that Thursday, I asked Chen if there were bathrooms at the courts so I could change into my gym clothes when we got there.

"Why don't you just change now so we don't waste time when we get there?" He insisted, looking down at his watch. I was reluctant to confess the real reason why I wanted to change at the court, so I made something up.

"Well, I have some assignments to finish before the game, and I don't want to leave them pending. I really want to get them done now. I need as much time as possible." The truth was that I'd feel over-exposed and uncomfortable wearing shorts and a t-shirt in a workspace. Chen looked a bit surprised: He had cleared me from the most recent task. But he was never one to push about any private matters unless I addressed them directly.

"Ok, Lea, no problem," he said. I was appreciative of his response. New Yorkers and Israelis would be on the other side of the spectrum, never letting-up until satisfied with the reason.

Both basketball courts were full. One of them had three-player pickup games on each side, so Chen and I decided to join in. We needed a third person on our team for the trio rotation.

"Hey Rey, you want to play with me and Lea next round?" Chen tapped a random guy on the shoulder. I turned around to a hunk with a dark complexion and slightly slanted eyes.

"Ok, sure," he said in a deep voice, scanning me up and down as he hopped in line.

It was finally our turn. Our opponents were attempting to secretly strategize, but their voices were loud and clear: "Are you kidding me, just guard HER, the girl's easy!" Rey and Chen eyed me expecting a reaction. No need. I was just waiting for reality to hit once we started the game! Rey didn't waste any time on the petty exchange either.

"Ready? Ball on!" he announced. At the onset of play, I unleashed my specialty shot— three-pointers— three times in a row!

"She dusted you again, put your hands on her!" one of our opponents shouted. It was the biggest guy— about six-foot-two and probably 200 pounds— who came onto me and began to shove and elbow me around my waistline. I was fearless, gyrating my hips with full force to box him out and lay-up over him.

"Back off her, stop pushing! That's enough!" Rey was furious. I was thankful for his defense, but I enjoyed this abrasive style of play.

"It's ok! I grew up playing like this! I'm used to it! We got this!" This is how the game was played in Israel. Taking on the guys meant that it was going to be rough and tough. No excuses.

Rey, Chen, and I won every game for the next few rotations. The guys on the other team gained respect for me and apologized for being so aggressive. Even Rey, the best player there, was amazed by my skills.

"Lea! Where did you learn to play ball like that?" He asked.

I was crouched over my bag, chugging water as sweat dripped onto the asphalt. "It's a long story, but I'd be happy to share it with you sometime!" How I still had the energy to flirt, I have no idea!

"Well, why don't you join us for dinner? It is YOUR win after all! And maybe you can tell us your story!" Rey asked, knuckle bumping my bicep.

"Sure, I'd love to!"

The three of us walked across the street together, ridiculing our opponents who underestimated me. "They were so angry! I can't believe it!" I exclaimed.

"Those guys were just intimidated once they saw those awesome three-pointers! They've got too big of an ego to let a girl score against them!" Rey downed a shot of tequila, "I've never met a girl who's so small and plays so well! I'm so impressed! Common, lemme treat you to a drink!"

I was flattered but politely rejected the offer. "Just seltzer please, thank you." Wow! I was parched! I downed the glass in one slurp. Rey took another two shots and Chen sipped on a Pina Colada. By midnight, we had all forgotten that it was Thursday— work tomorrow! Chen, Rey, and I made plans to play the following week at the same time.

"Thanks for playing with a girl, even though she dusted a few guys!" I joked and wished them good night.

Sore and stiff thighs confined me to bed for longer than usual the next morning. I finally got out of bed to take a shower and noticed black and blue marks all over my ribs and hips. No morning run. *How will I possibly walk to work in heels? Ouch!* With every step, I felt my leg muscles burning and bulging out of my short skirt. There was some sense of accomplishment there. I strode proudly into DW and settled at my cubicle. For once, I wasn't antsy. Around 11:00 AM, my work phone rang.

"Good morning, how are you feeling?" It was Rey. I was shocked to hear his voice.

"Good morning, nice to hear from you! I had a rough night, my body literally changed colors and my muscles are screaming for an ice bath!"

"Yes, the feeling is mutual, that was a tough one yesterday," Rey replied and cut to the chase: "Lea, I was going to ask you. Do you want to grab dinner with me on Saturday? We can go watch the Knicks game and eat dinner in the box!"

Wow! That was fast! I couldn't turn down watching the Knicks! "Yeah! That's a definite yes for me! Sometimes I watch Knicks games for two hours while running on the treadmill!" I revealed my secret, incapable of containing my excitement.

"Perfect. It's a date," said Rey. "I'll pick you up."

Rey lived all the way in New Jersey but offered to drive from his place to pick me up in Brooklyn, and then to Madison Square Garden for the game. I told him I'd be happy to meet him in the city. He insisted, "It's no big deal. I'll be at your place at five to come get you."

Part V The Single Scenes

7

Rey de la Cruz:
Love, Sex, and Friendship

T he Friday before my date with Rey, I met Tom for lunch. He had been on a work trip from Monday through Thursday, so we caught up on Friday with the usual weekly updates.

"Yesterday, I met someone named Rey de la Cruz when I was playing ball with Chen. Do you know him?" I was intrigued to know more about him.

"Oh... Rey de la Cruz...He's been with DW for over fifteen years," Tom glanced down at his salmon Caesar salad and took a deep breath. "Lea, de la Cruz runs a tight ship. He's tough, he's a fox. You're too innocent. Please be careful, he's a player." He took a small bite.

"A player? What does that mean?" I had never heard that term before. Innocence exposed.

Tom laughed, "Oh my goodness you're so naive!" and then retired to his serious voice. "Ok. Let me explain this to you: A player is a man who flirts with you and makes you feel special and like you're the only girl in his life when you're really just one of many."

"So what?" I challenged him, "Isn't that just like all the men swarming around me? What about you? Don't you make me feel special?"

"Lea, you're safe with me," he stated simply.

As our lunchtime talk evolved, Tom shared some stories about Rey in attempts to highlight his machismo and player-like qualities. It still didn't click.

At 5:00 PM sharp on Saturday, Rey rang the doorbell. As I welcomed him inside, the scent of Armani cologne permeated my cozy apartment. He wore a pair of dark jeans with a white dress shirt from which his shoulders and biceps protruded. I couldn't stop gawking.

"Would you like something to drink?" I offered.

"No, I'm alright. We'll be at the game soon. They have food and drinks there." Even if he didn't want anything, it was culturally ingrained in me to bring out just a little something. I steeped loose-leaf tea and set out a tray of rugelach cookies. "It's ok Lea, really, I'm ok," he said as I sat down.

"I know you're ok, drink anyway," I cracked a smile. Traditional hospitality.

We sipped and noshed for a short fifteen minutes, sharing our love for the New York Knicks. At around 5:20, we started wrapping up our conversation.

"Are you ready to go?" Rey prompted. I nodded my head with an eager smile like a kid in a candy store.

Ethnically Different, Ethically Similar

Along our drive, Rey told me about his background— born and raised in New Jersey, half Basque, half Filipino. Our ethnicities couldn't have been more different, however, we shared many common values and interests. Like me, Rey was close to his parents and older sister who built a life from humble means. He was the first in his family to attend college and work for such a prominent company.

"I've always loved working at DW, I've interned there since going to school. I'm always so grateful for that opportunity because it helped me support my parents and siblings," Rey stated. Although we shared similar careers and values regarding education, I was curious if we'd be able to fill our cultural, religious, and ideological gaps.

We finally arrived at Madison Square Garden. The box was filled with select Wall Street executives, directors, and their spouses or girlfriends. Beer and snacks arrived in abundance.

Rey introduced me to several of his colleagues, "Meet my new friend Lea, she's an outstanding basketball player! Her three-pointers are insane!"

I recognized a few of the guys from the game on Thursday. Drunken away, some began spilling out their initial impressions of me. "That small gal's gonna play ball? That's what I was thinking! Then she knocked us all out!"

"I'll show you how this small gal's mighty!" I chuckled with them and made plans to meet at the hoops again next week.

The Knicks' victory against the Golden State Warriors made the perfect conclusion to the evening. We exited the stadium bumping hands, sensing that we wanted to hold mine. I didn't make that move.

Rey turned toward me and asked, "Did you have fun?"

"The real fun would've been sitting on the floor behind the players or with the crowd. I'm really a simple person! But I had a blast, thank you so much!"

Rey winked at me as I buckled my seatbelt. "I'd much rather play basketball again with you, that would be real fun."

I flirted back, "Yeah! That's for sure!"

When we arrived at my place, Rey wanted to come upstairs. I could suspect where that was headed.

"I'm a bit tired, maybe we can meet up tomorrow?" I yawned. He nodded his head and walked me to the door of the building. I gave him a big hug goodbye. Our exchange of energy evoked a sexual sensation inside of me. I stared until his strong presence and model-like physique disappeared into the dark.

I finally closed the door and rushed upstairs. Straight to the shower! Crawling into bed that night, his figure's every tone and facial feature were vivid to me. Fantasies followed me into my dreams.

Lazuli's Take on Rey

I drove to meet Lazuli in Manhattan Beach the next morning for coffee. She was the perfect person to whom I could express my feelings about Rey. Perhaps she could help me understand them.

"Seriously Zuli! I haven't experienced that since what happened at the library! Remember when I told you about that? But now it's different, I feel this sensation AND I'm talking to him!"

She was blank for a moment, then prompted, "Well, that's great!

What attracts you to him?"

This got me thinking. "Well, he's nice and he defends me. I just feel like I'm missing the discussions that I had with Daniel or Bill. I just can't see myself having intellectual discussions or growing older with him. Besides, he's not even Jewish. But at the same time, I don't know how we could be just friends. There's too much sexual tension, I don't know…"

"Well, you guys could try having sex, maybe then you'll really know how much you like him!" Lazuli took a big gulp of her latte. This was absurd to me because in my mind, no social or emotional connection meant no sex, but Lazuli saw things differently. "Good sex is just good sex, and they're all good enough until the next one is better than the last! Lea, you're so innocent! Wake up girl, we don't live in Dagestan or the Middle Ages! So what if he's not Jewish?"

Wow, this girl is good— she pulled the 'so what' trick on me now. "Ah! Lazuli! I just don't think that way!" I listened to her perspective with open ears yet decided to restrain myself for now. The showerhead would serve me well until I could feel something deeper than lust for Rey.

Before Lazuli and I parted our separate ways, she told me that she'd be undergoing surgery to cut her protruding jaw. It was simply for aesthetic purposes.

"I won't be able to eat for six months, I will need your help," she clenched my shoulders for comfort.

"Of course, don't hesitate to ask, you know I'm here for you, whatever you need." I came in for a hug.

After my conversation with Lazuli, I dedicated an hour to journaling. There was a battle inside of me— a wildfire for sex burning restraint. *How can I contain my urge? Will I cave in? Will I really regret having sex with him if I did?* Regret was my biggest fear. *Is sex only a physical activity for pleasure? Or does it imply love and commitment?* I toyed with these concepts until indecisiveness exhausted me. Nevertheless, thinking before acting remained the number-one rule in my book.

I believed then, and still do, that the more you love someone holistically, the more love you can infuse physically. Building a friendship based on respect, personal-emotional connection, and intellectual conversations **first** brings additional passion to the intimate experience. Timing is key. 'JUST A FRIENDSHIP, FOR NOW,' I wrote in my journal. I appreciated Rey for the person he was, however, I was not looking for a long-term relationship with him. My purpose was to unpack the beliefs I held about sex while discovering my body's pleasures.

Developing a Friendship with Diverse Experiences

I invited Rey to shoot hoops with my brothers and me in the late afternoon. "Ready to kick ass?" He tossed me my sneakers. I nodded, laced up, and grabbed my car keys.

"Oh yeah! You'll love my brothers! I'm so excited you're getting to meet them! You're gonna hit it off!" And indeed, they did.

Rey and my brothers found many similarities amongst each other despite our religious and cultural differences. Like Rey, both Aidan and

340

Emilio were athletic, hip, and talked in the latest slang: "Pass, Pass! I'm here bro!" Our two-on-two matches were most intense and energizing. I felt respected and treated as an equal on a male-dominated court. There was no negative energy, demeaning language, or vindictive plays.

After the game, my brothers invited Rey and me to dinner with their girlfriends at Sahara, a Middle Eastern Restaurant in Brooklyn. Quick to shower and get dressed, we still had plenty of time to spare. That sensation came back as I waited for Rey to freshen up. I knew it would be wise to limit our time alone together.

"Wanna walk over to my parent's house before dinner? They'd love to meet you!" I'd ensure that before anything physical happened, he had a 360 degree view of my world— one beyond the fierce basketball player he knew.

My mother greeted us at the door, "Ah Luda, who is this?" She elongated my name as usual and looked at Rey with her head tilted, intrigued.

"Ima, Aba (mom, dad), meet my new friend, Rey." I was surprised that both of my parents seemed excited to meet him.

My brother, Aidan, introduced us to his girlfriend, a petite Italian-Catholic girl with long black hair, big brown eyes, and an effervescent smile complemented by red lip gloss. My mom and dad attentively listened to her share her devout roots, then Rey told us his story. I was shocked that they were willing to accept an Italian-Catholic, and maybe even a Basque-Filipino into the family. It became apparent to me that while they didn't want to assimilate themselves, their values of tolerance and kindness prevailed for their children. This put me at ease.

Sahara was packed. There was just one large table left that was open for the six of us. "Wow! I hear so many different languages, this is awesome!" Rey whispered into my ear as Spanish, Turkish, Italian, Russian, Chinese, and Hebrew flowed through the room.

Brooklyn itself is a small Cosmo, richness balanced by the rawness of it all. Every tenth blocks houses a unique cultural community where people's mannerisms, looks, shops, foods, and smells transition through the avenues. It's like Disney Land's 'It's a Small World' but real. Brighton Beach is filled with Russians whereas Sunset Park is home to the Chinese; Boro Park is populated by Hassidic Jews and just south lies the African American neighborhood of Crown Heights, where Puerto Ricans pop up in between. Turks nestled in Bay Ridge, Israelis in Kings Highway, and Italians in Bensonhurst. Poor and rich live together, dispersed across brownstones throughout the village. All co-exist with the singular goal of working toward the American dream while contributing to the collective good. And here was Rey de la Cruz, a Basque-Filipino, at a table with Russian Jews, Greeks, and Catholics freely discussing politics, religion, and sports through midnight.

Confessions Fostering Confidence

Monday morning. Back to work. My phone rang just as I was headed to lunch. "Lea, it's Rey, what are you up to tonight?"

On Mondays and Wednesdays, I took night classes at Baruch College. "My class finishes at half-past nine, it's too much of a hassle for you to drive from Jersey into the city late at night."

"I'll pick you up." He insisted in a low, authoritative tone, "Why do you ask so many questions? If I say that I'll pick you up, then I'll pick you up." We planned to meet at 9:20 outside the school's entrance gate.

That night after my class, Rey was waiting for me in his blue Cadillac Sedan de Ville. I jumped into the black leather seat. "Where are we going?"

"Unless you want to grab a bite to eat, I'll take you home," he pressed on the gas.

"Are you kidding? You drove all the way from New Jersey just to take me home?" At the stoplight, he looked into my eyes and stretched his arm around my shoulder.

"Why not? I really enjoy being with you, you're so different from all the girls I've dated before."

So, we're dating now? I had heard the 'you're so different' before, but Rey and me, dating? *Just ask a question.* "How am I so different?"

"Well, your family is different, you invited me to dinner with them and to play basketball with your brothers...and plus, you play ball with the guys and just kick ass." He turned to look directly at me as he made a right turn and said, "You're also beautiful, smart, and funny— it's hard for me to explain."

I was flattered but assured that he was sweet-talking as foreplay. Not tonight. *Just accept the compliment, don't react.* With Rey's speedy driving, we got to Brooklyn in no time. He helped me carry my bags upstairs. We sat on the couch drinking tea, discussing the class I was taking and my education in general.

"I couldn't go to college before because I was married to an Orthodox guy for three years." *Oops. That slipped.*

"Wait— you're divorced?" He didn't believe me. "I swear I am. I'll show you pictures." What I didn't believe was that "I'm divorced" just rolled off my tongue so casually.

After Rey finally left around eleven, I was exhausted yet desperate to journal. *Was it Rey's comforting character that prompted me to open up, or was divorce no longer my shame-ridden secret? Was I finally owning my past?*

Writing down my emotions led me to realize that my beliefs were shifting. How others judged me no longer mattered: I listened to their opinions, but always inspected them considering how a person's interpretation affected me. When sensing feelings of discomfort, I questioned whether it was necessary for me to accept, reject, or change my behaviors. If I felt hurt, or certain opinions prevented me from reaching positive outcomes, my solution would involve ownership and action.

My confidence sprung when sharing my narrative with full responsibility, regardless of weaknesses, failures, and mistakes: My responsibility to share, my responsibility to correct, and my responsibility to advocate for myself. There was nothing to be ashamed of because I realized that human beings are constantly developing to be their best selves and achieve their goals. Since all people possess weaknesses and strengths, managing weaknesses by correctly channeling energy to achieve purpose with inner peace is the ingredient to real strength. And confidence **is** real strength. Confidence— not so much how it's displayed externally, but more so how it manifests within— is the magical ingredient to happiness, success, and fulfillment.

Displays of Affection: Out of My Comfort Zone

Rey couldn't keep his eyes off me when he'd go the extra mile to pick me up from school almost every Monday and Wednesday. "Just to keep you company, just to hang out a bit," he'd say. It was a move of parallel play— content to simply share space with me— and I didn't mind it at all. I actually really liked it.

Driving from New Jersey to New York City and then all the way to Brooklyn was a two-hour ordeal. Some may perceive those doing this or accepting this as being needy or clingy, but at that stage of my life, I accepted kind gestures at face-value. Although our needs were different, we both enjoyed each other's give-and-take in the moment. We were like magnets, pulled together by the irresistible urge to be touched. To feel loved.

When Rey dropped me off on Wednesday, he asked me to ride the ferry with him on Saturday before watching the Knicks game. He called me again on Friday to confirm:

"Lea, I am looking forward to this evening. I was thinking that we could drive over to my apartment after the ferry ride, and then go watch the game later. Bring a change of clothes in case you know— you wanna get comfy or something." His tone tempted me. *Tonight may be the night. Set your boundaries.*

That was the first time I'd ever been to Rey's place. He lived in a boutique apartment building with six floors. The superintendent of the building welcomed us in.

"Gorgeous girl you got there, de la Cruz," he said in a heavy New York accent.

Rey winked at him, "Yes indeed," and introduced us, "Lea, meet Tony. Tony, Lea."

Rey and I proceeded upstairs to his thirteenth-floor unit. It was spacious, organized, and modernly decorated. Rey gave me a quick tour and went to take a shower. I gravitated toward the large window overlooking the skyline, appreciating New York City's beauty from afar. I imagined what my life would look like in a couple of years in this colorful city of dreams. A city of vast opportunity. *Will I still be working on Wall Street? Still living in Brooklyn? Living with a man, or somewhere else?* I had no great aspirations to climb a career ladder and become some elite executive. For me, as a woman, that would never happen: there were hardly any women in executive positions at DW. For now, I was just happy to have a job and attend school part time. Through self-discovery and a dedication to my passions, I'd steer my life's direction and make the best out of it wherever it would lead me.

A warm presence from behind startled me. I turned, and instantly Rey's lips were around mine. He kissed and held me tight, then tighter, and tighter until I could no longer resist.

"Let's take it slow," I pleaded. His moves only intensified. *Distract.* "Come on, let's go to the game! We can't be late!"

"You know I want you," he whispered, slowly pulling back. I grabbed his hand and led him out the door.

We took our seats in the stadium box surrounded by couples. They were all touching each other. Rey began to touch me as they were, tightly clasping his hand around my thigh; then, he inched closer to wrap his arm around my shoulders. I would have been ok with this if we were at home. This public display of affection irked me. *Everyone else is doing it. Is it*

weird that I feel uncomfortable? I did nothing to stop Rey but didn't play along. I tensed up. *What beliefs are making me feel this way?* In my culture, a couple's intimate relations are reserved for private spaces to respect the lovers' privacy and the respect of those around them.

It was nearly midnight when the basketball game was over, but our night was just getting started. On the drive home, Rey persisted with touchy gestures and sweet-talk.

"I'm so in love with you." He caressed my hand.

I felt uneasy, maybe because I wasn't so much in love with him, and sexual chemistry was all I could feel.

"I care about you too. I love spending time with you. But I just came out of a long-term relationship and I'm not ready to commit yet." I confessed, "This is why I'm restraining myself from having anything physical right now." Honesty always. *Play the waiting game, give it time.*

"I'm patient, Lea. As much time as you need." He read my mind. I smiled at him, sensing that he deeply valued our friendship. We kept chatting about our relationship as Rey zipped through the dark, empty highways and across the Brooklyn Bridge. When Rey dropped me off, he placed a gentle kiss on my forehead and wished me goodnight.

"Thank you, I had fun as always, I'll see you soon," I said. He gave me a nod of assurance.

For the next few days, there was only silence from Rey.

Ball Up!

I did not hear from Rey until Thursday. Chen and I walked to Battery Park City to meet the regular crew for a game, and I spotted Rey walking intensely towards us from afar.

"Hey Cocktease! Are you ready to ball up?" An aggressive whisper from behind startled me. It was Michael, one of the top traders at DW.

"I'm always ready! But what does cocktease mean?" I chuckled to avoid embarrassment all the while genuinely curious.

"Michael, shut up. Common guys let's just play." Rey suddenly appeared next to me. "Lea will show you how to ball it up," he said, pinching my shoulder. The old Rey was back, defending me once again. All of this happened so fast. I was still wondering what that word, "cocktease" meant. "You too, Lea. Don't be like Michael, don't stall the game. Can you just shut up for a change? Let's play, I'll tell you later." His fuse was short.

"Ok, let's go! Ball-up!" *It's better to avoid pissing him off for now. Just follow his advice and play the game.*

We played three-on-three: Chen, Rey, and I versus Michael and his teammates. Dribbling past defense towards the hoop, Michael hovered and jumped on top of me. I fell and tumbled down, letting out a short cry of pain. The entire left side of my thigh was scraped up by the asphalt. Rey ran at Michael and shoved him to the ground with his hip.

"What was that?! HUH Michael?! HUH?! We don't play like that here, man!" Rey scolded and punched his shoulder.

"Please, let it go, stop!" I shouted, wiping the fragments of rock and blood off my skin. Chen gave me a hand to get off the floor, but I dusted myself off and jumped back up like nothing happened.

"You sure, Lea? You don't need a break? Your leg is all bloody!" Chen pointed to my scraped-up leg in concern.

"Nope! I'm good! Ready, come on guys, let's have fun, there's no need to ruin the game!" I grabbed the ball and rallied my team to set up for the next round. Playing with the guys meant being one of them—

rough, tough, and fun. I passed to Rey, him to Chen, then back to me for the lay-up. In the end, we all had fun, but I was still confused as to why such hostility surfaced on the court.

I repeatedly asked Rey about that slur at dinner. My confusion erupted like word vomit. "Rey, what was all the commotion about? Was it the cocktease slur? I'm ok with their shoving, that's part of the game! So what? What's so bad about cocktease? I just don't get it, is there something I did wrong?"

"Lea, these guys are too cocky, they have big egos." Rey set down his beer and explained, "Michael is one of the top traders at DW. People like him can't take it when they lose to a team with a girl."

I understood that, but cocktease was still undefined to me. "Rey, for the last time, what is cocktease? Why did you get so mad when he said it the first time? And why did you hurt Michael after he pushed me? That's a part of the game—"

Rey cut me off. "You're so loud! Keep it down!" Then he cackled, "Cocktease! Ha! Are you really that naïve? It means cockteaser. When a girl turns a guy down, some big guys with big egos call the girl a cocktease. It's quite simple." Rey terminated the conversation sternly.

"Oh really? I kind of see that as a compliment!" I giggled to diffuse the seriousness, trying to be cute. He didn't seem to lighten up. Many of these American slang-terms, like cocktease, and their derogatory nature were foreign to me. "Rey, I just don't pay attention to labels. Plus, I'm used to it. I had similar experiences with guys in Israel as a teenager. Don't be bothered by it. I can handle them."

"Common, Lea, let's go," Rey sighed as he signed the check. He placed his hand on my lower back as we exited the restaurant. We walked toward the subway in silence; I awaited Rey's response. Finally, he spoke.

"Lea, you think you're strong. But Israel isn't America. Let me handle these jerks. I know them, they work for me. They just want a piece of you."

"Thank you, but I'm a big girl, don't worry about me."

"Listen to me, Lea." He grabbed my wrist as his countenance stiffened. "You have a bit of a reputation. Cocktease is an expression for a girl who teases guys and plays with their feelings but doesn't sleep with them. Basically a player."

"So just like you?" I spun it around and teased, "I've heard stories about you playing too!"

He was still serious. "I haven't dated anyone since I met you, do you understand? I want to be with **you**." His authoritative tone was intimidating.

"No, I don't understand," I played stupid and laughed it off, "Cocktease is a compliment then! At least I'm not called a slut!"

Rey's brows furrowed, his eyes narrowing with disdain. "Ok, I'm done here." He turned his back to me and headed left toward his train. I ran downstairs to catch the B-line to Brooklyn.

Cockteaser: A Compliment or Condescending?

Time alone on the subway gave me a chance to reflect. *So what if these men call me a cock-teaser? I'm not sleeping with any of them! How could I be leading them on?* A gender issue, perhaps. This reminded me of how Tom, too, claimed that I was misleading men. It was either a self-construed misconception of my bubbly personality or a way to manipulate me. I later realized that arrogant men who face confident

350

women who refuse to give into their needs or don't satisfy their expectations pin these offenses on them to feed their ego. It's a means of arming themselves with nasty slurs to weaken women and lure them in.

I found compliments attesting to my confidence, warm character, and gregarious personality in these labels. Enjoying my experience was all that mattered, and I refused to let a few arrogant guys control my behavior or ruin my fun. I'd continue showing up with the brightest smile, being kind, and honest to those around me. The beliefs, words, and actions of others were out of my control— I could only control myself, be assertive of my intentions, and attempt to influence. Internalizing the beliefs of others and letting them define our own means that we value their opinions above our own. I was ready to take on any offenses struck at me.

Speak Your Truth and Throw a Bone

I arrived home around eleven to a voicemail box blinking with messages from Daniel, Lazuli, and Rey. Daniel confirmed our dinner plans for the weekend, Lazuli wanted to get coffee, and Rey seemed to be feeling guilty. His message: "Hey gorgeous, sorry for snapping at you. Call me when you get home."

I wasn't tired, so I called him back. "Hi Rey, what's up? Are you ok?" I asked, unpacking my bag.

"Thank God you called back. I'm so sorry for what happened tonight, I really am. I want to take you out on Saturday. My treat, sweetheart."

"Rey, it's ok. Nothing happened. I had a great time!" I brightened my pitch to comfort him. "I'm planning to see Daniel on Saturday; he's visiting from D.C. over the weekend. How's Sunday?"

There was a moment of awkward silence. Then Rey asked, "Wh-Why do you have to see him? Isn't it over?"

"Daniel and I are just friends, and he's still going through a hard time. I'm here to support him, that's all."

"He still wants you back," Rey persisted, "Why do you need to see him? You should tell him that it's over."

"I already told him that it's over. I'm not responsible for Daniel's feelings or actions, only for my own."

He interrupted me brashly, "This is precisely why you should cut it off! Lea, don't you get it?!" His tone amplified. We were going in circles, and my patience was short-fused.

I interjected, "Why can't you just accept that we can still be friends after a breakup?" I thought that this very moment would be the perfect opportunity to speak my truth and throw a bone to Rey— sweetener to a souring relationship while maintaining integrity. Throwing a bone involves harsh truth, but adjuncts a compromise that intends to uplift the other person.

"Rey, I've had enough, please accept that I will continue my friendship with Daniel. I do not and will never interfere with your female friendships. But let's do Shabbat dinner at my parent's place next Friday. If you want to grab lunch on Sunday, we can. Would that work?" I needed him to say "yes" so we could conclude the conversation with a slight diversion and end on a positive note.

"Yes, sure, I would love that." Rey sounded reluctant.

"Ok perfect!" I jumped in before he could utter another word. "I'm looking forward to it. I am very tired, so let's talk tomorrow?"

"Hmm...ok. Good night."

This conversation was certainly bitter-sweet for Rey. However, the principal tool that carried me through everything was putting truth above all. My truth. Truth is about respect, which conveys strength and freedom. Knowing your truth and expressing it clearly to others opens the opportunity for them to understand you. When challenged respectfully, both parties acquire what is needed to strengthen the bond. Unfortunately, many often deem any challenge or confrontation as an attack. So, when sensing discomfort in a contentious conversation, speak your truth and throw a bone to end the discussion graciously. Take a breather and come back to collaboratively resolve the root of the issue once both partners have had time to clear and calm their minds.

Seeing Daniel: A Bitter-Sweet Reality Check

That Saturday night, Daniel and I met at a casual restaurant in Brooklyn. We updated each other about our past few months, where he shared experiences from Capitol Hill.

"Lea, it's nice there, but I just feel like everyone has someone. When I walk to work, I think about that, and I just feel so lonely. I miss being with you." He looked down at his soup, and then up at me with puppy eyes. "What can I do so we can get back together? If therapy is what it takes…"

No way. This cannot be what he came here for. I gently cut him off and said, "Daniel, I am so grateful for the relationship we had. You opened me up to a different part of this world— the arts, your amazing family— and showered me with unconditional love. I've moved on, and I know you can too." I tried to comfort him as much as I could, but he didn't seem to take it. Daniel pushed his bowl away with pursed lips. I felt bad, but there was nothing I could do but be honest and provide support. He wouldn't value my empathy as I thought he would, or at least not at that moment:

I put both hands on the table and leaned in subtly, "I'll always be here for you as a friend, never hesitate to reach out."

"I know, Lea, you're always there for me. But I want more. I want what we planned." Daniel kept reminiscing on the good times we shared and how we could correct our missteps.

"I'm sorry, Daniel, I really want to keep you in my life as a friend. Friendship is all I can provide."

Our evening concluded after some appetizers. Daniel's appetite was conquered by discomfort and longing for me. To him, 'just friends' was a disappointment, but was something he'd accept eventually. I was at a point of no return. Time heals all wounds.

My dating experiences revealed a correlation between gender and perceptions of relationships. Even after a romantic relationship fails, many women seek to maintain the friendship, but most men deem the friend zone meaningless if they want or wanted more. I could be wrong about this correlation; perhaps it was just me. At this stage of my life— a stage of exploration— I held a strong need for friendships and sought to maintain them no matter what; besides, conflicts between friends are an opportunity to strengthen the bond. I gravitated towards those who fostered opportunities for self-discovery to build my identity and self-esteem. I knew that those I shared relationships with were still interested in me despite the trials and tribulations we endured together. There was no reason to give up on the bond altogether if we liked each other to date in the first place and nothing severe caused our rupture.

Speaking my truth to Daniel was essential. To show him respect, I had to set his expectations so he could decipher his future investment in me on his own. I also secured my boundaries and increased my confidence because I left the conversation with nothing withheld. That's liberty: My role was clear and all decisions for our friendship were in his hands.

It's All About Sex, Baby! But is it Really?

Before Shabbat dinner that Friday evening, Lazuli and I met at Bucci, our favorite café in Manhattan Beach. She was still recovering from her surgery but could messily slurp on a cappuccino.

"How are you doing? How do you feel?" I gave her a warm hug, careful not to bump into the thick bandage around her chin.

"I'm ok! I can talk, at least! I'm just drinking Ensure shakes and coffee for now. But enough of me! Let's get to you and Rey!" Her voice still rang with the same enthusiasm. Of course, that's Lazuli— eternally selfless and spunky!

"Alright, alright. We have much to talk about!" I began by telling her about Daniel, then about how Rey was upset that I met him for dinner. "I really like Rey, but he seems possessive at times. Maybe he's offended or confused because I won't touch him."

"So just have sex with him! She burst with foam all over her lips, "Who cares? It'll feel so good afterward, just enjoy it!" Her words were slurred. I couldn't take her seriously.

"How? I know I ask you this every time, but I still don't understand how you can just have sex with anyone!"

"Listen, Lea. You have to understand that sex doesn't give people ownership over you. Think of it as a sport— you're a runner, right?!

355

You're just running, now with a partner!" We both bent over with uncontained giggles, then Lazuli got serious again. "Lea, for real. I have a sex outing tonight, and I've only met the guy once— just briefly last week. I need the sex! Is it ok for men to have their needs satisfied while women cannot?! I'm not kidding you! This is ridiculous! Lighten up Lea, sex is not a man's license over you, it's yours over them! Just go and f*ck the guy! You know what— let's make a deal. I'll f*ck two guys tonight if you f*ck Rey!"

Oh my goodness, this girl is crazy! "Ok, ok..." I gave in.

Although Lazuli's philosophy clashed with mine, it did resonate. My promise to her was not superficial. Many thoughts provoked me: *What if I don't enjoy sex with him? Will I regret it? What exactly will I regret? What if we break up after having sex? What is up for gain or loss?* These brief moments of reflection relayed that if I had sex with Rey, I had nothing to lose, and everything to gain.

While deeming sex a product of serious relationships or a signal toward marriage, my purpose was to explore my body and experience passionate sex driven by physical attraction. I wanted to test if sex alone— without true love— could ignite profound pleasure.

Rey would not be my life-long soulmate, but our deep investment in each other seemed worthy of unleashing our fantasies for. Since I trusted him, Rey was the perfect person to do this with. These criteria filtered out potential regrets. My commitment to self-discovery and accepting responsibility for my actions regardless of the outcomes stood strong. However, cultural barriers placed around my sexuality imposed a preliminary obstacle.

Restraint and Reason to Avoid Regret

7:00 PM hit. I was slipping into a black fitted dress and heeled boots. Dinner was in half an hour. Rey rang the doorbell and came in as if no time had passed. I came out of my room to greet him.

"Hello, how are you? How was your week?"

"You look so gorgeous tonight, I missed you." He ignored my questions, just kissed me. He smelled of that delicious Armani cologne. "I love you. I want you," he whispered and lured me back to my bedroom. I followed. *Was I under his spell?* The temptation was getting to me. I had to stop myself:

"Rey, I really don't want any commitments right now, is that what you want—"

He cut me off, "Is it because I'm not Jewish?" and looked into my eyes fiercely, "I'd be willing to convert."

"No, Rey, it's not that. I told you I'm just not ready to commit," I stated. At that moment, Rey didn't care, and my body signaled to my mind that neither did I. Before I knew it, my promise to Lazuli was being fulfilled. I had to set terms to avoid any misunderstandings. "Rey, listen, I'll make one commitment to you. So long as I'm having sex with you, I won't have sex with anyone else. If you want this to work, you must promise me the same in return. All I'm asking you is for the freedom to hang out with whomever I want. The same applies to you."

"Shhh," he whispered, his hands cupped around my cheeks and thumbs pressing on my lips. He kissed me again, a seal to our deal. I looked up and caught a glimpse of the clock. It was 7:30.

"Everyone's waiting, we're late!" My saving grace.

Rey squeezed my hand on our walk over to my parent's house. I could hear my dad and brothers shouting at each other from a block away (not abnormal!). We let ourselves in and were greeted by my parents, their neighbors, friends, and family.

"Shabbat Shalom, man! How ya doin'?" Emilio greeted Rey. My brothers and Rey exchanged their classic bro-hugs and fist-bumps. "Finally, you're here, Luda! We've been waiting for you!" said Aidan.

My mother called everyone to the table to light shabbat candles. Twenty of us huddled around my parents conducting the ceremony, singing loud, passionate twists on Jewish tunes from Tat culture. My father conducted the Kiddush, a blessing over the wine, followed by the Hamotzi, a blessing over the Challah bread. Unlike the Ashkenazi tradition— to gracefully slice the loaf of bread, salt it, and pass it around the table— my father would rip pieces and throw them to each guest. After our short ritual, my mom laid out overflowing platters of grains, salads, stews, and cakes, across two long tables. Be te-avon (bon-appetit, in Hebrew)!

Dinners with my family never lacked substance: Special rituals, an abundance of food, interesting company and heated discussions were guaranteed. After discussing the weekly Torah portion, we'd choose a theme for the evening. Each person at the table would fight just to get a few words in to express thoughts on that theme, bombarded by rambunctious interruptions, bombastic comments, and explosions of laughter. Hearty discourse was encouraged, and we found humor in drama, all forgotten within twenty-four hours. No matter your identity, where you came from, or your opinions, each person was embraced in full.

This Shabbat dinner transported me back to my days in Israel and Russia. It was not until I moved away and was experiencing life myself that I fully appreciated how unique and special my family truly is. While with tribal mannerisms, my family's gracious hospitality and value for diverse human connections were ingrained in me. Today, my daughter stands as a beacon of this cultural legacy, preparing traditional foods for the holidays, relishing in intellectual conversations, and leading discussions at our dining table among friends and family.

I helped my mom wash dishes and clean-up while Rey was schmoozing with my dad and brothers. Once we finished, Rey and I hugged my family members goodbye, and we walked back over to my apartment.

"Can I come upstairs?" Rey asked as we approached the building.

"I am super super tired…" My voice dwindled with fatigue. We fell into a soft kiss.

"I want you. I want to be close to you," he held me tight and whispered, "Please, let me have you."

"I want you too, and we are close, Rey— very close. I just need a bit more time." He pulled away from me disappointment. I leaned in and touched my lips to his' again, then whispered, "Good night, Rey, let's talk tomorrow."

I went up the stairs, took a shower, and crawled into bed pondering yet again if I'd regret having sex that did not lead to a serious relationship. Living life with no regrets was a priority at the genesis of my transformation. I had to bring myself back to weighing risks and rewards, along with the ability to accept responsibility for the worst-case scenarios. *Would potential negative outcomes serve to develop inner-strength and strengthen self-esteem?* If so, I'd forge ahead with risks in mind and a reliable action plan. To stay true to myself, I had to eliminate any prospects of shame to stay true to my purpose. If Rey wanted sex, that was fine with me for now, so long as he was sexually loyal to me. Only me.

I heard little from Rey over the next few days. It was strange that he hadn't called to discuss our agreement from that night, which I considered closed. He hadn't introduced me to his friends or family. *Does he have any?* With Daniel, I found my connections with his social circle enriching our bond. If Rey wanted a serious relationship, a dip into his world would have been important. *Perhaps it was another cultural gap. Maybe Rey just needs a breather from me.* I let it go.

Lingering over Rey exacerbated my anxiety. Maybe my proposal turned him off; maybe he was thinking about it; maybe he expected more, beyond sexual commitment. But I had communicated clearly, and I wasn't about to compromise my boundaries because he was confused. I maintained my routine and continued branching out to free my mind. Exploring in moments of anxiety or confusion can elicit new opportunities and conclusions with time to reflect. I thought about where I stood just three years prior— humiliated, shattered, and hopeless; liberation seemed impossible. The more I focused on how my feelings and my values aligned, the more mature my actions became.

Beyond Lust

Men became easily accessible to me— disposable, even. I enjoyed being a hunter-gather, seizing opportunities to engage, learn, and move on. With sex comes an additional layer to the relationship: Intimacy, an embedded physical-emotional connection. So, for me, physical safety and mental certainty were requirements to any sexual experience.

As pursuing a sexual relationship that did not culminate in marriage would be sacrilegious to my traditional norms, I had to dismantle them. I asked myself, *can sex for the pure joy of intimacy, shared interests, and physical attraction be respectable? Are physical passion, lust, and fun justifiable reasons for adding sex into the equation?* Yes: My balance and boundaries had to be individually defined. I never had sex for fun or pure pleasure before, and Rey was the ideal candidate to help me explore. I was prepared to withstand any criticism from my family, friends, or the outside community. Since my ultimate purpose was self-discovery, any outcome of the experience— positive or negative— would serve as insight.

I waited for Thursday: Basketball Day. Rey and I planned on grabbing a quick dinner after the game. We quickly changed our clothes and headed to our usual spot across the street from the courts. The staff knew us there, so our food arrived in no time. Rey was relatively quiet, taking small, thorough bites of his burger. It seemed as if he was avoiding conversation.

"Are you ok? I have not heard from you for a few days. You seem…umm… preoccupied," I prompted casually while nibbling on one of Rey's French fries.

He finished chewing and swallowed deeply, "Well, it's disappointing to me that we can't be more than friends. It's been months of spending time together, and I-I just don't understand you." He sighed, then continued ranting. I listened patiently.

"I want to be with you too, Rey. Do you understand how hard it's been for me to be together and restrain myself?"

Rey's usual French fry-ignited smile was absent. In fact, this time, he let me have all his French fries whereas other times, we'd usually be fighting over them like birds. His face dropped— deflated and defeated.

"I do want to be with you... trust me." I put my hands over his and peered into his eyes, "I just need a bit more time. A bit more patience." My voice tempered to a rare softness. Rey slowly pushed his unfinished plate aside and signed the check.

"Common, let's get out of here," he murmured and led me outside. We walked toward the subway station, but not holding hands as usual. I hugged him before we parted ways.

"See you tomorrow at my parent's house. Good night."

"I want you," he whispered, holding me tight.

I whispered back, "I know," arrogantly with a grin.

Just Lust is Prone to Rust

Shabbat dinners with Rey were a usual ordeal at my parents' house. Flares of unleashed passion occurred afterward, debuting with long foreplay culminating in lavish lust through early morning. Although sore at times, Rey was the best lover I'd had until now. I became familiar with once foreign sources and feelings of elation.

At his place, Rey would surprise me with lacey black lingerie neatly placed on the bed. It would rarely make it onto my body. Our pleasure-pain ritual became an obsession for Rey to the extent of foregoing our outings. We began to skip our Thursday basketball games. On the weekends, we would go out for a short dinner and immediately head home for a night-long of sex. On the few occasions that we went to see a show, Rey would smirk and say, "It's so boring to sit still for two hours.

Let's go home and have fun." This even happened when we had tickets to a Nets game, a spectacle both of us had always been eager to watch.

Our sexual rituals became arduous for me as the novelty dissipated: Fun and games of foreplay bored me, my body felt overused, and my libido was diminishing. My feelings indicated to me that the infusion of **true** love— a combination of intellectual, social, and emotional bonds added to the physical— impassions sexual interplay. With Rey, the social and physical bonds were tight, but the emotional and intellectual ones were not. Without each of these pillars sustaining the relationship, lust is prone to fade away.

An Erosion of Love & Joy

Unbalanced sexual appetites did not serve our relationship well. Although I enjoyed our intimacy, it became apparent that Rey was craving more while I was begging for less. He was struggling to foster my growth beyond his demands, and clearly, I was failing to foster trust, safety, and confidence in him. I offered to make dinner at my place. Agreed.

"Rey, you know I care for you and truly enjoy our relationship. However, over the past few months, it's been all about sex. It's a lot on my body! I feel like a machine! Wear and tear are about to break it down!" We erupted with laughter at my ingenious analogy.

"Hmmm… I understand Lea, I'm sorry. I just love being with you. I want you to build a family with you, and I want you to have the life of a queen in a big house overlooking the lake in Long Island."

Wow, that's a lot. I dropped my fork. My jaw dropped. "Rey, that's so generous of you, but that's not **my** dream. It's not what I need at this point in my life. I need the freedom to keep exploring, discovering, and understanding me and the world around me."

"Seriously?" He interjected in contempt, "The world around you? You mean keeping your old boyfriends? You mean dating other men? Don't you love me!? What is it that I do not do for you?" He couldn't stop ranting. I could hear his pain.

"You have to understand my perspective, please," I tried reasoning with him, "If you really loved me, you would trust me. If you believed that we had a strong foundation and nothing could break it, you wouldn't impose these rules on me, right? The last thing I want is a possessive man— been there, done that! I want someone who trusts me so we can grow together, and I'm still trying to find myself. This is why I'm not ready for a committed relationship yet. Do you get it?"

Rey clenched his teeth, the anger bubble burst: "No! I do **not** understand you! No, Lea! This is not acceptable!" He jumped out of his seat and pushed his chair aggressively. "I am done, that's it," he stated walking toward the door. He slammed it behind him.

This was an enlightening moment. Somehow, I felt liberated in Rey's rejection because he refused to accept my priorities. With unmendable disparities in our needs and values, he made the decision to shatter our construct as is. This made it especially easy for me to move on.

There was no sign of Rey over the next few weeks. I also refrained from calling him. It served me well. It was a much-needed break for physical and emotional healing as I lost desire for a relationship centered on sex alone. All the while, the relationship had achieved its original purpose. Over nine months, Rey and I developed a beautiful friendship founded on common interests which entrusted me to explore my body and sexuality through him. Promising myself to engage in such relationship allowed me to discover what my boundaries were. Disciplining my head and heart to act in unison cultivated personal growth. To Rey, however, my discipline was a red flag because it prevented me from satisfying his sexual appetite. He also resented that I kept in touch with Daniel, that I continued to date, and that I wouldn't commit to him.

I'd soon learn that when expectations are not fulfilled, disappointments morph into resentment and vengeful behavior. Other than shouting matches, silence is a form of displaying resentment and often indicates something hidden beneath the surface. By breaking the silence, both parties can voice needs, priorities, and values to diagnose disconnects. Assertive communication is key to seeing clearly and being seen clearly to make value-based decisions for the relationship.

The Anchor Sinking in Rancor

Thanksgiving was a time I had spent with Daniel's family over the past few years. Since neither Rey nor my family made plans that year, I accepted Schwartz's invitation. I called Rey to wish him a happy Thanksgiving and to notify him of my plans. I also wanted to understand where our relationship stood, sensing that it was falling apart.

Rey remained unresponsive for the next few days. Worried that something happened to him, I decided to stop by his place after the holiday on my way back from Long Island. Around 9:00 PM, I rang the doorbell from the lobby. There was no response. He could've been working out or playing ball, but it was late. I went to the lobby to find Tony.

"Tony, would you please let me upstairs? I'm here to surprise Rey."

"Sure thing, darling," he winked sharply as usual and pressed the elevator button for me. I arrived at the fourth floor and knocked on Rey's door. No response. Sure enough, the door was unlocked. And there he was...

"Rey! What happened to you!" I exclaimed. He was passed out on the sofa with an empty bottle of Vodka on his chest. I tried to lift him gently, testing his level of intoxication.

"You're ruining me... I don't understand you. You confuse me... I can't go on like this," he mumbled with his eyes half-closed, somewhat conscious.

"Rey, what happened?" I nestled close to him after helping him sit up. "Please, tell me."

He shook his head and begged, "Please, stay here with me, stay the night." He flopped back again.

"Ok, I'm here for you, don't worry." I had none of my belongings with me, but Rey was more important.

Time for Closure

I scrambled some eggs and toasted two slices of bread for Rey the next morning. Hangover recovery. Over breakfast, he shared his aspirations— much different from mine at this stage of my life. He was in his mid-thirties and ready to settle, whereas I was a twenty-eight-year-old butterfly, fluttering freely for the time being. He was still failing to understand my side of the story.

"What don't I do for you? I showed you love endlessly, when is enough, enough? I want you to be my girl, mine!" He shouted, pounding his fists on the table. I jolted back in my seat. *Just keep calm, keep reasoning with him.*

"Rey, I really care for you and our friendship, I'm just not ready to settle yet." Trying to comfort him with a gentle kiss failed. He pushed me away. "Ok, Rey. How about we take a break? I'm so sorry for the pain I have caused you, but if you want to talk or need anything, please call me whenever you're ready." I saw no compromises or resolutions materializing from this discussion. It was my time to go. Time for closure: "I care about you, Rey, see you soon." He didn't say a word, crunching angrily on a piece of toast.

I journaled upon arriving home from Rey's that Sunday morning. *Can I just move on? What will I say to him? Can we still be friends, without benefits?* I didn't think so: Rey's possessiveness was a deal breaker for me. Rather than an expression of passion or love, I felt his possession as a control mechanism. I could not live like this; his actions also spoke louder than his words. Giving him time to cool off was my game plan. My purpose had been accomplished. That's all that mattered for now.

To Seek Truth or Trust Signals?

Rey's behavior toward me changed: "Lea, I cannot pick you up from school this week... Lea, I cannot play ball this Thursday.... Lea, I cannot see you this weekend, I'm busy." These sequential "I cannots" persisted with "I'm busy at work, I have other things to do." I was certain that his priorities had shifted as passion between us dissipated. *Why is he keeping me in the dark? Am I being deceived?* I began to suspect that our original agreement was breached. *Do I really need to know the truth? Or are his words and actions telling enough?*

I decided to call Rey. Only direct truth, from the source, would eliminate festering anxiety. No matter how far I'd fall when reality hit, I still wanted to know. This knowledge was integral to making responsible decisions to forge ahead.

A week and a half passed with sparse communication between us. He rarely picked up and never returned any of my calls. We made no additional plans to see each other. I left him a few messages: "Rey, if you want to start dating others, please let me know. Based on our terms, if you're having sex with other women, I would like to end our relationship."

I began to lose trust in Rey and refused to be kept in the dark any longer. Perhaps I didn't need to seek truth, deeming the relationship to have achieved its purpose and fizzled out based on Rey's dynamic. However, my curiosity and inner need for closure convinced me otherwise.

Surprise Surprise!

On a Thursday around 8:30 PM, I decided to surprise Rey. Like the time before, nobody answered when I rang the bell in the lobby. I looked for Tony.

"Hey Tony, have you seen Rey? I forgot my key and Rey told me to come over tonight. Could you please open the door for me?"

"Of course, darling."

Nothing changed about Rey's unit— tidy, spotless, and rich with the scent of that intoxicating Armani cologne. His phone and credit card bills were spread on the coffee table. I skimmed them over. Something was odd: The same number appeared several times daily over the past month.

I scribbled it on a sticky note and stuffed it in my pocket. His transactions were even more suspicious. Hundreds were spent at high-end restaurants and Broadway shows; I found checks for thousands poured out at luxury brand stores including Tiffany's and Hermes. On my break from scavenging around, I opened the fridge for some Pellegrino. Inside were boxes of fancy chocolates from MarieBelle (he hated chocolate!) and expensive wines. He had some explaining to do. *I won't leave until the case is closed.* I retreated to my car awaiting his return.

At quarter-till midnight, a royal blue Cadillac rolled up behind me. Out came Rey accompanied by a tall, lean woman in a black mesh body-con dress and red stilettos, shiny blond curls bouncing around her snow-white face. *I knew it!*

"I can't believe you! Is this what you're doing instead of being honest?" I yelled, slamming my car door. His mouth fell wide open. I wanted to punch my fist inside of it.

"What are you doing here? You're crazy!" He shouted.

"Yes, Rey, I'm crazy. But you're a liar!"

He tried to divert attention by telling his side-chick that everything was ok. "Come on, let's go inside, she's insane."

I hopped back in my car and drove home well-high over the speed limit. This was uncharted territory for me, however, the uncertainty I was experiencing made time for self-examination and resolution. Although my exit from this relationship was final, there was still a missing piece to conclude it on a satisfactory note. The truth was ugly as betrayal always is, but I got what I wanted: closure.

Trailblazing for the Whole Truth

I decided to further investigate before drafting an action plan. The following evening, I called the phone number registered on Rey's phone bill. A sweet voice answered, "Hello, this is Mary."

I couldn't believe she picked up. "Hi, I think we have a friend in common, Rey de la Cruz."

"You play ball with him, don't you? I've heard lots about you. Lea, right?" she said casually.

I told her about our relationship and remarked, "It looks like he called you frequently, but he never mentioned you to me."

She cleared her throat and admitted, "We were dating a couple of years back, but we just started up again two months ago."

I thanked her for her honesty. "Mary, just so you know, my sexual relationship with him is over and I'm moving forward." I was curious to know more. "But let me ask you, are you the girl who came out of the Cadillac last night with Rey?"

The line went silent. After a long pause, Mary finally spoke. She was sniffling. "What? No, that wasn't me. I worked the night shift. I'm a nurse." Then she bombarded me, "What happened last night? Who was that girl? What did she look like? What were they doing?" Sniffles turned to sobs.

After a lengthy conversation discussing what had transpired, truth came out. She swallowed, then spoke: "Lea, I am so glad you told me your story and that we were able to figure this out. I'm done with him too. I hope we can meet one day."

"I do too, thank you for your time and honesty. Best wishes, Mary."

I hung up the phone and plopped on the couch, emotionally drained but mentally liberated. Truth is key to who I am: it fuels my emotions, feelings, expressions, and actions. Seeking truth always imbues one with knowledge, and speaking truth frees me mentally while providing due respect to those around me. When lies accumulate and trust is breached, relationships fall through void of grounded trust. A relationship I'd accept had to be transparent and sustainable, beyond lust alone. Not with a player: *Now I know what that means.*

Profound Passion or Toxic Obsession?

Rey and I hadn't spoken since the incident, four days ago. My intercom beeped bright and early on Saturday morning: "Hi Lea." *Oh my!* It was Rey. I ignored it, but he kept ringing.

"Please go, it's over," I responded through the microphone. Ten minutes later, he banged on my door and busted in. "Oh my goodness! What are you doing? It's over, Rey!" I exclaimed.

"You ruined everything! I did everything for you!" His teeth clenched as he braced my shoulders.

"It's your doing! You lied to me! If you don't stop, I'll report you at work!" I threatened, pulling away. He tried to trap me. I kicked him and pushed my elbows into his stomach, then bolted out of the apartment, down the stairs, and sprinted toward the playground across the street. I sprinted as fast as I could to find an area surrounded by people.

"Stop running! I won't hurt you! Stop!" Rey shouted and tugged on my shirt from behind. We were both winded.

"You need to stop!" Breathing heavily, I sat down on the asphalt and fired back, "I hate liars! It's over!" I yelled at him looking up from the ground while removing the granules of rock from my bare feet.

"I'm sorry, Lea, I'm sorry." He extended his hands to help me up. I pushed his hands away.

"You ruined our love," he whispered scathingly, wrapping his arms around me. I pushed him again.

This had to end: I no longer sought Rey's affection or an apology. His mild aggression brought flashbacks from my relationship with Mendy. Red flag. Despite my instinct to move on, I retained a visceral craving for closure from him directly.

"We can talk next week after work. We just need to give each other a breather." I got up and we walked towards my building. "See you next week, maybe Wednesday?" I suggested. He nodded and we parted ways.

Comparing Relationships Reveals Toxic Patterns

While I realized that Rey was different from Mendy on so many levels, there were several parallels between them. Both men were obsessed with exerting control, manifesting with oppression and aggression. I was initially confused about what constituted love, but as I compared my relationships thus far, I had a clearer picture. Ironically, when I thought about love, four words interconnected with control popped into my mind: Passion, possession, oppression, and aggression. I sought to understand how these words played a role in perceptions of love and relationship dynamics.

Romantic relationships take flight with electric energy and intense attraction, labeled as passion. Sometimes, obsession and possession are indistinguishable, both expressions of a passionate relationship. But will the obsession yield passion or oppression? Could a passion so strong—obsessive, even— strengthen the bond? These questions are answered as the relationship evolves, whereby one examines their feelings and whether the dynamic is hindering or fueling personal growth. In my relationship, passion turned to possession, then oppression; restrictions were imposed on me, thwarting my journey of self-discovery. The behaviors in my relationships felt toxic, and I refused to normalize a dysfunctional dynamic that left me miserable, alienated, and destined to shatter moving forward.

When possession flares with aggression, an alarm rings to confront the issue. Depending on the situation, one must question whether to amend or abandon the relationship. The energy and attraction between two people may steer one in the direction of ignoring the issue or staying in an unhealthy relationship, but oppression must never be confused with compromise.

Energy and attraction morph into passion, but do not define love. Romantically, lust and love go hand-in-hand. They are not synonymous though. Although attraction can energize the relationship, it should not be the foundation of the relationship: Lust can take possessive forms and disrupt love based on other factors such as friendship, intellectual connections, or emotional bonds. The disparity between the needs of an individual seeking freedom and another seeking control fosters a power struggle. This battle lends itself to unbridled reactions and potentially, physical altercations.

I discovered that the person exerting aggressive tactics lacks constructive tools to gain control of what they can. These unhealthy behaviors do just the opposite of what the controller seeks, hurting those they love in fear of losing control in general, control over that person, or plainly, losing that person entirely. In the mind of the controller, control can be translated to impassioned love, but true love requires maturity to nurture growth in oneself and others. Through a respectful, balanced, compassionate relationship tied by a knot of trust, each dances freely toward their purpose— whether those goals are related or not. Recognizing that periods of disharmony are inevitable, common principles to resolve issues conduct the path to overcoming obstacles, gaining clarity, and building a stronger bond.

Now, I had redefined love by three pillars: Care, compassion, and commitment. Love is to grow with someone, not under someone. Caring for one's individual goals and communicating with compassion is encompassed by the commitment to nurture one another, together. I wanted to be with someone who trusted me to explore, experience, and evolve so I could realize my full potential. I wanted someone who took responsibility for their actions so we could resolve conflicts constructively.

My reflections led me to consider what type of relationship I sought next. Clearly, I was craving sustainability, balance, and freedom. My search for a soulmate— someone I could spend my life with— had begun.

Our Last Supper: Amend to Peaceful Ends

I was looking forward to my last dinner with Rey so we could set each other free. Honest, amicable conversations are mechanisms engineering self-liberation and inner peace. By explaining the motives behind our behavior and gaining insight to hidden details, we could accept the disparities in our needs and affirm that our relationship was not compatible.

Rey and I met Harry's Diner with a nonchalant greeting. He had no athletic pep in his step. His eyes and smile were dull. I began with small talk about his day and proceeded to share mine. I then moved to addressing the situation, comforting first before confronting.

"Rey, you have been a shining light in my life over the past year, and I am grateful for all the outings and experiences we've shared like basketball with the guys, dinners with my family, the sex— sex to my pain point— we had so much fun!" I tried to brighten his mood with a light-hearted giggle. "I really do want you as a friend, and I enjoy your company, but we have far too many gaps that set us apart. Our cultures, our lifestyles, our ages, our needs, timing... Plus, I'm not ready to commit to anything serious yet. I'm young and I'm still exploring. You're almost seven years older than me, so I get that you want to settle. The timing is just off." I set it all on the table; my little speech liberated me.

While every muscle in my body relaxed, Rey's eyes filled with tears ready to burst. He rested his forehead on his palms, and he began wiping his face. I had seen him upset before, never sad. His sadness tugged at my heart strings a bit. However, this was no excuse to avoid last week's incident.

I softened my tone with compassion, "Rey, we've had such wonderful times together and I've had experiences with you like nothing before. For those and more, I am grateful. But why lie, Rey, why?"

This elicited a reaction, but not one of bursting tears. His sadness turned to rage. "Don't be stupid, Lea, I don't want to have this conversation. I see where it's going. Let's stop this. I don't need you to make me feel good. I'm not interested in being friends with you either!" He was almost spitting at me with barred teeth. Rey yanked his wallet out and slapped a hundred-dollar bill on the table and walked away. We had barely ordered— just a salad to share— and barely touched it.

My instinct was to follow him out and talk more to gain a clearer understanding. I stopped myself. *Restrain yourself. Let it go. Nothing good will come out of this. Not worth my time and energy.* I closed-out the check and went home.

375

Did I mess up? I did not expect the evening to end so bitterly. *Maybe I said something wrong.* I'm not sure what. All the while, I achieved inner peace because I launched my best efforts to seek truth and mend our differences compassionately. My intentions were pure. I had no control over his emotions or reactions, only mine. There was nothing more I could do besides focusing on what I learned from the relationship. He enabled me to recognize patterns of behavior in relationships, helping me understand my likes and dislikes for a future partner. He was also the vessel through which I tried to unbind sex from love, leading me to discover that sexersise was simply not in my DNA. Lazuli's ways were not mine: I did not need sex to feel loved or bolster my self-worth. To me, sex remained a sacred seal on true love. I could wait.

I pondered my sexual aspirations more and more. The quantitative side fascinated me: Generally, sex is only a sliver of the relationship pie, whereas other activities the couple pursues compose the bulk. A highly sexually active couple may have sex for one hour a day, totaling to seven hours weekly. Over time, the intensity and frequency of sex reduces to about three times a week. I wondered what weight should be pinned on sex if the average couple engages sexually for three to five hours a week. [8] Based on the data, sex should hold less weight. However, this exercise of intimacy involves a profound connection between two people, which is precisely why its quality and significance is essential. Sex can certainly be pure fun but can also indicate the health of a relationship by conveying unexplainable feelings.

Sex drives must be balanced for a healthy relationship. American psychiatrist Dr. Gail Saltz says, "If your sex drives are out of balance,

---

[8] Luscombe, Belinda. Time, 26 Oct. 2018, "Why Are We All Having so Little Sex?" *Time*, https://time.com/5297145/is-sex-dead/.

your aim is to meet in the middle, having sex a bit more than one partner likes, but probably a bit less than the other likes." Disparities in desires and expectations must be verbally communicated to build trust in the relationship. Awareness of my physical passions and aversions allowed me to leverage my sexual needs as the cherry on top of desired qualities in a man. Moving forward, sex would constitute a small criterion when searching for a life-long partner, and it would surely serve as an authentic expression of love. Confident that there was still much that I did not know, I supposed that my next adventure would fill in the gaps I was missing.

PART ◆ VI

My Soulmate:
A Sustainable Relationship

1996 - Present

1

An Unexpected Encounter at the Turn of the 21st Century

I t's rather trite to say that the unexpected changes our lives. We can't always preach 'expect the unexpected' because, so often, the unexpected is unimaginable. As for me, I eliminated expectations from my rule book after my break-up with Rey. I had no intentions or big plans. I saw dating as a gamble— playing the slots of a new network, riding on high self-esteem, and sometimes, getting lucky. I didn't expect to hit the jackpot, at least not for now. It was a numbers game: The more you fish, the more options on the table. Practice makes perfect. I had mastered skills to initiate small talk, narrate my story proudly, set boundaries, expand beyond my inhibitions, and above all, exude confidence that blended striking features with genial friendliness. "You're so exotic, you have such an authentic smile," men would say, "you have incomparable charm."

While the attention I drew from Wall Street men was flattering, my inability to settle was disappointing my family. Every time I visited my parents, they pestered me with the classic "are you ever going to settle?"

My mom would ask, "how many men do you need to find just one?" An unexpected encounter would soon reverse the fate they feared and truly, change my life forever.

That chilly November afternoon happened to be my boss, Rob Walt's, birthday. During my thirty-minute lunch break from work, I rushed to Century 21, one of New York's finest department stores, to buy him a gift. Choppy winds nearly blew the Cossack black fur hat off my head as I ran across the street between honking cars. I reached the entrance and pushed through the entrance brimming with people toward the men's section. My eyes caught sight of a woven navy blue-striped sweater.

"Do you like that sweater? Who are you shopping for? You know this is a men's sweater, right?" said a voice from behind as I grabbed it. I turned around to a handsome young man with jade green eyes.

"Yeah, that's kind of an odd question, that's why I'm holding it!" I replied sarcastically.

"Well, who are you shopping for?"

"I'm just trying to find a present for my boss."

"What size is your boss? Maybe I can model it for you!"

This guy is crazy. He can't be serious. I could barely move. Before I knew it, this man shoved between a cluster of people and pulled the sweater over his shirt. He began twirling foolishly amongst the crowd, making funny faces, striking dozens of ridiculous poses. *This is quite strange.*

"It might be a good choice, it looks great. Thank you," I said nonchalant, trying to get him off my back. My ridiculous encounter led me to the opposite side of the store, the watch section. I examined various options, and yet again, heard that voice behind me.

"Excuse me," he tapped my shoulder gingerly, "I am really good with accents, but I can't place where yours is from."

That pick-up line, again? Classic. "Oh, I'm from Israel," I replied, fixated on a Bulgari.

"Really? I was born there! You don't have an Israeli accent though." Neither did he! He seemed American as apple pie with his light complexion, green eyes, strong bone structure, and mild mannerisms. *Maybe he was Swedish?* Despite my doubts, I played along.

"You're from Israel? You don't have an accent either! No accent at all! And you don't look Israeli!" I joked, "What's your story anyway?"

"Well, I was born in Israel, but my family immigrated to Mexico City when I was six. At eighteen, I moved to California for college, and I've been living in San Diego since then. Anyway, I'm going to my cousin's wedding tonight. Do you know what I should bring as a gift?"

Ok, random. I'll just answer his question. I gave him a few pointers: "Well, it depends on your relationship with the couple, but the gift should at least cover the cost of your plate, usually ranging about a hundred bucks per person. If you're giving money, it should be a multiple of chai." Chai means eighteen in Hebrew and symbolizes good luck in the Jewish tradition.

I wondered what morphed my aversion to interest in this silly guy. Perhaps it was our shared Israeli and Jewish backgrounds. I mean, he was handsome too. I noticed that he had no ring on his finger yet wanted to make sure he was still single so I could craft my communication to suggest interest.

"Who is going with you? Adults? Kids?"

"Just my cousin and me." Yep. Still single. Good questions are the best form of foreplay. He beat me to it.

"Where are you really from?" He diverted the subject, "You have quite the mixture of accents, you must speak other languages."

I insisted that he guess but had to give it away as usual. Our conversation about my upbringing was soon interrupted by a young lady.

"Oh, meet my cousin, Ally. And by the way, we never formally introduced ourselves— I'm Vick."

"Lea. Nice I meet you," I curtsied with a smile as usual. "Nice to meet you too, Ally." We shook hands.

I peered down at my watch. Quarter till 2:00; fifteen minutes until work. "I really have to go, but here is my phone number, I have to get back to the office." I scribbled it down on a random slip of paper from my handbag. "If you want to meet up, just let me know."

"Wait—" he blurted out as I turned away, "the wedding is tonight, and my plane back home takes off at 4:00 tomorrow afternoon. Can we have an early lunch?"

My frantic side came out. "I'm in a bit of a rush, my sister is coming into town tonight. Let me check my schedule. Talk tomorrow?"

"Sure thing." Vick nodded.

I ran back to DW in my tall, black heeled boots realizing that my boss's gift had been long forgotten. No big deal: I could buy it after work, on my way to class. *Hopefully that sweater is still there!*

Reflections with My Mom and Sister

I jumped on the B-line headed back to Brooklyn for dinner with my mom and sister. Betty had just arrived from Israel in search of a get-away. She had been adamant about divorcing her husband for quite some time;

she and her husband, Zohar, had been fighting for years. Zohar was one of my best friends growing up. I had fond memories of going to soccer games and playing basketball together. He even tried to teach me how to swim (I never learned)! It was difficult for me to disconnect my relationship with him while giving Betty advice, but I remembered my life in her shoes. I remembered how it felt to be trapped in vicious fight-flight cycles. I remembered feeling like a prisoner in my own marriage— a prisoner in love, incarcerated by fear. I remembered that moment in the mirror— shattered, and pieces of myself scattered in an empty vessel. Betty needed to know that she **did** have options. It was up to me— someone courageous enough to break the divorce taboo, the first in our family to do so— to help Betty liberate herself.

"I know how you feel. It's awful. You have to do what is best for you and your children. You guys fight five days a week and have two days of truce. The numbers just don't add up to a happy life. Ask yourself what it is that you're looking for—"

She interrupted me, "Luda! How am I going to support myself with three kids? It makes no sense!"

My mother comforted her, "You don't have to pay rent until we sell the old house. We will help you. But Betty, Zohar is a very good man. Don't think that there is a better man out there."

"Betty, listen," I interjected, "Mom and I are not in your situation, and cannot make any choices for you. Please think hard on what you want, then make your decision. Don't compromise your life, never compromise you." I pointed at her, advising assertively with Jewel at the back of my mind.

Debunking my mother's traditional views was an essential step to Betty's well-being. Although my mother meant well, she would be ashamed to have another divorced woman in the family. She was stuck too, trapped in a normative thought bubble— mentally and physically— since the age of thirteen. Her paradigms were so confined in this bubble that her life-time struggles had emerged because she could never pop it.

"Ah Luda, Jon! Papa is in Israel, not here, and it's even worse! Why is he so worried about what I am doing? I am alone! He calls me every day, calls me bad names, asks me where I am, asks who I'm with… He thinks I'm having an affair! He sees a movie that does not exist! He's driving me crazy! I don't know what to tell him." My mother's voice rang with despair and her eyes swelled. Tears sank into the maroon rug beneath her.

My father was back in Israel building a three-story home for my brother, Aidan, and his wife. Traditionally, the eldest son lives with his family and his parents to take care of them, like how Mendy and I lived in a brownstone with his parents back in the Boro. Change was challenging each of my family members on different fronts but listening to my sister and mother ramble on gave me much insight about their issues. Although different on the surface, they shared roots.

"Betty, what are the things you are willing to change to have a better life? Ask yourself what you're willing to accept, reject, and change. Why would you make decisions that benefit others over yourself? You must be responsible and take charge of what YOU WANT. That's being free. Ask what risks and rewards there are." I continued, "And mom, we are not living in Dagestan, right? You can keep living your life here, you're doing nothing wrong! Do what you want— go out, see friends! Just ignore him!" I hoped that they each recognized how they contributed to their own inhibitions.

My mom looked at me, perplexed. She could hardly utter a single

386

word. Although my mother loved my father dearly and admired his amazing qualities, his accumulated moments of craziness made her life miserable.

"I cannot leave him," she finally spoke. "He will never let me be without him. He needs me. If something happens to him, I will feel guilty all my life. You are kids, you will never understand me." More tears fell. Although her response was kind and compassionate, she probably sensed that I was acting as some martyr who had foreseen her destiny to save her from it.

"Mama, all I'm trying to say is that I feel your pain, and I saw it." I moved next to her on the couch, cuddling for comfort. "I understand you and the traditions we come from, but I wouldn't encourage anyone to endure pain. That's why I got divorced. I don't care what people say. My happiness comes first— nobody but me will come and fix my life, and men cannot make me happy if I am not happy myself. That's why I'm telling Betty that she needs to decide for herself. And you, mom…don't stop living!"

I was grappling with the idea of a sustainable relationship composed of 'opposite' people. It seemed as if different characters, energies, expressions, wants, and needs would culminate in proliferating conflicts— yelling, screaming, revenge, retaliation, abuse, manipulation, etc. Only if both people shared similar priorities, principles, and personalities could the relationship last. As for Betty, personality was the main ridge.

"Luda, Zohar drives me insane. He is so lazy and moves slow, it's like he has all time in the world for everything. He doesn't! I can't stand it, and I just don't think I can live in peace with a low-energy person anymore!"

This was exactly my point, but I reversed her statement as I usually did in moments of confusion. "Betty, they say that opposites attract, so how does that work in a marriage? You probably drive him crazy with your intensity too, right? Not everything can be on one person's terms in a marriage."

"Yeah, that makes sense, I get it." She hesitantly nodded her head in agreement, then asked, "Maybe if two people are too similar, it can cause issues too?" We both needed to think more about this. The question lies in what you prioritize most in a partner and whether you have the skills to remedy conflicts. Nobody will possess every trait you desire.

Even after much reflection, we couldn't come up with an exact answer. However, I hold true that personality (different from character) and pace can make or break relationships. So, when choosing a life-long partner, a person's intensity and energy should play a strong role because a radical imbalance may rupture the harmony. For many, a harmonious dynamic is easily found between two people who share cultures, beliefs, and values.

In addition, relationships fall apart because issues accumulate and erode people's tolerance for one another. To truly love someone means that you have the patience to nurture them through any obstacle. The purpose behind love is eternal persistence for another person's growth with radical compassion. As the dance of relationships endures inevitable tumbles and tribulations, the duo who embraces them as opportunities to bond and evolve locks in a life-lasting partnership. Only by bridging differences with a solution-oriented mindset can opposites indeed complement each other.

My mother, sister, and I continued chatting through the night, laughing over my funny experiences on Wall Street with Lazuli, Maggie, and Michelle. *Oh my!* I forgot to tell them about the strange man had I met at Century 21! Who knew if he'd call... probably not. At around 4:00 AM, we finally crawled into bed.

His Proposition, My Persuasion

My phone rang. It was 7:00 AM. "Lea, good morning, it's Vick Soffer, we met yesterday at Century 21." *He proved me wrong!*

"Hello, Boker Tov, it's good to hear from you," I replied in Hebrew, still rubbing my semi-shut eyes.

"Can we meet for brunch today, maybe around 11:00 or so?" he asked.

"Works for me." Pure excitement was my coffee replacement. I jumped out of bed and ran into the quiet living room. My mom and Betty had just woken up. "Mama, Betty! I forgot to tell you about yesterday! I have to get ready to go soon!"

My sister began bombarding me with questions, fatigued but enthusiastic. "What's he like? He's Jewish! You met him shopping for what?!?!"

From the sofa, my mom reached to grab my hand. "Ha levay, Ha levay," she preached.

"Please, don't expect anything. I'm not sure how this will turn out." I didn't want them stringing a fictional narrative together as they often did when a prospective gentleman seemed promising.

I arrived to pick up Vick a few minutes early. He was already waiting, dressed in dark blue jeans and a white-collared shirt. Punctual, sporty, elegant— I liked what I saw. We exchanged greetings as he took a seat in my car.

"Before I start driving, what would you like to eat?"

"Anything that swims, fruits, and veggies," he said.

Great! Just like me! I suggested the fish market in Sheepshead Bay, a great place for seafood that Vick had never explored.

"How was the wedding?" I pressed on the gas and prompted a conversation.

Vick delved into a detailed explanation of the Orthodox rituals. "I'm really amazed by how long and deep each blessing is, it was so unique. Just all-around beautiful."

"Yes, the rituals are very complex," I affirmed. Before the opportunity escaped me, I brought up, "Actually, now that I think of it, I had a wedding like that too! I was married in Boro Park to a religious man, then divorced a few years ago." It came out so easy, no hesitations.

"Wow, how interesting! Tell me more!" Vick found the stories from that period of my life fascinating.

We took a table with a view of the bay. Over a platter of oysters accompanied by grilled Sea Bass atop roasted greens, Vick and I spent the next three hours discussing our upbringings, religion, and their infusion into our modern lives. I enjoyed his company, from which I sensed a breadth of intellect, wisdom, and thoughtfulness. His green eyes glimmered with unexplainable meaning, a magnet of trust and comfort. He projected a manliness that was not masochistic, but passionate and protective. The similarities between us ignited unimaginable chemistry; I could see our differences as healthy elements bonding us close. Not only did I like what I saw so far, but what I heard and how I felt.

Vick's phone rang at around 2:00 PM. It was his sister, panicking over missing their flight which was boarding soon. "Give me a minute, I'll call you back." He hung up.

"Ok Lea, my flight leaves in a couple of hours…I'd love to continue our conversation and get to know you more. If I stay in New York until Friday, would you be interested in spending more time with me?" He assured me that he'd make arrangements with his partners so he could take a few days off from work if I did the same.

"Sure, that could work, my mother and sister are staying with me, I can manage." A fuzzy feeling of belonging returned. Oh, how I missed it!

Vick flagged the waitress and suggested that we head back to his hotel and inform his sister and business partners. I offered to pay, but he handed her his card before I could even take out mine.

"All on this one, please," he insisted.

I thanked Vick for a lovely lunch and dropped him back off at his family friend's apartment. He promised to call me after sorting out flight and work logistics. "I'll be here for the next few days for sure, just give me an hour. I'll see you soon."

I drove back with a glowing smile. My mother and sister were standing in the kitchen anxiously waiting for me. "What's that smirk on your face? Where have you been? What happened?" Betty asked, hands on her hips.

"Uhh, nothing…" I giggled and proceeded to share the news.

"Maybe this will be the one, Ha levay." My mother clasped her hands together looking up at the ceiling, thanking God for her daughter's fortune. "When will we meet him?"

"Soon enough, mama. Soon enough."

Introducing My Date to the Family

Vick called at around 4:40 PM that same day. "Everything's been settled. I'm free anytime." I invited him for dinner, looking to my mother and sister for approval. He gave a hesitant "yeah, sure" seemingly shocked by my invitation, considering we met just the day before. Maybe my warm welcome was premature? Not to me, not in my culture. Even someone befriended in the streets was welcome.

I gave Vick my address and confirmed, "I'll see you around 6:30."

My mother and sister lit up with immediate purpose. "We have fish! I'll make stew and mejadra!" My mom bust open the refrigerator with all her strength and began scavenging for the best ingredients: red peppers, zucchini, and tomatoes, among bunches of fresh parsley, cilantro, and dill. Betty turned up the stereo and rummaged through a packed spice cabinet for cardamom, cumin, and fennel seeds. We danced to our favorite Israeli tunes as we whipped up a tabbouleh salad and stuffed cabbage. The hours passed at lightning speed.

Ding-dong. The moment of truth— introducing my date to the family.

"Shalom! Come in, come in!" My mother immediately offered Vick tea or something to drink as she laid out an assortment of cookies, dried fruits, and nuts. Noshing and slurping away, Vick shared that his parents were Egyptian Jews and that he spoke five languages fluently: English, Spanish, French, Hebrew, and Arabic.

"Egyptian? Really? You look like a Swede!" Betty said bluntly and laughed.

392

"I get that a lot," he smirked. My mom was smirking too, giving off a slight smile that sparkled through the room. This man had her blessing.

"Salmon is ready! Let's eat!"

The meal-time conversation flew frictionlessly, touching on diverse topics of our personal lives, backgrounds, childhoods, politics, and beyond. Vick blended seamlessly into the family tapestry, as if he'd been a part of it for years. Our cultures, values, and shared language were certainly key factors fostering such strong connections. Following a five-course dinner, my mom quickly changed our plates and prepared mint tea, her most exquisite homemade strawberry jam, and set out trays of baklava. About six hours had passed since Vick arrived. It was nearly 1:00 AM. We made plans to meet again later in the evening.

2

Getting to Know Vick

The next few days were spent touring the city, from Carnegie Hall on 92nd street and Y to the Jewish Museum on Fifth. Vick and I continued our deep discussions at fine restaurants among coffee shops and local delis. We shared culturally rooted paradigms; we compared and contrasted differences among Jews, Russians, Egyptians, and Mexicans. What a colorful combination!

On Tuesday night, we hopped off the subway near the Hotel Empire. We wandered around the Upper West Side until the rich, earthy smell of dumplings lured us into my favorite restaurant, Shun Lee. Waiters circulated with bamboo baskets filled with steamed buns. I sampled new varieties each time a waiter came round. Vick and I bit into a discussion over my past marriage and got tastes of each other's dating philosophies, too.

He was fascinated by my previous experiences but seemed apprehensive when I asked him about his prior relationships and dating situations in California.

"You know that it's against the rules to ask about prior

relationships," he remarked.

"Huh? Rules? What rules? I didn't read any rule book, and don't care about rules anyway!" I jested.

"I'm serious, I try to follow that rule," he said.

I didn't understand why it was normative to keep our exes concealed. I deemed it important to share successes and failures in previous relationships to better establish future ones. "Why is that rule in place? Why should we keep our exes concealed? Don't they give an insight to who we are as people? Shouldn't we own our past and share those stories to learn from them?" I asked.

He reflected for a moment, then replied, "I guess it's a rule that single people follow, out of respect for their date. Shouldn't we be sharing our own lives, apart from our exes?"

"Well, we have." I challenged him again, "And plus, aren't our exes a part of who we are?"

Vick stared at me for a minute, then finally confessed, "Yes, that's true. I am actually enjoying our conversations since they are authentic and different from any of my other dates."

I smiled at him, took a scrumptious bite of my shrimp dumpling, and began: "Living through extreme cultures has made me realize that most rules are not universal. They're formed within communities to create a common standard. They aren't usually principle driven either. They just serve those who set them up. So that's why blindly following somebody's rules is pointless unless they help me accomplish my goal. If I followed them out of 'respect' then I would be compromising my own self-respect. Respect is about honestly sharing life experiences with one another."

He was gawking at me, riveted in my thought-process. "Huh, how'd you figure that out?"

I told him about my commitment to 'know thyself' and how I used journaling to rationalize my emotions, resolve inner conflicts, and devise action plans moving forward. "I live my life to be happy and fulfilled, that's all. If I am going to follow a rule, it should achieve my goal, improve my outcomes, and eliminate worst case scenarios. That's my rule to following rules!" I concluded confidently.

Vick set down his chopsticks and admitted, "You're right," then added, "In a way, I can't make any valid counterclaim because I wasn't much of a rule-follower myself. I was, let's just say, a mischievous kid. I built makeshift bombs in my garage and exploded them near embassies or at neighbors' doors to scare them." He swiveled his wine glass, took a sniff, and took a short sip.

"You made what?! Makeshift bombs?!" I nearly choked on my water, cracking up. "We should have met earlier! We could have been partners in crime!"

It was about 11:30 PM when we finally walked out of Shun Lee. The perfect balance of humor, emotion, intellect, and push back filled never-ending conversations. The city was sparkling with lights and vibrant with life, just as I felt. We headed towards the subway and hopped on the B-line.

Defying his own rule book, Vick confessed that he had broken up with a girl who he'd been dating for five years. "I wanted someone who was Jewish, and she wasn't." He later revealed to her that he started dating someone new: Me.

I was shocked. This only reinforced what I had learned from my relationship with Rey: When men are no longer interested, they often make no effort toward closure or an explanation, but when they are interested, they go the extra mile. The sincerity of one's words and actions may confuse more than provide closure. However, this doesn't mean they don't love or care for you. It points to insecurity and a lack of self-awareness, which we all have, often manifesting as thoughts failing to follow through with words, or words failing to follow with action. While difficult to own and resolve this misalignment within, I had to understand the psychology behind it after my divorce and through my next relationship.

To Persist or to Quit?

Vick happens to be skeptical about everything. His skepticism comes in the form of an instinctual 'no' to anything new or outside the norm: The abnormal poses a burden, a risk, or a hindrance to any objective.

Vick and I met for lunch on Friday, shortly before his flight back to San Diego. He used the Oreo cookie tactic to basically sum up how our relationship could not work.

"I had the most wonderful time with you here. I enjoyed meeting your family and exploring the city for the first time," he stuttered, "b-but I've been thinking, I simply don't believe in the long-distance thing and another reason is that—" he paused, searching for words. "The opportunity cost for you to move to San Diego or me moving here would be too high for the both of us. You have your career, family, and friends here, while my business and entire life are in San Diego. I just can't see this working."

My eyes followed his attentively. Amused by his choice of words— "the opportunity cost" being "too high"— I prompted, "So you see your dates as business propositions... hmmm." I wasn't really laughing. He was.

I realized that Vick did indeed evaluate relationships as business opportunities, attempting to minimize the margin of error for relationship failure. He was an engineer by training and a business owner after all, so I tried to match up to his lingo.

"I get you, but I'm not a business deal. If you want to evaluate personal relationships as business deals, we can negotiate the terms to realize a very profitable endeavor." I winked.

From his responses, it also seemed like Vick was projecting his own insecurities onto me. However, before relenting to my assumptions, I was curious to gain his direct perspective. "So, Vick, what are the obstacles that you see beyond logistics? If anything, please do not worry about my career, family, and friends."

"San Diego isn't New York... you know what I mean." Vick showered me with doubt, reiterating shallow concerns.

I challenged, "Don't you think it is premature to consider moving for now? Let's take it one step at a time...when we need to cross that bridge, we can talk about that." I figured that peppering positivity onto his negative convictions may open his mind. "People go through life to find a strong connection where there are alignments of values, cultural background, intellectual stimulation, and emotional bonding. What else would you need to explore our relationship further? Why wouldn't it work? Just geography?"

"I know. You're right about that, but I don't want to get into a situation knowing that there are so many barriers from the onset." He remained unconvinced. It became apparent that my plays of persistence would not succeed in a single conversation. Time was running out.

"Let's talk when you get home," I concluded the conversation. With a luscious kiss we parted ways. He hopped on a yellow cab and waved me goodbye.

Encountered Skepticism:
To Pursue or to Withdraw?

Vick was pretty much what I was looking for in a man: Self-made, hard-working, intellectual, generous, high-integrity, Jewish— you name it! While smart and business savvy, his emotional intelligence needed some sharpening. He seemed to follow some normative rule book, however, felt comfortable breaking it with me; he remained firm in his beliefs, yet relished learning with a ravenous appetite for philosophy, intellectual discussion, and knowledge of any sort. *Is it worth trying to influence a skeptical man? How can I do it?* I had to test the waters. Although changing people is impossible, the art of persuasion can leverage some behavioral shifts via savvy influence.

In the past, I deemed my elite moral dogma an effective permit to change people. After reflecting in the mirror at twenty-three, I understood that high morals were only a sliver of the pie. My direct style of expression was perceived as arrogant and forceful, yielding a loss of credibility and disappointment. My moral character and good intentions were ignored. As I was failing to achieve my intended purpose time and time again, a new strategy was required.

I began to think of influence as an art, whereby a plan is sketched and then carefully painted over with many brush strokes. These many brush strokes take various forms, analogous to tactful conversations that infuse trust and confidence in another person. First, one must listen attentively and inspect a person's belief system; then, one must follow up with logical questioning so that person can re-examine fallacies or consider new paradigms. After understanding Vick's point of view, I sought creative tools to dismantle his concept of a relationship as a business proposition. Perhaps that would reel him into my rule book…

Hooked With Books

I brainstormed ways to crack the code of a skeptical businessman. I came up with a great idea, one that would credibly challenge his paradigms from several angles. *What better way than to send him a few books?* The following morning, I headed to Barnes & Nobles to purchase three books that had influenced my own beliefs: A Man's Search for Meaning by Victor Frankl, Emotional Intelligence by Daniel Goleman, and The Road Less Traveled by M. Scott Peck. I highlighted sections relevant to Vick's fallacies and dedicated each book by writing bullets on the inside of the cover page. Each bullet pointed out his skepticism contrary to the author's philosophy. Then, I indicated pages of relevant sections and added follow-up questions. For instance, 'How would you reconcile the disparities between the author's philosophy and your belief?'

In short summary, I sought to highlight the existence of love despite physical distance through A Man's Search for Meaning. Goleman's dissertation about healthy relationships was my attempt at shifting Vick's concept of relationships. Scott Peck's opening sentence, "life is difficult," aimed to cement the fact that "we must negotiate the curves and corners of our lives" to embark on a journey filled with opportunities, growth, and love.

I wrote Vick a letter to go along with the books and concluded, 'If you want to discuss any of these philosophies, please call me. Lea.' All wrapped up in taupe packaging and a red bow, I shipped the books to San Diego hoping they'd be the key to his heart.

On Saturday morning, my phone rang: Vick followed up on his word. "I just got home, and all is well with me. It's a sunny day in San Diego. How's New York?"

"Lucky! It's freezing here! I'm going out with my mom and sister soon for breakfast.

"Sounds good. Go enjoy your day. Tell them hi from me!"

Just about to hang up, I was eager to reveal my surprise: "Hey, by the way, I wanted to keep our conversations going, so I sent you a little something in the mail. Let me know when you get it!"

He stuttered, "Wh-wha-what surprise? And um— just know that I don't really like to talk on the phone that much, but yes, let's talk soon."

"Yep, you'll find out eventually."

These books were a gift to me rather than to him, as it was my endeavor to influence a skeptic through philosophical interactions. I hoped that this connection would pave steps towards true love through common values, the ability to engage in hearty discourse, and the commitment grow through our differences together. Physical distance did not seem to be the real barrier; it was nothing but a logistical setback to overcome as the relationship matured.

I was clueless that these three annotated books would propel our relationship. Such emotional and intellectual ties left us on the phone for four to five hours daily, with some conversations even lasting for days at a time. One phone call literally went on for fourteen hours; I was stuck in my apartment for an entire weekend! So much for "I don't like to talk over the phone."

My principal lesson from this was to pay less attention to what men say and rather focus on the connection between their words and actions. Vick's skepticism is a deeply embedded personality trait, manifesting as cautionary decision making rooted in a high sense of responsibility, integrity, managing risks, and fulfilling his commitment to others. Learning to understand and address others' hesitations, concerns, or weaknesses is integral to developing trust and cultivating strong relationships. With Vick, I began to listen attentively and ask questions intently. These open-ended questions validated all his personal experiences, beliefs, and feelings. They kindled discussion instead of provocation, enabling me to graciously embrace his opinions and attempt to influence from there.

3

My First Visit to San Diego

Our relationship flourished in no time. "Why don't you come to San Diego for Thanksgiving?" Vick asked casually over the phone one morning.

I could not contain my excitement. "Are you serious!?" I planned to take time off from work for a week.

I got off the plane around 8:00 PM. Vick greeted me with a big hug and a soft kiss. It was dark outside, but the weather was pleasant and cool— a stark difference from New York all around. Coming a dense and urban city, San Diego seemed like a paradise on earth. In the car, we chatted about the flight and noted differences in scenery between our two worlds. I'd never seen palm trees so evenly spaced, swaying lyrically in the calm breeze. Streets were quiet, clean, and manicured— more and more as we approached the serene suburbs. We stopped in front of a wrought iron gate surrounded by green vines and a mosaic waterfall. A sign read 'The Golden Triangle.'

"We're home," Vick said as the gate opened. He turned into the corner home.

"This is so beautiful, so magnificent."

I had never seen anything like this. Vick's home emitted an eclectic style: Luxurious but not opulent, refined with detailed fabrics and warm colors.

"Would you like to eat and drink something? I have some pasta and salad made," he offered.

"I am ok, thank you though. I don't usually eat this late. Just water, please. I'm a bit tired and want to take a shower." My eyes were closing.

Vick lifted my suitcase up the stairs. I followed behind him, dragging my tired legs. The bedroom was plain. Walls and shutters were white-hued yet colored by quilted pillows, blankets, and a barber rug. A touch of dark wood surrounded the bed frame. Vick showed me the closet and drawers among other storage areas for my things.

"Would you like to share the bed or sleep in a different bedroom?" he asked.

"As long as we don't do anything, you know, I'm fine sharing the bed. I think I trust you." I grinned.

He cracked a laugh and assured me, "You have nothing to worry about. You're safe with me."

During my time in San Diego, I began to imagine my life here, cloudless of worry and bright with love like the California sun. Spacious surroundings, peaceful with politeness, and a man with whom I could grow old. But settling wasn't my goal quite yet. Vick and I would travel between coasts at least every couple of weeks. I remained focused on building a social-emotional connection with Vick through our shared values and bridging philosophies. He did the same, affirming that our needs and expectations aligned.

The culmination of expressions, actions, and verbal promises dictated the pace of our relationship. We communicated terms and conditions for one another which built mutual trust and stability. Our commitment to one another would come naturally, the most authentic seal to love there is.

Trust: Honesty Absent of Jealousy

Three months into our long-distance dating, Vick called me from Mexico City. He was attending his business partners' son's wedding. I was clueless as to what his colleagues had in store for him besides their opinion of me: Too outspoken, not a good match for a reserved, elegant guy like Vick.

"I just want to let you know that my partner, David, wanted to introduce me to a girl here. I hope you don't mind. I'm going to meet her for coffee on Sunday." I was a bit surprised by Vick's transparency and casual framing of intentions. It didn't seem like he was asking for my permission, however, I was delighted that he was being honest with me.

"Sure, go ahead, be my guest. And let me know if she is better than me," I replied confidently with no choice but to accept.

I recalled that when Vick started dating me, he told me that he had been seeing another woman for some time but didn't inform her that he was seeing someone else (me). Like with Rey, I explained to Vick that the same terms applied to me— the term being that I had the same freedoms to explore as he did— and that we'd be transparent about who we were meeting and how we felt about them. Fortunately, both Vick and I viewed sex as a sign of commitment.

Communicating directly, honestly, and clearly is key to developing relationships based on trust and respect. Setting up expectations, terms, and conditions allows for mutual understanding, where each can exercise their self-made rules equally. Many relationships deteriorate because of expressions that deceive, distort, or deflect from the truth. It is far easier to accept, reject, or change boundaries in a relationship where each has the chance to voice their own needs and establish terms. That is respect: being transparent and intentional with your communication. If your partner or date is still exploring potential relationships, it may mean that he/she may still have some doubt about you— which is OK! Instead of being upset, free your partner to explore, and liberate yourself to do the same. This allows one to determine the following: (1) what is acceptable and how to accept it, (2) what is risky and should be rejected, and finally (3) what is within your control, what can be changed, and how to change it.

Confidence: Be Curious, Courageous, and Calm

Vick and I talked on Monday morning. "How was your weekend in Mexico?" I asked generally, most curious about his set-up.

"The wedding was beautiful. My date was nice as well, a Mexican balabusta (a Jewish housewife)— very domesticated and impressive. But not as expressive and fun as you. And by the way, I bought tickets to New York. I'll be there next weekend. Are you around to see me?" *Told you so!* Answer granted.

"Yep, I'm around! I'm looking forward to seeing you too!" A smile crept on my lips. Obviously, Vick wasn't interested in the girl that his business partner introduced him to or any other girls he had met. Remember: A man will fly thousands of miles to see you if he's interested

408

and will come up with hundreds of excuses to avoid it if he's not.

Many women would be turned off by Vick's conduct in my situation— we had been dating for three months already. *What do you mean you're "meeting another girl?" Now?* But think about it: I would have been even more upset if I had found out about this woman later and Vick didn't tell me. After my divorce and single life, I vowed to never enter or create a possessive relationship with anyone. Suffocation engenders a toxic cycle of deception, resentment, explosive reactions, and guilt. It may be difficult to grasp, but the mutual freedom to explore establishes a profound level of respect with trust built upon it.

Our open conversation benefitted us both, especially me. Regardless of the outcome, it was important for me to be aware of what qualities Vick liked and disliked in a woman. The full truth is essential to evaluating standing in the relationship and making high-quality decisions moving forward. Confronting small dilemmas from the onset also reduces the possibility of additional problems and provides two people an easy way to resolve them before they escalate. I appreciated that Vick and I prized values of honesty and integrity, integral to remedying any issue and growing from it together.

Taking "No" as a "Yes"

On a Saturday in May, Vick and I sat on the rooftop of Manhattan's fine restaurant M for lunch. "We've come a long way in the past several months, it's like we've known each other for years," he stated.

"Yes, it's incredible how much we have in common. I was dating so many guys in New York, but it's funny that I found someone all the way from California! I've really been looking for someone just like you!" I could see our lives progressing together, but only on the same coast.

Sleepless nights due to endless phone conversations and stress from traveling back and forth were taking a toll on my health.

"Vick, I do love what we have, but my stomach hasn't been doing well and I've hardly been getting four hours of sleep. The past couple of months have been really hard for me," I confessed. By this stage, and after weighing risks and rewards, I was ready to bring the relationship to a more serious level: The challenges created by our long-distance relationship were greater than my fears of moving. "Our honey-moon stage can't last forever; we need to start thinking about our next steps."

Vick looked at me puzzled: "Well, umm, I don't see how either of us can move, I mean, you have everything here and I have everything there. It's just not ideal. You remember when I told you that I don't believe in long-distance relationships, they're impossible to maintain over time. You have your job, family, friends—"

I interjected to cut-off his circular reasoning, responding by validating his concerns then debunking his perceptions: "Vick, I get it. But finding someone who shares culture, values, and principles is far more important than logistics. I can take a leave of absence from work and move to San Diego to see if things can work out. Plus, I can find a job anywhere. You don't need to worry about me."

"Hmm...You're not afraid?"

"No, I'm not. It seems like you're really worried about me— don't be. I won't hold you responsible if things don't work out."

The conversation took an interesting turn as Vick brought up a new subject: "Well, you know, if we were ever to build a family together, I'd want to have intellectual discussions with our kids."

What? That's so random! I broke out in uncontrollable laughter. "You must be kidding! All those hours on the phone! What do you mean?

We are constantly discussing articles, books, and philosophy! Is that not intellectual? What are you trying to say?" I craved clarity.

Vick put his fork down and began to stutter, "You-you, you see, you need to finish college and get your bachelor's degree."

"What about my mom? She read every Dostoyevsky book but didn't even finish high school. Does she not qualify as being intellectual?" I challenged him jokingly. He tilted his head and squinted his eyes. I had stupefied Vick because he perceived academic intelligence as the umbrella under which intellect falls. To him, a degree secured your credibility regardless of your intellectual activity outside of it. However, I knew that emotional intelligence and people skills were of equal or even more importance to academics. Knowing oneself, how to listen, how to question, how to debate, and how to apply the knowledge gathered from experiences to daily life are the pillars of wisdom. These skills can be integrated with a college education, and of course, are not mutually exclusive. At this moment, although his request of me was valid, my degree should not have been a deal breaker. Besides, I was working on it! Rather than expressing my disagreement further, I decided to share my story:

"Vick, I know that's important to you, but I am working toward my degree, but you have to understand that my life's situation didn't allow me to complete it so fast. After I moved here, I was married for four years and wasn't allowed to go to school." I placed my hand on top of his and looked him in the eyes. "Trust me, whether it be here or in San Diego, I'll get it done. I'm just doing it slowly."

"I get it." He nodded but was still skeptical. "Lea, I just really don't think you moving right now is a good idea. If you're already enrolled in school and have your career, I don't want to mess that up for you and I don't want to be responsible for that." He was still making assumptions.

"Vick, you don't have to move. I am, I want to, and again, you are not going to be responsible for me. Let's figure it out together and decide when. I'm a big girl, you don't have to worry about me. Just think about it."

There was no need to push more for now. He needed time to digest the information slowly. I couldn't grasp where Vick's skepticism was rooted, yet to understand that it was all in genuine care for me and my personal growth.

Persistence Despite Resistance

Vick and I spoke over the phone a week later. I casually brought up, "I just wanted to tell you that I'm ready to move. I hope you've had time to think about it since we saw each other last." He held the same reservations.

"What about your car? Your apartment? Your family?"

"Vick, I'm ready. Are you?" I promised him that on my end, everything would be fine.

Talking to someone who fires "no" at every idea or suggestion can be extremely frustrating. One may feel shut down and devalued. Learning to manage skeptical personalities is essential as they inevitably emerge in our personal relationships, friendships, and in the workplace. Through my experience, I've learned that one can indeed convert a skeptical "no" to a "yes." While difficult, it creates opportunities to understand and be understood, thereby strengthening the relationship. Inspecting the validity of a person's beliefs, fears, and doubts helps both sides gain confidence and comfort in their discomforts.

Persuading Vick came through the grinding technique: Rounds and rounds of open-ended questioning ensued to dismantle his perceptions. I asked, "What are your concerns about me moving?" While projecting hesitation, after many conversations, he'd surprise me. These surprises indicated that seriously considered my move.

"I just spoke with my sister, her boss is hiring Y2K developers, so you might have a job waiting for you," he confirmed.

"Wow! Thank you so much! The only thing I would need is a car, but we can shop for it when I get there."

He had even closed the loop on that detail, too: "I have my old Nissan Maxima, you can drive it. Everything is set for you to move here, just arrange the leave of absence with DW."

Arrangements had been made to eliminate any margins of error in my transition. I was amazed that Vick organized everything behind the scenes.

"For all these weeks and months of saying no and that it wouldn't work out— you arranged everything for me? Thank you! I am beyond grateful." I was thrilled to embark on this new adventure.

4

Packing and Helping Me Move

I packed my belongings into boxes (more liked shoved). Not the most meticulous person, I aimed for practicality— just for nothing to break or fall out. I used my clothes to wrap picture frames, dishes, and fragile items. Unlike me, Vick has a knack for making sure that "everything is in order," as his father says. He is one of the most meticulous people I know, graced with thoughtfulness and generosity. He flew to New York and helped me ship all my boxes through DW's interoffice delivery system. I stayed in New York for two weeks before moving so I could transition my projects to my replacement.

I took the time to journal during my flight. My toolbox was slowly filling up with powerful techniques I could employ to advocate for myself and influence skeptical people patiently. I felt empowered and at ease.

Upon arriving in Vick's San Diego home, I would enter paradise once again. All my belongings were perfectly sorted. My suits were all ironed on hangers and arranged by color; my documents were labeled by category in identical stacks. Maybe it was just Vick's OCD, but I saw this as a labor of love. Taking his first "no" as a "yes" was worth every risk and granted great rewards. It is said that words may show a man's wit, but their actions show their true intentions. This certainly rang true for Vick: All I had to do was plant the seeds, and he followed through with deeds.

Lost In Paradise

Looking up at sunny San Diego's clear blue skies reassured me. Snow-white clouds projected a protective halo over my head— *everything will work out in the end*. At first, I was enamored with the serene west-coast lifestyle— the antithesis of New York city's rough edges— and graced by Vick's presence. However, the extreme shift from a city that never sleeps to a quiet town was a total shocker. The novelty would soon wear off and I'd be lost in paradise, disenfranchised from the superficial beauty that the golden coast emanated.

I tried to re-establish my usual routine: exercising in the mornings, working during the day, and going out with Vick or new friends in the evenings. He **did** warn me: "San Diego is not New York." There wasn't a soul on the streets past 8:00 PM! There were only so many museums, shows, beaches, and restaurants to explore.

Depression spiraled. I could hardly make friends, stemming from a communication barrier between myself and the San Diegans I was meeting. We spoke English, but our words held alternative meanings. Positive or negative labels were attached to every word or phrase. Many topics were sidelined as taboo, those of which happened to be my three favorite subjects to discuss: Politics, religion, and sports. Too controversial. Agreeing to disagree was foreign here like back in Boro

Park. I wouldn't hold back from being myself. I wouldn't hesitate provoking stimulating discussions to better understand people's perspectives and incentives. I'd learn to manage, push back, and convey my message tailored to my audience.

5

Compulsive Order Creates Disorder

A dapting to Vick's rule book in the household was extremely challenging (it still is!). I felt obliged to follow it at first, as his unconditional generosity left no room to disappoint. He set me up with a job, gave me his old car, and bought me new summer outfits from Nordstrom and Ann Taylor. So much for a guy who "didn't want to be responsible" for me.

While Vick's OCD would seem to keep things in order, it caused moments of disorder in our relationship as my bad habits irritated him. My bad habits weren't all that bad, but to Vick, leaving a glass of water on the table was a grave sin. It was a sin— like the sky was falling: "Lea! Why can't you pick up your stuff! You could live in dirt, and it wouldn't even phase you!" I used to ignore it thinking no big deal.

These episodes intensified over time. Vick wanted cleanliness on his clock and to his perfect standard. After exhausting days of work, I'd take off my suit and leave it beside my closet as a reminder to put it away after I relaxed. "This is dirty! Why is it here? Put it back!" he'd assert in frustration, "I can't function when things are all over the place." I'd tell him nicely, "I'll do it in a few minutes, I just got back, let me lie down for a little bit."

That fell short of his needs. His tangents exacerbated, and so did my reactions. Already depressed at the time, his fits derailed my well-being and triggered rash behaviors from my previous marriage. "I can't do this anymore! You need to stop!" I'd erupt in anger, pack my stuff, and threaten to leave.

This was the first time I had ever seen Vick's aggressive side; it was probably the first time that he saw mine, too. Basic cleanliness was all I needed, but it was clear that an immaculate living-space was a priority of his. Although our priorities were misaligned, it wouldn't be wise to argue or leave him over it. It would be pathetic for these trivial issues to ruin our relationship— a relationship tied by common cultures, values, and intellect. The qualities I loved about Vick surpassed those I wished would change. Acknowledging that I couldn't change his compulsive habits and that our honeymoon period wouldn't last forever, I'd learn to manage my behavior and reactions. Until today, disparities in our household habits remain a work in progress for us both.

When You're Fired, Find Freedom

I'm a mad scientist in the kitchen. When it comes to cooking, I throw absurd combinations of vegetables into a pot and take bites of the concocted outcomes as I go along (oftentimes they're really tasty!). My gourmet recipes can never be duplicated, nor can the mess I make. Vick, on the other hand, cooks like a Michelin-star chef who follows mise en place to the tee. Every ingredient is carefully selected, measured, and prepared to perfection. Most importantly, when it's time to eat, the kitchen must be spotless. While we each love the methods to our madness, they repel under the same roof. Vick's tantrums over my messy habits shifted toward my culinary technique as well. Sadly, my gastronomical experiments would be no more. As our time together passed, he'd insist more and more that we go out to eat.

I rushed home from school to prepare a nice dinner for us one evening. Just as I was greasing the pan, Vick came into the kitchen and said, "Lea, please put everything back in the fridge."

I set the olive oil down. "B-but I washed the veggies and everything. I'm just about to start cooking. Are you sure?"

"Let's go out, it's easier, don't worry about anything." He helped me put everything away and wiped down the counter like a windshield wiper.

We drove down to George's by the Cove, a rooftop restaurant overlooking the La Jolla shore. After placing our orders, Vick prompted, "Lea, you have so many skills and talents, but you know, it would be better if you dedicated your time to your education and career. You don't need to cook and clean."

"I honestly enjoy coming home and cooking after work. It's therapeutic sometimes," I assured him, "it's no big deal for me." This was the first time someone— especially a man— told me that I didn't need to contribute to household affairs. *Wasn't my role, as a woman, to carry out domestic tasks?* "This is the way I was raised," I added, "and it's the least I can do to thank you for everything you've done for me."

Yet again, Vick repeated that it was a lot easier if we eat out and that I should focus on my profession and academic pursuits.

I was offended at first. *Does he dislike my cooking? Are my contributions falling short? Maybe there's something he's not telling me.* After going in circles, I just let it go. *Maybe I should just embrace this.* Weighing the risks of being offended versus the rewards of freedom from responsibilities comforted me. Vick once told me that I'd always be his queen, but now, I felt like a princess with no duties in attendance.

Fired from the kitchen, I found the freedom to rearrange my schedule. I'd work longer hours, take extra classes at the local college, explore new projects, and network with people I took interest in. So long as Vick was happy with this resolution, it was fine by me. I found liberty in rejection once again.

Overheated Reactions Flare Up

Being fired from the kitchen was great, in theory. It was merely a band aid for our underlying communication gap. Vick and I still struggled with each other's organizational habits and how we went about household duties. Shouting matches occurred more frequently, each one over a more trivial issue than the last. We couldn't seem to confront situations collaboratively.

One evening after an argument, Vick brought up the subject. "Lea, we need to find a way to resolve these issues because when you yell and scream it makes things worse."

My explosive reactions hindered solving problems like in my past marriage. However, I had to curtail my flaring emotions and apply a solution-oriented mindset. "I know our priorities are different, but I would hate for these silly things to ruin our relationship," I responded, "I know, it's hard for me to contain my anger sometimes, and I cannot seem to meet your cleanliness standards." I paused and thought about strategies that could help me prevent lashing out. "Writing helps me contain and reason with my emotions. Maybe we can write to each other when we disagree about things, for this and in general."

Vick peered down at his napkin, squinting his eyes in doubt. "Writing? How would we do that? I'm not sure what that will accomplish," Of course he was skeptical!

"Common, let's give it a try, just trust me on this one."

A couple of days later, I stopped at CVS and bought a small black notebook. It was intended for Vick and me to communicate our gripes via letter. My experience with this process was especially unique. When I noticed myself heating up, I'd immediately scribble away in the black notebook. This outlet calmed me and helped me leverage my emotions by articulating my feelings and beliefs rationally. After reading a few sentences, I'd often realize that I was overreacting, and that Vick wasn't at fault: I was. It was me taking out my internal conflicts on him.

Reading Vick's notes enabled me to understand his point of view. Once I was fully aware of his emotions, needs, and objectives, we could devise a solution with both of our priorities in mind. After a few months, I no longer needed to write. The routine practice of thinking before I reacted was literally engraved in me. From here on out, it was here to stay.

My love for philosophy infused with a quest for self-betterment led me to personalize philosophies over solely intellectualizing them. Transferring my solo-journaling to a partnership inspired my life-long process of personal growth and career. I strive to endow others with liberating methods to make empowering decisions for themselves and in their relationships. One can only make wise choices when free from self-imposed rules, social norms, and the opinions of others. Sometimes, reflecting on our feelings is all it takes to regear our beliefs. We must trust in the little things— like a small black notebook or even just a few written words on a sheet of paper. Just one meaningful word, gesture, or action can buy and transform the entire course of a journey.

6

You Took My Cousin Away from Me!

Think of a time when someone you love or a close friend began branching out to new social circles. Think of the feelings and questions that flooded your mind: *Did I do anything to create distance? I don't think I did anything wrong.* Many feel rejected, jealous, and resentful. These emotions are natural, but love is not a competition. We must own our feelings, express them calmly, and seek to understand what created that degree of separation. Our loved ones, as close as we think we are to them, may need time for themselves or a breather from their relationship with you. Asking questions that take their feelings into consideration is essential. This sets heated emotions aside so one can maintain the relationship despite the distance.

While this scenario is common in friendships, it also resonates in conflicts with in-laws. In my relationship with Mendy, I recalled his mother constantly telling me, "He will always be my son, mine. He will never be yours." I experienced tremendous power struggles with her, my father-in-law, and of course, Mendy. I wanted more from my husband at the time but failed to ask myself what my goal was. Jealousy of Mendy's relationship with his parents morphed into my resentment toward his whole family. At the age of nineteen, I lacked the maturity to manage Mrs. Wolfson's snarky comments; I let her control my attitude and actions toward Mendy. My divorce taught me to never repeat this behavior with anyone. It was my responsibility to block out other's opinions and act in accord with my principles to debunk my perceptions of love as possession. That's why my purpose— reaching a liberated state in a sustainable relationship— failed.

Vick's cousin, Ally, saw him as her safety net, biggest ally, and best friend. Before I moved in with him, they did everything together, from weekend road trips to biweekly sushi nights and morning beach walks. I also had a nice friendship with her while still living in New York; even upon my arrival to California, she was kind and generous to me. Ally helped me find work at her company, we took our lunch breaks together, ran on the treadmill side by side, and spoke on the phone almost daily. She was my first real friend in San Diego after all.

Within a couple of months, Ally's behavior radically changed. She stopped reaching out and ignored my phone calls. This was unlike her. I wondered what happened. Maybe something was going on in her personal life; I didn't want to meddle in between. However, her passive-aggressive behavior shed light upon festering jealousy.

Ally and I had a colleague in common who had just given birth. I wanted to send her a gift but didn't have her home phone number or address since I was new. I decided to reach out to Ally hoping that she'd have our colleague's phone number.

"I'm not going to give you her number, you just keep stealing my friends."

"I can't believe you're saying that, why would you?" I replied, clueless as to what I had done to make her feel this way. I barely had friends! She hung up the phone and went completely silent for the next couple of months.

It was clear to me that Ally deemed her friendships scarce. She felt the need to compete with me for attention. At the time, I didn't have the knowledge to understand why she acted this way, considering her inability to verbalize her emotions. I should have asked her directly. Years later she admitted, "I didn't know how to control my jealousy, I was Vick's best friend before you moved, and I felt like you took my brother away from me."

When I became a part of Vick's world, his time and attention to Ally were split by my presence. She felt sidelined. As I mentioned at the beginning of this chapter, this feeling is normal: Human beings have a visceral need for intimacy, all on a journey searching for love and connection. This need is greater in people who harbor underlying insecurities, as personal weakness corrupts their methods to matching their intentions and goals. Had I reacted angrily toward Ally, our friendship could have dissolved long-term. Letting her get some air gave vitality to the relationship.

Ally's attempts to keep her friends close only did more harm than healing. Rather than respectfully integrating herself in outings with Vick and me, which we would have been happy to share with her, she expressed hostility rooted in resentment. The once warm dynamic between us chilled, exactly the opposite of what she wished for. It's ironic that the person who employs possessive tactics to keep their loved ones close ends up pushing them away. Ally's coping mechanisms (like mine in the past) signaled that her behavior had nothing to do with me.

She herself was unable to fill the void in her life, which is why she saw me as competition. I would never let her make me believe that I was stealing her friends. I would never harbor the belief that I was competition. It was all in her head.

While able to mend our differences eventually, these repeated episodes would leave our bond at a looser level. Ally is and always was a good person; her insecurities propelled possessive fears. The young and naïve me never fathomed that someone so kind would act this way toward me. By now, I have experienced these situations enough to know that insecurities manifest in endless forms. This is why we must examine our own and other peoples' actions while observing how we/they tailor their personality in certain situations or environments. Different settings and interactions can elicit unexpected reactions and qualities which point to insecurities worthy of acknowledging. Such awareness is essential before acting or diving deeper into a relationship.

I was surrounded by people who acted differently in the household versus in public a decade prior, back in the Boro. Rather than a self-contained group whose actions revolved around their image in certain spaces, this entire city's culture was based on it. In San Diego culture, communication and mannerisms are constantly being tailored to please others. Saying what I thought and doing what I said got me in trouble. I'd soon learn that it was necessary for me to tweak my behavior if I wanted to accomplish my goals. We can change momentarily on the outside, however, 'to know thyself' means that we're aware of what we're changing, when we're changing, and for what purpose.

7

Communicate to Motivate, Manage to Your Advantage

You can take a wolf off Wall Street, but you can never take Wall Street out of the wolf. That's where my experience in corporate America began. I hadn't lived anywhere else in the United States besides New York. Wall Street's concrete jungle was all I knew— crowded and chaotic, yet with some mysterious order behind it. Hierarchies are distinct, roles are strictly assigned, and tasks are executed methodically: Double time. *Want to get from A to B?* Take the direct route, no time to waste. Some may perceive it aggressive, nonetheless effective. What you're told is exactly what you need to hear: Blunt, direct, straight to the point. No B.S.— just get the job done.

Getting the job done in San Diego is done much differently. *Want to get from A to B?* Well, you're about to go on a treasure hunt! I was handed clues with no clarity and a key with a code that was foreign to me. For answers, one must delicately dance around the shadows of nicety. Any phrase or action out of line with this smooth, lyrical choreography is deemed offensive. My style did not match. Yet another social norm on the golden coast I was not used to.

I enjoyed working as a consultant for large utility companies. The job required tremendous analysis and I also managed teams of ten to sixteen people. While thriving in solo-tasks, I struggled in group projects. Many team members took offense to my directive communication, frustrated when I insisted that they deliver top-notch projects on time. I considered myself assertive and responsible, but to my dismay, most San Diegans did not: "You're overpowering. You're so intense," they'd say, "just chill out!" I wondered why I'd need to 'chill out' if I was on the job. *Isn't our goal to get things done quickly and to the best of our ability?* A few months into this leadership role, my group stopped cooperating. It didn't make sense to me.

Fortunately, my IT director was not a San Diego native but a born and raised New Yorker. He called me to a meeting well-aware that my forthright style had no personal implications toward my colleagues.

"Lea, I can understand what you're going through. I see the root of the problem clearly. I've worked in many different environments too. San Diego is one where you can't boss people around. They get offended too easily."

"My intentions are always in good faith, I just want to deliver quality tasks on time," I assured him. He nodded his head and pulled a book out of his drawer, The New One Minute Manager by Ken Blanchard.

"Here Lea, this will help you, trust me."

From reading The New One Minute Manager, it was evident that San Diegans operated leisurely compared to New Yorkers. I had previously assumed my leadership role as a license to direct my team with authority. Because I was in charge, I expected tasks to advance under my methods and at my pace. "You're too intense" was their way of telling me, 'Your pace is too fast, slow down.' To generate results, I would have to adapt by tailoring my attitude in the workplace. This surfaces in personal relationships as well, where personalities clash due to differences in habit and lifestyle.

Ken Blanchard emphasizes that when people in a workspace are knowledgeable, a manager does not need to tell them how to work. Instead, a leader must inform them of the objective, why it's important, and allow the team to engineer ideas toward that solution. Giving others the opportunity to create brings an influx of ideas. Disagreements surrounding those ideas inevitably surface, however, they are beneficial to the task if the manager and team handles them correctly. I had come a long way in learning to ask questions apropos my colleague's thoughts and methodology. Open-ended questions in the workplace shed light upon the construct of your team— from their expertise and their shortfalls to their work ethic and beliefs. Blanchard writes, "You can expect more when you inspect more."

Another line that resonated with me was, "People who feel good about themselves produce good results." This held true for me: My team improved tremendously after I altered my style, a heavy burden lifted off my shoulders. I no longer had to act like a policeman, my team was happy and confident, and we were delivering quality tasks on time. A win-win solution.

The most important lesson from this book was that the greatest leaders are not authoritative but democratic. They employ a style of guidance that aims at creating opportunities for growth and remedying conflicts with an integrative resolution process. Presidents, executives, and managers are not the only leaders: We are **all** leaders. Each one of us takes on a leadership role every day in some aspect of life, whether it be navigating through a sticky situation with friends, managing a team at work, or being a parent. I'd soon apply this principle among other techniques from the New One Minute Manager to my marriage and motherhood, where my core purpose was to establish constructive relationships with my family members. Just as I committed to never force my team into a decision because I was their manager, I'd never tell my daughter that she had to do something because I was her mother. Never.

8

Ringing in a Respectable Woman

It took several months before fully adjusting to my new life in San Diego. Between daily exercise, work, and school, I kept busy under a solid routine. While missing my friends and family back home, we kept in touch through daily phone calls. My mother was anxiously waiting for the day that I'd inform her of my engagement: "When are you getting married? It's about time, Luda, you're already thirty-three. The clock is ticking."

Connecting with people and groups who shared my similar interests and background eased the transition. Vick and I were a part of San Diego's tight-knit Israeli and Jewish communities. We socialized with different people from each of them at least once a week. Friday night Shabbat dinners were dedicated to sets of friends who enriched us with new perspectives and intellectual conversations.

An older couple we saw frequently had befriended Vick many years ago. The Adelmans met Vick through the Jewish community, where Mr. Adelman and his wife sat on the board of our local synagogue. One

Saturday night, Vick and I were invited to attend a lecture there. The Adelmans greeted us as we exited the hall and picked up a friendly conversation.

"So, tell me, when are you going to make her a respectable woman?" Mr. Adelman motioned at Vick. Vick chuckled with no answer.

I interjected with a big smile and my arms wide, "I already feel respectable, more than married women, actually! I get treated so well! I have all the respectability I need!"

Mr. Adelman's old-fashioned slur was familiar to me, commonplace from Derbent to the Boro. In the Jewish tradition, if two people are living together and aren't formally wed, the woman has yet to be made respectable through marriage.

Mr. Adelman pushed, "Well, you should definitely get a ring on her finger either way." His wife remained quiet as usual, her scrawny arm linked around her husband's. She took part in our laughter and friendly conversation until it got dark.

"We'll see you guys soon, let's get together for dinner." Vick waved.

"Yes, at the wedding! Make it happen! Don't make us wait that long to see you next!" The old man shouted as we parted ways.

My hand met Vick's as we walked side by side, looking up at the stars and then into each other's eyes. "Lea, it's time to get married," he whispered.

Many people deem the symbolic wedding ring and the husband/wife label as a bind to their bond. It may have that effect, but I saw no need to formalize our relationship at the time. I was content living under the same roof as Vick and enjoyed his company. We both had the freedom to work in professions we wanted, arrange our own schedules, and see who we wanted to see. These were liberties I seldom had and couldn't be more grateful. Over time, providing each other the resources and support to grow independently brought us closer. Time is the currency of relationships: Time invested in a relationship pays off well when wants and needs fall into place naturally and mutually. Time invested in a relationship determines the pace, intensity, and path that the relationship will take.

Within days of our conversation with the Adelmans, Vick would constantly bring up the 'I want to build a family' discussion: "Lea, we're not getting any younger, and I want to have kids."

I wasn't so sure about kids, but I loved Vick too dearly to leave his dreams unfulfilled. Without marriage, there would be no kids or family. The knot had to be tied.

9

Never Let Turmoil Spoil

O
ur commitment to each other grew over five years of living
under one roof. There was no cute proposal like the ones in
movies. Marriage would simply serve as a license to build a
family. We bought our rings together and proceeded to plan the next
stages of our life as a couple. Before officially tying the knot, Vick and I
bought a new home. We drove several miles north from La Jolla and
stumbled upon the beautiful suburban neighborhood of Carmel Valley.
The cul-de-sac housed many couples raising children and building their
families. Many were Jewish. Beth Am, the local synagogue, happened to
be just around the corner. This seemed like the perfect spot to settle
before embarking on our married adventure.

Wedding plans were underway after weeks of traveling to buy
furniture and moving-in. We approached the Rabbi of our congregation
who charmed us with his charisma and asked him to officiate our
marriage.

"Yes, it would be my honor. In fact, I do something very special for
couples," he said, "each of you will write a piece to each other,

undisclosed of course, and I will weave them together with philosophical and biblical elements and read the final piece at the ceremony."

"Great! That's amazing!" We gave Rabbi Ridel definite nods of approval, ecstatic to append such a unique accent to our wedding.

From that December through March, Vick and I had weekly meetings with the rabbi. After the third one, I noticed a very interesting pattern in the Rabbi Ridel's behavior: He'd ramble on about himself for the first fifty minutes and left only the last ten to discuss our wedding. I sensed something suspicious but followed my rule of giving three to five chances before jumping to conclusions. After five or six meetings, it was clear. I shared my concerns with Vick, and he dismissed them.

"You're just getting into your head, it's nothing. He's been doing this forever. Just trust him."

Ok sure. "Uh-huh." I went along.

Vick and I decided on June 17th, 2001. Mid-March came, and we met with the rabbi to confirm the details. At the tail-end of the hour, he casually mentioned, "By the way, I'm available on June 17th, but did you check the synagogue's schedule? I believe there's a Father's Day event."

What? No way. And he's telling us now? We checked, and he was right. We frantically called every other synagogue in San Diego. Not even one was available that day. Now, just two months before the wedding, we had no venue! We had already coordinated with all our friends and family! To say we were upset would be an understatement. My intuition was correct after all.

A New (Crazy) Idea

We had Saturday night dinner plans with a few Israeli friends at Japengo, our go-to sushi joint. Golan and Tali Sason were world travelers, with businesses in Turkey, Dubai, Israel, Greece, and the United States. "We're looking forward to the big day, finally, after so long! Is everything ready?" Of course, that was Golan's first question! He was just like Mr. Adelman. Vick and I looked at each other in disappointment and shared our unfortunate situation.

"Why don't you guys get married in Italy?" Tali proposed. "You're doing your honeymoon there anyway." She turned to Golan and mentioned, "We know of a beautiful synagogue in Florence, too."

Vick reacted, skeptical as always, "No way! Are you insane?"

"Vick?! Why not? Let's do it!" I loved the idea. Despite Vick's resistance, I took their suggestion seriously and inquired about the details. More information to fill in the gaps often incentivized him to give in. Vick concluded the dinner conversation ended with, "Yeah, I'm sure we'll figure something out."

I brought up the subject on the drive home. "So, what do you think? Getting married in Italy could work out!"

"Lea, that's impossible. How are we going to get married in Italy? We have to change everything now!"

"We're planning to be there for our honeymoon anyway! And how awesome would it be to get married in Italy? It's a once-in-a-lifetime experience! What do we have to lose?"

In days to follow, I'd convince Vick little by little without causing an argument, armed with the grinding technique. It took two long weeks until Vick acquiesced: "Sure, whatever. We can try." It was our only choice.

Our new arrangement took a toll on Vick's sanity. He'd pace about the house rambling, "We're going to have to cancel the photographer, the caterer, tell all our guests to cancel their tickets to San Diego— what are we going to do?!?! This is such a mess!"

"Vick, it's ok, what's the big deal? We'll just tell them the truth and move on. There's nothing we can do. What other options do we have now?" I tried my best to calm him down by understanding the source of his anxiety. I've found that stressful situations often tear relationships apart but asking the right questions to refute worries and doubts can reinfuse trust that was lost.

The next week, we began making phone calls to inform our guests that the wedding would be relocated. "Ok, where?" they asked. "Um, Florence. Florence, Italy."

Some were livid. "What?! You can't be serious right now!" They had already booked plane tickets to San Diego and made hotel reservations. Fortunately, though, many were compassionate toward our situation and even came with us! In the end, we flew about sixty members of our family and closest friends to Italy.

Rabbi Ridel from Beth Am in San Diego still offered to officiate, claiming that his Rabbinical certification was applicable to our local synagogue or any other. I was the skeptical one this time, but Vick insisted that we have somebody trustworthy come along "to have insurance" and manage logistics. We were also looking forward to the special speech he composed about us having sent him our pieces a few days back.

Deceived and Left Hanging

Upon arriving in Florence, Vick and I settled in the Il Salviatino, a boutique hotel perched on a hilltop overlooking the city. Rabbi Ridel assured us that everything would be set up after he came into town within the next couple of days. To our dismay, the seal to our insurance plan was canceled. Our insurance plan became his!

Over the next forty-eight hours, there was no sign of our rabbi. Since we were covering his expenses for the trip, we knew his travel plans and which hotel he was staying at. We called the reception desk in concern. He was totally MIA. *Maybe something happened to him?* We knew little that Rabbi Ridel was living a secret sumptuous life in his five-star suite and indulging at Florence's finest eateries. Had he done his job we wouldn't have minded it. Just days before the wedding, Rabbi Ridel's intentions became crystal clear.

We met with the chief rabbi of the synagogue in Florence where our wedding was to be held. He broke us terrible news: "Unfortunately, Rabbi Ridel does not have the necessary certifications to orchestrate a wedding at an Orthodox synagogue. He can still serve as a witness and read one of the seven blessings."

This must be a mistake. "Why is that?" Vick asked.

"So let me show you here," the Italian rabbi pulled out a pile of documents. "I checked his Rabbinical certifications, and your temple, Beth Am is conservative, not Orthodox." He pointed to the discrepancy, "It is different, you see, there are different types of certifications. Those of your rabbi do not apply here, but with pleasure, someone from our congregation can marry you, no problem." His heavy accent rang with assurance, but we had no idea what to think. Vick thanked him for letting us know and told him that we'd call Rabbi Ridel to sort things out. If only he'd answer.

We called Rabbi Ridel's hotel morning and night for the next few days. Nothing. I still couldn't believe that a man with so-called honor would lie to us about his credentials. Vick and I prayed that this was a miscommunication and that he would follow through with his promises.

Trolled, Not Trampled

Our procession would begin at 5:00 PM on July 4th, 2001. There was no sign of Rabbi Ridel until our photography session at 4:30.

"Hey guys! You both look amazing!" he exclaimed, interrupting the photographer, and coming in for a hug. I received him coldly but tried to be friendly.

"Where have you been?"

"All is well, all is well." He brushed it off and changed the subject, "By the way, Lea, I got your piece, but Vick, I don't have yours."

Vick was shocked. "I sent it via email before we left, a couple of weeks ago. Are you sure?"

The Rabbi peered down at his shoes then looked back up. "Well, I don't have it, and I need something from you to put it together." He was frantically digging through his suit pocket. His eyes widened as he pulled out a tissue of some sort. "You remember the idea of it, don't you? Just, um, just write something here."

"I don't have the piece with me, I can't possibly rewrite it." Vick's face flushed. Left with no other choice, he was scribbling remnants of once carefully crafted words on a wrinkled napkin. Our photo session was long gone.

Meanwhile, Rabbi Ridel stepped closer to me, trying to start a conversation. "Stay away," I snapped, "you've done enough damage!"

He tried to calm me down, "Lea, don't worry I will put them together right now, everything will be fine."

I ignored him, too upset to even speak with him. I had put so much thought into my writing and can only imagine how thoughtful Vick's piece was. He was a perfectionist, wise and thoughtful with words. We were both so keen on having Rabbi Ridel deliver this special address, but there was no way we'd be getting what we wished for.

One of the Florentine rabbis conducted our ceremony. It flowed beautifully in such an elegant, emotional language. Rabbi Ridel was still scheduled to read our seventh blessing in conjunction with his dedication. He uttered a few cliché words from a napkin, one ear and out the other for me. Nothing special— far-short of profound and philosophical. But there was no way I'd let this situation ruin this precious moment for Vick and me. Ridel could be dealt with later.

In days after our wedding, I was amazed that we were able to enjoy such an enriching marriage despite the whole fiasco. With Rabbi Ridel absent, his job became ours. Vick took on the role of master planner. When Vick plans, everything must be perfect— perfect to a golden standard that not even event planners and designers could achieve alone.

Table settings, flower arrangements, and food platters had to be impeccable. Furnishings had accents of reds and golds like our Ketubah, and dishes were tasted time and time again to meet Vick's Michelin standards. The procession had to be precisely scheduled, all its components in a particular order to infuse meaning. Every single object, word, and ritual held profound symbolism tailored to our personal qualities and the cultures we were bridging together. Most important was preserving the historic traditions that shaped our unique Jewish identities. Vick always had the concept of legacy in mind: "So our children remember and follow in our footsteps."

10

Masterpiece Matrimonio

Clearly, the journey to marking our legacy was not so easy. In addition to the hunt for a destination, venue, and an official rabbi, we had other battles to tackle.

In ancient Jewish marriages, a wedding certificate called the Ketubah was handcrafted on parchment by an artisan scribe. Even today, Jewish families sign some form of a Ketubah for official documentation. Of course, Vick wanted a parchment original. When we first met with the rxabbi in Florence, less than a week before our wedding, Vick inquired about an artisan who could create one for us.

"Hmmm…There is one guy," said the rabbi, "But he is very far away, I am not sure if he will be able to make it in less than four days, but you can try." This artist happened to be the only person in all of Italy who still produced them. Our wedding was on Wednesday.

Bright and early Sunday morning, Vick and I took a four-hour road trip down a dirt road to the quaint commune of Sovicille. I felt teleported back to the Roman empire as we drove between ruins and skinny archways surrounded by identical salmon-pink homes. We could hardly decipher which alleyway to enter; our car could barely make it through. Up narrow aisles of cobblestone was the artisan's humble abode, a boxy studio enveloped in a blanket of lush greenery.

The old man trod down the rustic steps with a beaming smile, "Ciao, bonjiorno!" His scruffy white beard quivered with his shaking jaw, "Matrimonio! Matrimonio!" He welcomed us inside.

"Si, si! Molto gratzie!" Vick replied as we followed him up the stairs and into his home.

The place was miniature. It was spacious enough to house two, the artisan and his wife. They invited us to sit on the couch just inches from the door. From their cube-sized kitchen to the right came a smell larger than life— oregano, thyme, garlic, and basil simmering with cherry tomatoes, onions, and roasted peppers.

"You like to mangiare? To eat?" the curly, gray-haired woman offered showing-off her skillet of parmigiana di melanzane, or eggplant parmesan. We kindly declined; it was too early for us. "Limonada!" She insisted brightly, waddling to her garden, and picking some lemons from the tree.

So, there we sat, sipping on freshly squeezed lemonade crammed on the sofa across from the ninety-year-old craftsman. He showed us flipbooks with pictures of the Ketubahs he had made. We smiled in amazement and marked those that appealed to us. Neither he nor his wife spoke a sentence of English or Hebrew— just broken phrases. It was relieving to have found a way to understand each other using facial expressions, hand gestures, and mixed languages despite the barrier. Fortunately, Vick spoke Spanish, so he gave Spatalian (Spanish and Italian mixed) a try!

446

"Como este, (like this one here)" Vick pointed to a red toned Ketubah in the frayed album.

"Certo," the artisan assured, "Yo fare, yo fare."

"Gratzie, molto gratzie." We thanked the artist profusely for accommodating us, and his wife for such warm hospitality.

A handmade Ketubah takes a couple of weeks to create between the draft, the scripture, and the artwork. Ours was produced within just three days, and we didn't even have to drive back to Sovicille to pick it up! The artisan made a special trip to Florence on the morning of our wedding to deliver it. My heart filled with joy knowing that an appreciation for love and culture could override gaps in communication and foster treasured connections between people.

I found myself at the Mikvah two days before the wedding. Traditionally, a Jewish woman immerses herself in a pool of sacred water to purify herself before marriage. I was obliged to do this before marrying Mendy, but not this time. For some reason, I chose to enter the Mikvah on my own before marrying Vick. I flipped through my journal and saw the words, *preserve your heritage and roots, that's the most important.* Rather than viewing this ritual as one mandated by Orthodoxy, I had matured enough to link my past to my present with a higher purpose.

Often, people focus on differences rather than similarities. The perspective by which one angle their focus— how you see something rather than what you see in plain sight— is what counts. Gaps between secular and religious communities or between different cultures may be vast, but common customs never fall short of uniting them.

Matrimonio Memories

Paging through our wedding album feels like restitching a quilt of old-fashioned fabrics interlaced with modern-secular threads. That was our ceremony: A blend of past and present, an amalgamation of colors, characters, and cultures. By the time Vick and I were married, we had both morphed into secular Jews despite coming from Orthodox backgrounds.

I stumble over a picture of Vick placing an ornamental ring on my finger, artifacts which we borrowed from the synagogue on that very day. While we still had conventional wedding rings, we requested to marry wearing ancient ones like in historic times. [9] Engaging in this tradition reminded Vick and I of how humbly our ancestors were married— grounded in our roots and tradition.

Each snapshot of our celebration brings memories of the vibrant tunes that filled us with joy. The music we selected personified diversity between Vick and me. We danced the horah upon entering the hall; a mélange of Middle Eastern, Russian, French, Israeli, and Mexican instruments accompanied the klezmer violin. Visuals were the most unique aspect. I embraced my past in a color of ownership, a symbol of fervor for the future. Rather than wearing white, which represented innocence and purity, I walked down the aisle in red. Yes— I was a stained woman from my previous marriage and past mistakes, but I deem these stains of strength. These imprints on my identity inspired my courage enough to move forward and marry with renewed passion. Also in red was our glass goblet, decorated with a strip of baby pink flowers.

---

[9] Back in historic Florence, most commoners didn't have enough money to purchase rings, so they were lent out.

It was handmade by an artist from Sovicille, like our Ketubah.

My takeaway from my wedding is to never leaving beginnings behind and use them as catalysts for growth. The hallmark of this blossoming period in our lives was the moment when Vick stepped on the glass under the chuppah (wedding canopy): We took it upon ourselves to reconstruct the vessel after our honeymoon. No matter what would shatter in our relationship, we would always work hard to piece it back together. Surrounded by the warm climate of love, those flowers could always blossom again.

As we had planned, Vick and I embarked on our honeymoon adventure straight from Florence. We drove through the Italian countryside down to the Amalfi Coast, explored the South of France and Monaco, and finally traversed the border from Spain to Portugal. These three-weeks marked our last moments of freedom as a married couple. Our responsibilities would soon mount again in a totally changed life. Vick says, "July 4th is the day that America got its independence, but mine was taken away." I claim much differently, in that America got its independence, and mine became a product of it.

The ability to see the world through another pair of eyes is not only a rewarding gift, but the most liberating privilege. Motherhood has allowed me to nurture and be nurtured through inspiring and being inspired in return.

Motherhood: Through My Daughter's Eyes

2002 - Present

1

The Alien Invasion

O h boy! An alien invaded my body! I was honestly a bit vain, always fixated on feeling good, looking good, eating healthy, staying active, and having fun. Going from running seven miles a day at dawn to waddling uncomfortably out of bed every morning was a change in routine I could barely fathom. Everything I had focused on and everything I enjoyed became impossible.

Typical pregnancy ailments left me ill and confined to my bed as the months passed. Tortured by agonizing aches, I freaked out when sharp kicks thumped against my inflated stomach. Nausea left me an endless snacker, thinking that eating more would clear the episodes of brain fog and fatigue. "Don't even look at the scale!" Vick used to say when we went in for check-ups. Intense weight gain took a toll on my energy levels and my motivation plummeted. More than the alien inside of me, **I** felt like the alien detached from my body and unable to control my situation.

While pushing myself to stay active and social, Vick noticed a complete change in my behavior. I seldom realized the impact of my misery on those around me— normal for a moody pregnant woman, I guess. But I didn't want Vick to take my short temper personally because my irritability had nothing to do with him. I communicated my feelings assertively, so he knew that I wasn't feeling well and didn't intend to take it out on him or on others: "Honey, it's not fun to be pregnant. I'm anxious, agitated, and lethargic. I'm sorry if I'm crabby, just know it's not you." By sharing your challenges, you can own them, liberate yourself, and find those willing to support you. Then, you can focus on solutions rather than lingering on the pain.

After communicating my feelings to not just Vick, but others in my social circle, I decided to learn about pregnancy and styles of parenting. Not only did this take my mind off the physical discomfort but filled me with knowledge that I could apply to the next chapter in my life. Besides, there was nothing I could do besides take medicine until the baby was born.

As my baby bump rounded-up, my female friends would constantly ask me how I was feeling. My classic response was: "Not so great, being pregnant isn't fun. I feel like an alien invaded my body!" Their countenance would often tighten, "Oh my goodness, don't say that!" with an unnerving tone, "the baby can hear you!" *Really? That's ridiculous,* I thought, *is it just me who feels this way?*

Contrary to my perception, many women enjoy pregnancy because they feel bonded to the little thing growing inside of them. This bonding sensation was absent for me: I was honest about it. Another emotional burden was the last thing I needed, and these women's attempts to shame me wouldn't triumph. Journaling about how these women made me feel and how I truly felt as a pregnant woman influenced my new response: "I am so happy that you feel or felt bonded with your baby. I wish I had the same experience, but we're different. And that's ok, isn't it?" This may sound a bit snarky, but I was not willing to endure humiliation. I wouldn't try to change how I was feeling or communicate otherwise. I'd stay true to myself and those around me, displaying myself with confidence despite my discomfort.

While I didn't exactly bond with my growing alien, I bonded with those who embraced me, respected my honesty, and provided unconditional support to help me push through this journey. To them, I will be forever grateful, but it was I who had to be my biggest cheerleader. Family, friends, doctors, therapists— you name it— are all great help! However, the help of others can only take effect to a certain extent. There are internal conflicts and physical challenges that only oneself can manage. Some situations may be impossible to change which is why the power of positive attitude is essential.

To cope with struggles in my own hands, I directed a new level of kindness towards myself. Sluggish and awkward with each pound I gained (all 58 of them!), I never let myself down or pretended that it was easy. I was religious about my hygiene, dressing nicely, and working out. Although honest about the raging discomfort, but my smile never faded. To boost my mood on the inside, I'd have to elevate myself on the outside. Smiling really helps! Fake it 'till you make it!

Pre-pregnancy, I felt my mind, body, and spirit aligned. However, my physical setbacks forced me to grow mentally. I was coming to 'know thyself' in a position where my body was out of my own hands. Transforming my mindset and spirit to thrive was the only option: It didn't have to be all or nothing. Despite the whirlwind of changes, my daily needs remained stagnant. Running seven miles sounded great, and so did late-night outings with friends, but my physical state would not allow it. *What could I do to fulfill those needs and stay happy?* I could still work out and I could still socialize, just at a lower intensity and frequency. Even in moments of dire fatigue, I remained active by opting for lower impact exercises at the gym like light weights and the elliptical. To continue networking, I signed up for new moms classes. This period of my life propelled me to explore new activities that satisfied both my needs and condition.

Breaking routine is hard. I had moved mountains to find my optimal schedule and climb to my peak: My endorphins were high, plans rolled out as they should, and I had no complaints. Life, however, always looms over with a storm of challenges. Once the damage is done, getting back to that peak seems impossible. I certainly felt this way. Acknowledging that my condition was out of my control and making the best out of it helps me weather personal storms until this day. I can always come back to my peak with grit, the ability to adapt, and learn from the situation. Then, I can focus on solutions and take swift, appropriate steps forward.

Iterated in my story many times is the 'insurance plan.' Experimenting with various routines, and prioritizing them based on preference, the insurance plan sets up a safety-net to fall on. From a young age, I've recognized that a plan B is just as important because one day, plan A may be taken away. Pregnancy never felt good even with a plan B in place, but I achieved my purpose by making the best of it. While plan B may not be ideal, it can become your savior when left with no choice.

2

What Kind of a Mother Will You Be? Eyes Paired by Mutual Tears

My mother used to ask me what kind of mom I wanted to be. Tomboyish, high-energy, and impulsive, she had little faith in my ability to patiently nurture another human being. For a while, I believed her. I pondered how I'd remodel into this new loving, compassionate, and tender character. It was, again, my turn to look in the mirror and decide which qualities I sought to reflect and those I would not. Could my biggest weakness become my biggest strength?

During my stay at the hospital, an older nurse with light eyes came to my bedside and said, "Just remember, when your baby is crying, it's because they need something." She rested her hand upon mine and continued, "Until they're eighteen months, attend to their needs. Change their diaper, offer them food, or just pick them up."

As I lay in the delivery room ready to burst, my mind traced back to a book I read a few weeks prior: The Wise Baby Theory. It was one of the many pieces I flipped through while I was pregnant. The book describes a method to regulate babies' sleep cycles, allowing them to cry in increasing five-minute intervals until they stop as they'll fall asleep eventually. *How wise is this 'wise baby theory' really?* It seemed a bit abusive to me.

The nurse's philosophy seemed sensible because we all have methods by which we ask for things that we need. Babies don't speak adult language, so we must be compassionate toward their calls for attention. Their crying signals a need for emotional or physical support— whether they're hungry, in pain, or just want to stay by your side. Adults do this too, just quietly.

I gave birth that cold November morning with a vow to never leave my baby crying. Adopting this practice from the dawn of motherhood would bond me closer to the alien that was finally on my same planet. The six-pound creature resting in my hands bore a blue, cone-shaped head. We thought something was wrong with her. "All is normal," the doctors assured us.

Vick and I took our baby home knowing little how dreadful the next twenty-four months would be. Unabated shrieking toiled with my sanity. Changing diapers and breast-feeding sucked the life out of me, quite literally! With an unpredictable routine and planning nearly impossible, I lost control of my schedule. I longed for the day I'd return to the office and work with my consulting team. My brain was drained.

I'd eventually take pride in being a mother as our little princess, Sabrina, grew older. Her conehead did indeed round-up, and her cheeks inflated with youthful joy. After an enervating first year-and-a-half, it became easier for me to understand her needs as our connection evolved. Preventing the crying spells early-on enabled her to develop attention-grabbing signals, knowing that I'd be there to unconditionally protect and provide. When a baby knows that when they cry, mommy will be there, their trust strengthens. With age also comes maturity, whereby maturity shapes intentions and clear communication. Clear communication from mother to daughter and daughter to mother fulfills the asks of any new parent. Well, there is one more thing a mother may ask— and that's love in return.

A Different Love: From Mother to Child

I rarely cried, and rarely do until this day. However, tears got to me shortly before Sabrina's second birthday. My memory falls short of what specifically ignited this emotional moment, but an epiphany hit me: I realized that the way parents love their kids is much different than the way kids love their parents.

A portrait of my mother crossed my mind as I imagined myself in her shoes twenty years prior. Motherhood swept her adolescence and identity into a vacuum. Fearing this fate for myself, I began to weep uncontrollably. To paint the labels of 'mother' and 'wife' over all my work through the years petrified me. I was finally feeling happy with a high sense of self-respect. I was proud of the principles, activities, work, and relationships I was cultivating. Meanwhile, I had yet to understand that my identity was like a revolving door, constantly redefined by the elements entering and exiting my life. As Sabrina matured, her entrance into my door would transform my views of each panel, inspire my perspectives, and influence my decisions. That element of love I yearned for would step through and fill my world in due time. I was able to receive it by channeling unconditional patience, compassion, and collaboration into my parenting. As a new mother, I had to understand that self-sacrifice is required to establish a relationship of trust with my child.

I Make More Money Than You. Stay Home.

Reading every morning and mingling in mother's groups didn't quite fulfill me. I was a full-time mom too, but my brain wasn't operating as it was used to. I grew irritated with stagnant intellectual exercise. I longed to think with people, engage in stimulating discussions, and innovate solutions. One day, I got lucky.

My friend, a prominent IT director in San Diego, called me: "Lea, the communications between engineers and business services are overwhelming! I could really use your help."

"Yes! I'm in. When can I start?"

Seven months later, I was back working full-time. The long hours tore me between my new job and my precious princess. Vick also spent full days in the office, and out of the country— from Mexico to China— frequently with his colleagues. I was often left alone with Sabrina for weeks at a time. The mother-career struggle became intolerable. Vick and I searched for babysitters and live-in nannies to help us out. Until then, we needed a quick fix: daycare. I called to ask about her every few hours. The caretaker's response worried me:

"I don't know. I think she's ok, let me go check on her," she said. I could overhear Sabrina wailing in the background. Obviously, she was not ok. There was no way I could trust just anyone with my baby. Who would have thought that my motherly instincts kicked in!

While on our search for live-in nannies, I needed to start

brainstorming more sustainable solutions. After returning home from work one evening, I discussed the daycare situation with Vick. We were at a major crossroads, both thriving and leveling-up in our careers. Indeed, money talks big in the face of tough decisions. Practicality is the priority.

"Lea don't take this personally," Vick tried not to offend me, "I know you love your job, but I make more money than you. It's best if you stay home and look after Sabrina for now, I will give you whatever you need to be happy, just take care of our little girl."

I understood where he was coming from. My baby always came first, so I had to make a sacrifice. I knew little that my role as a full-time mom would encourage new projects toward a line of work inspired by my daughter.

Defiance Spews During the Terrible Twos: What to Do?

The terrible twos are inevitable, so they say. I was warned countless times, "Lea, be prepared, it won't be easy." A two-year-old is like a blender without a lid, a reckless rule-breaker who makes endless mess. This is rooted in a child's curiosity to explore a new world exposed to them by pushing boundaries in it. This was me: Since my childhood, I've questioned the validity of people's opinions, beliefs, or decisions, and argued when things did not make sense. Accepting the terrible twos as a normal state of kids' behavior— absent of tools to address it— made zero sense to me. This would be contrary to my purpose. My purpose was to understand my child's behavior, contain it, and teach her to redirect her energy.

I was confident that there were ways to shift this paradigm from the terrible twos to the terrific twos. Why? Because I saw a different reality at her preschool: I found that Sabrina's terrible twos dagger only pointed at me. Sabrina would listen and follow everything asked of her at school but resist at home.

"She's such a good kid! Sabrina is darling," her preschool teacher told me one afternoon at pick-up.

My eyes widened. "Really? I'm sooo glad! At home, she's so defiant. She doesn't listen to me! Every time I ask Sabrina nicely to pick up her toys or to come home after an hour at the park, she fires back, 'no, you do it!' or no, you go!' I just don't get it!"

"It's normal," her teacher assured me. "Toddlers tend to listen to their friends and strangers but not their parents, it's a phase. Just the terrible twos."

Yeah, I've heard that one before. I refused to accept it. If my daughter could follow her teacher's instructions, there is no reason why she could not follow mine. I ventured to my mother, sisters, and friends for input. Their response— referencing the banality of the 'terrible twos'— was no different. *How can I raise my child under the belief that it's ok to rebel at two years old but not later?* If I lacked simple tools to guide her now, this pattern of defiant behavior would persist and escalate through her teenage years. *Would I accept the moody, teenage years as 'just a phase' too?* This seemed wrong.

It baffled me as to why an authority figure held more power and influence over my daughter than her own mother. For reasons of safety beyond school, I knew that it was I who needed to have the final say on her influence and decision making. Knowing myself as a toddler, I would've interpreted the 'OK' to defy my mother while listening to others as a signal to take other people's advice over my own parent's. Only parents are guaranteed to have their children's best interests in mind. Others may have their own agendas and may guide a child toward their personal gain. The thought of my daughter being manipulated horrified me.

If Sabrina ever landed in a bad situation, I wanted to be the first one to know and help her overcome it safely. Creating an environment in which she could confide in me was necessary because her well-being was my number-one purpose. I was determined to communicate effectively with Sabrina, so she'd understand what to do, why doing so was important, and what strategies worked to resolve a particular conflict.

3

Parenting School

Sabrina's preschool offered parenting classes called 'Redirecting Your Children's Behavior.' Before my first session, I pulled out my journal to cement my objectives. From now on, I'd be responsible for her growth. I supplemented my bullet with three questions to answer after the class:

- What are my roles and responsibilities as a mother?
  What am I currently doing wrong?
- What tools and techniques do I need so I can guide her with LOVE, not fear, to make good decisions?
- What values and tools shall I equip her with so she learns to make responsible decisions?

The seminar was worthwhile overall. I reflected upon the techniques presented and complemented them with additional research. What resonated with me most was "treat children with respect." It got me thinking about the differences between child and parent views of respect.

My exposure to various relationships and cultures reminded me of how "respect" holds opposing meanings to different people. In Israel and New York, a child who challenges authority is deemed respectable and intelligent, whereas in Russia or San Diego the child would be considered disrespectful. These differences prompted me to create a personalized toolbox that equipped her with self-reliance and knowing right from wrong. Looking at the world from my child's eyes was my first step. Understanding exactly what my child needed and her patterns of reaction in voicing a particular need made the toolbox process far easier.

When Sabrina refused to pick up her toys or follow my instructions, I would now step in her shoes before reacting. *Why would I, as a kid, want to pick up my toys after playing with them? Why would I want to leave the park if I was having fun on the swings with my friends?* I decided to channel my directive tone into a collaborative and empowering method. For instance, I shifted "you do it" to "let's do it together, let me help you." I shifted orders to posing a question: "How can **we** agree?" or "How can I make it up to you if we leave now?" This was the magic pill. In the toy situation, Sabrina's defiance transposed from "no mommy, you do it," to "no mommy, I can do it myself!" By the age of three, I had instilled Sabrina with some awareness as to why listening to her parents mattered. Shaking my head with a smile, I'd ask, "When you have a problem, who will you come to?" Her instant response: "Mommy! I go to mommy!" Then I asked why. "Mommy wants what's best for me," Sabrina exclaimed.

A blind faith in mom was never the outcome I wished for. I wanted Sabrina to challenge and be honest with me, as she always had. Over the years, I began enhancing my message: "Sabrina, you don't always have to follow and do what I tell you, but if you are not going to do it, the only thing I ask is that you tell me why and explain yourself. I only care about your safety and well-being. I am ok for you to try things so long as you're safe. Will you promise to be honest with me?" Her big eyes peered into mine and she smiled, "Yes mom, I promise, pinky promise." This seemed like an empowering moment for her. The combination of guided freedoms and compassionate communication eliminates much of the combative resistance parents experience as their child seeks independence.

Authority Isn't Always Right

The 'terrible twos' weren't just a phase for Sabrina. She has always been one to challenge, embrace challenges, and project herself with confidence. Immersing her in various activities elicited this behavior at the age of five and beyond. As she twirled and slid across our home's marble floors in bright pink fuzzy socks, we had no choice but to enroll her in ballet.

One afternoon, she arrived at a group lesson with a new pair of ballet slippers. I sat just outside the studio before the session, observing her leap around the room with her friends while waiting for the instructor, Mrs. Tanya. Finally, Tanya, an older Russian American woman, came in to set up the music. The kids scurried to their positions, standing still in a straight line. Tanya approached Sabrina, crouching down, and pressing on her toes. All I could see from the window was Sabrina showing off her slippers, hands on her hips, and a smirk on her face.

Tanya marched out of the room and confronted me, "Lea, your daughter just talked back to me. Very disrespectful. In my twenty years of teaching, no kid has ever spoken to me in this way."

I was shocked. Sabrina never had a history of disrespecting teachers. "I'm sorry, she is usually very well-behaved, can you tell me what happened?"

"Well," she peered down at her watch and scoffed, "Listen, Ludachka. You are holding me up and I do not have time for this. I told Sabrina that the new shoes she was wearing didn't fit so well. She told me that they are comfortable and refused to change."

What was so "disrespectful" about that? Maybe it was her tone. "Was Sabrina rude to you? Did she yell? How did she talk back to you?" I asked.

"She just told me that the shoes fit very well, and she didn't want to change, but I checked them. They are too big. A child should not refuse to follow directions from a teacher!" Her heavy Russian accent reminded me of the strict discipline by my Russian piano teacher in Israel who told my mother, "Don't waste your money on her, she is restless and has shpilkes in her tush!" I would consider myself to have had musical interests, but the crack-down instruction discouraged me altogether. However, ingrained in this culture— and in the traditional lens of my parents— is that the teacher rules, uncompromised. I had to explain to Tanya that I had always raised my daughter to challenge authorities if she needed to, so long as she was not rude.

"I want to teach her to be assertive," I stated, "I know in some cultures we expect kids to follow authorities blindly, but I see that as a risk because as a mother, I want to ensure my daughter's comfort and safety. That's why I encourage her to express her feelings and opinions respectfully. I am sure that Sabrina didn't mean to disrespect you in any way. She was just being honest and telling you how she felt."

468

Tanya shook her head and rushed back to the studio. Kids were running wild. My message probably did not resonate with her based on her reaction, but I was glad to have discussed this with Tanya anyway. She needed to know that my daughter's feelings and opinions mattered. She needed to understand that children who express themselves opposed to authority are not necessarily "disrespectful." Just because adults are adults, and kids are kids, it doesn't mean that the adults are always right. If Sabrina felt uncomfortable or violated, she could inspect the authority's claims or assumptions. So long as she stayed under my roof, I wanted her to know that she could express her needs to anyone; Sabrina needed to know that if she was ever retaliated against, I would be her best ally and advocate. Eventually she would mirror this trait, becoming a staunch voice for herself and for others.

Part VII Motherhood: Through My Daughter's Eyes

4

From a Bully to a Buddy

S abrina was always the last one off the playground. She was hidden in a miniature cluster of giggling kindergartners, the smallest and youngest among them. After a few months, something changed. She'd hop in the car right when the bell rang and complain about bullying more and more.

"You've been doing great! You've made so many friends! Tell me, what's happening?"

Her cheeks swelled and her eyes puffed up. "No Mommy," she shook her head anxiously, "I don't wanna go back to school."

I encouraged her to tell me what happened and assured, "I promise, we will take care of the problem together."

Sabrina's tears and sniffles wouldn't stop. I gave her time. Finally, she confessed, "He is big, and I am small. Rex," she wiped her face, "Rex is laughing at me, he pushes me in the sandbox."

I had met Rex and his mother on the first day of school. Rex was a seven-year-old kindergartener. He had been held back a grade. Sabrina, on the other hand, was only five having skipped a year of preschool. While an easy target for bigger kids, bullying was something she'd never experienced this before.

"I'll call Ms. Wilson tomorrow. Everything is going to be ok." I hugged her tightly. She was still young, and I could not let her 'just suck it up:' Rex's actions were not merely verbal. Safety first— always.

It was a battle getting Sabrina to school the next morning. Around lunchtime, I called her teacher, whom I knew well. "Good afternoon, Rachel. It seems that Sabrina is having an issue with one of the kids in class. Are you aware of this?"

She seemed confused. "The kids love Sabrina from what I've seen," and affirmed, "she's very outspoken and confident. I think she would tell me if something was wrong. But I'll keep my eye on her and let you know if I see anything."

A couple of days later, Ms. Wilson called me back with no news of any incidents. Meanwhile, Sabrina's daily complaints about Rex persisted: "Mommy, he says, 'you're not even five yet! You can't play with us!' and then pushes me." She wouldn't stop crying. It pained me to see her dreading a place she once loved. A place she used to never want to leave.

In moments of conflict, my most useful tool is to go straight to the source. I couldn't confront a seven-year-old boy, but I could call his mother: "Hello Christie, how are you? It seems that Sabrina and Rex are having a little issue. Are you aware of it? Is everything ok on your end?"

"Hi Lea, yes, everything is good here. I'm so sorry Sabrina is going through that. Let me talk to Rex about it," she replied. This happened to be a silly case of bullying, but a more serious solution to this issue had to be devised.

"I have an idea, Christie. Since Sabrina and Rex both love the playground, maybe we can organize a playdate for them? We could grab coffee and sit nearby to chat? I think it would be good for them to be in the same space while we're there, so they learn to get along," I proposed. She welcomed the suggestion.

Rex immediately apologized to Sabrina at the playground on Monday after school. "I'm sorry for pushing you in the sandbox. I won't do it again. I promise," he said. Evidently, his mother had talked to him.

Sabrina was receptive yet remained hesitant. She cracked out of her shell bit by bit as they began to play. "You want to swing?" she shouted to Rex from across the playground.

"No, I want to climb," he shouted back. He continued racing up and down the ladder as Sabrina swung on her own.

Christie and I laughed over the kids' total disinterest in each other's activities. That was totally ok! So long as Rex learned to respect Sabrina and Sabrina respected Rex despite their differences, nothing else mattered. "Cheers to that!"

Civility and respect establish a relationship which can be strengthened into a friendship by common values and interests. Even if no interests are shared, the acquaintance is good enough too! In addition to helping the kids to mend their differences, I wanted to exemplify the course of navigating issues to my daughter. The steps I took built Sabrina's trust so she could easily confide in me, even when I immersed her in a situation where she felt uncomfortable. Knowing that she was safe, I could convey that all conflicts take courage to confront and can be resolved.

Part VII Motherhood: Through My Daughter's Eyes

5

Make Your Children Your Masters

Introducing Sabrina to Disneyland might have been a mistake. She fell head over heels for Disney princesses and drove me crazy asking for every princess dress: Cinderella, Belle, Mulan— you name it— she was wearing them everywhere! *Cute, right? Sure.* But this cuteness warped with total chaos.

I'd walk into Sabrina's room every morning to see her trying on dress after dress and leaving them scattered across the floor. Despite extreme frustrations, I was able to curb an emotional outrage.

"Sabrina, dear, it's time to leave for school, common, let's get dressed and clean up this mess! Let's pick up together, we're going to be late!" I encouraged her cheerfully. But the magic pill— suggesting that we clean up the mess together— didn't work this time. My little girl still couldn't decide which princess she wanted to be for that day, throwing dresses in the air while I was frantically refolding them.

This reoccurred for weeks until the stress became intolerable. She even wrecked her closet at the crack of dawn on weekends. Maybe a sit-down conversation with her would help. I could explain how this situation was negatively impacting both of us and brainstorm solutions together. I planned to gently raise the issue over breakfast.

One Saturday, Sabrina came downstairs in her Jasmine princess pajamas. She was lured into the kitchen by the savory aroma of toasted bread and fried eggs permeating the house. Vick made her a royal platter of his famous love eggs atop buttered toast, cinnamon-spiced Mexican hot chocolate aside side.

"Good morning," Vick greeted proudly as he served his culinary creation. Without a word, Sabrina jumped onto the barstool and shoved down three big bites right after the other. Crumbs of toast were all over her mouth and egg fragments made their way across the granite counter. While her manners weren't so princess-like, I'd have to treat her like a princess so she'd cooperate.

"How are you this morning?" I asked, "what are we doing today?" I waited for her to chomp on her last piece of toast before prompting the conversation.

"I want another dress! I want to be Belle!"

Oh my! Another one? Vick is going to flip! But I had to keep my purpose in mind: To gain her trust and resolve this issue. "Ok, we can go after finishing breakfast, getting dressed—"

She cut me off, "Really!?!"

Sabrina dashed upstairs at the speed of light. I came up a few minutes later. With no surprise, dresses were sprawled all over the floor. "Sabrina, can we clean up this mess?"

She initially refused, "No mommy, I'll do it later, let's go now!"

This would be the perfect time to discuss this issue since we weren't rushing anywhere. "Sabrina, mommy really needs your help. I'd say yes to doing it later another day but today, we must clean now. Can we talk?" I said, kneeling next to her. Her eyes lit up with curiosity. I continued, "You know, mommy loves you very much and I want us to have a good relationship. When you change your clothes so many times in the mornings and don't put them back, it leaves a big mess, and it takes me lots of time to put them back. I get stressed when I see the dresses all over the floor." My tone remained lighthearted. I gave her an opportunity to respond but expectedly, Sabrina was silent. So, I tried again.

"We are late for school almost every other day and it's really hard for mommy to drive in a rush. I want to make this easier for both of us. What do you think we can do?"

She looked up at the ceiling and then back at me. "I don't know."

I made a few suggestions to get her mind running. "How about you wake up earlier to have more time to clean up? Or you can choose between only two or three dresses? Then, in the morning, you can get dressed without making a mess and we can get to school on time! Does that work for you?" I gave her a minute to gather her thoughts.

"Well mommy," she paused and looked up at me, "Maybe I can choose before daddy tucks me in at night?"

Wow, I was impressed. "Good idea! Let's do it!" I summarized the new plan to her, "So each night after your shower, we will go to your closet and decide on a dress. Then you can put it on your bedside table waiting for tomorrow!"

She got it: "Ok, mommy! Let's clean up this mess and go get Belle for Monday!"

After coming downstairs, I informed Vick that we were heading out to run errands. "Want to come with us?"

"Where are you going?" He asked.

Sabrina jumped up and down pulling on my wrist, "Belle dress, Belle dress!"

Vick turned to me, astonished. "Another dress?! You have so many, you don't need another one!" He crouched down to Sabrina's level, hands on his hips.

"I promised her, it's ok," I said, "Common Sabrina, let's get in the car!"

Spoiling vs. Rewarding

Vick was facetious to avoid upsetting our daughter, but we've always held different philosophies when it came to buying her things. Like most parents, he considered buying children their desired material goods as spoiling them. "You're just raising her to be entitled," he'd say. Admittedly, Sabrina was materialistically privileged, but this didn't mean that she would grow up to be entitled and disregard the value of money.

The parent must place boundaries around what is being purchased and explicitly explain the reasons why— whether the item is too expensive or not needed. In this case, the princess dresses were inexpensive, and I treated purchasing them for Sabrina as rewards for her good behavior or accomplishments.

Ingraining Sabrina with the tools to independently organize herself made me more than happy to honor her collaborative spirit. She was learning through a method of earning what you worked for. Kids **do** learn this way! Sabrina meticulously prepares her outfits the night before until today, at nineteen years old. Later, she'd apply this habit to scheduling, scrupulously planning her weeks in advance with daily priorities in place.

See Your Child as an Equal

Sabrina has never been one to simply comply with my suggestions. Since she was a little girl, I've always seen her as an equal in our conversations: Her needs, opinions, and priorities count just as much as mine. Just because I am her mother, she is younger than me, and lacks years of life experience, I have no higher power than she does. A young girl also sees important elements from a different perspective that an older woman may not.

I refused to dictate with authority under the premise that I was her mother so she should do as I say: In my childhood, I instantly refused, defied, and resented my dad because he thought that he knew what was better for me than I did. My rebellion came from feeling disrespected and misunderstood. However, this is not to say that children should not be reined in— they should. Reining in must be done with a collaborative approach where the child feels respected.

A major epiphany from the parenting class I had taken a couple weeks ago trickled back to me: "Respect your child" means to make kids feel that they are equal to the parent, empowered with the opportunity to explain themselves and be understood. This not only resolves the situation smoothly but strengthens the parent-child relationship because the child feels valued.

Part VII Motherhood: Through My Daughter's Eyes

6

Avoid a Flare, Just Repair

A﬇er a busy Sunday morning, the whole family drove downtown to celebrate Vick's dad's birthday. We decided to eat lunch at his favorite seafood restaurant overlooking the Coronado Bridge. My laptop had broken down a couple of days prior, so Vick suggested that we stop at the Microsoft store inside the central mall after lunch since the restaurant was relatively close by. Sabrina was in the backseat listening with no complaints, happy as a clam.

We settled in the car after a lovely lunchtime birthday celebration. I confirmed the Microsoft store plan with Vick. "Microsoft store" didn't seem to digest well with Sabrina.

"Microsoft store!? What?! No! I want home!" she burst.

"Sabrina, I am going in and out, it's on our way home. I promise I won't take long," I explained.

She began kicking her legs against the driver's seat. "No! I want home! Now!"

"Sabrina, stop. Please, stop!" Vick twisted around and demanded. The fit only intensified— her kicks stronger, her cries louder.

Out of nowhere, Vick grabbed her lanky legs with one hand and squeezed them together. "Sabrina enough! Stop it now!" His teeth clenched; he squeezed tighter.

Vick continued driving, still holding her legs with one hand and the other on the steering wheel. Sabrina was furious, but grabbing her legs was not helping. She continued whining and shrieking sporadically. I found it odd for Vick to hold her legs, so she stopped kicking. Shouldn't he have used his words to influence her? I also wondered why Sabrina was so upset. This had to stop.

"Vick! What are you doing?!" I tapped his hand, "Let her go! Today you hold her legs, but what are you going to do when she's seventeen? Talk to her so she understands, please! Let me handle this," I reassured him. He finally let go. He said nothing. Sabrina was bawling. Instead of stopping at the Microsoft store, Vick sped straight home as the commotion overwhelmed us all.

Upon entering the house, Vick shouted, "Sabrina! Straight to your room! I'm taking away your toys!" He marched up the stairs with a garbage bag threatening to throw her dolls in the trash. I could hear her screaming, apologizing, and begging him to stop. I tried to stop him again.

"Lea, we need to be a united voice! What do you think you're doing?" He erupted, "You're too soft with her! She can't just run to you every time she does something wrong thinking that she'll get away with it!"

"Vick, I'll handle it. I have my ways."

I went upstairs to see Sabrina curled up in a ball on her bed with her entire head covered in a hoodie. "Sabrina, come here. Come downstairs when you're ready. Mommy wants to talk to you." I left that request with her, hoping that she'd agree once she was ready.

About ten minutes later, Sabrina plumped on the downstairs sofa, tomato-faced and watery-eyed. I said, "You know mom loves you. I'm just trying to understand why you didn't want to go to the Microsoft store," I inched myself closer to her on the couch.

"I don't want to talk. I'm too mad," she muttered peering downward.

"Ok, I just want to know so that next time you can tell me why you were so upset without banging on dad's seat." I gave her two options: "You can tell me, or you can write me a story about what you did and how you'll act next time. This is very important," I enunciated my words, "You made both daddy and me very angry," then paused waiting for her reaction. She crossed her arms, still silent. "What about we can talk later? You can write the story tonight or tomorrow," I suggested.

As always, Sabrina wanted to get things over with. Without a word, she grabbed the binder from my desk and began scribbling away.

Opening the Door for Expression Welcomes Consensus

Since Sabrina was five, I sought to create a constructive conflict resolution process for us. I did not believe in punishment or the traditional method of 'grounding.' Rather, I wondered how to instill her with value-based decision-making skills and teach her to learn from her mistakes. Developing an authentic, compassionate, and assertive way for her to express her feelings, thoughts, beliefs, and needs was my priority.

The little black journal Vick and I used to communicate our gripes crossed my mind. I thought to convert the concept into a kid's friendly template whereby Sabrina could share her side of the story and brainstorm methods to solve any problem. She would write what she did, why she did it, who she impacted, and finally, what she would do next time if placed in the same situation. This 'Share Your Story' template was eventually converted to 'Sabrina's Diary,' which would not only give Sabrina the opportunity to assertively express her thoughts through writing, but to discuss the problem and solutions as a family.

Kids may initially resist writing their story: Sabrina surely did. Sometimes, I had to tell her that she could not go to her playdate or horseback riding lessons until she wrote it. However, kids can eventually discover the benefits of writing their story for several reasons: First, it is better to spend 20-30 minutes writing a story and having a discussion with parents for another 20-30 minutes than being locked up in a room wondering when freedom will be granted. Through writing, children can also discover and examine their feelings, beliefs, and reactions. Engaging in a constructive way to manage situations can inspire a child to continue applying collaborative methods to conflicts outside of the home and in any situation.

After Vick calmed down a bit, all three of us settled in the sitting area. Prior to the conversation, I read what she wrote about her uproar in the car. It dawned on me that Sabrina was too tired to go to the Microsoft store that day and just wanted quiet time. She feared her excuse was inadequate to get her way. Vick's belligerent reaction blew the issue out of proportion, and Sabrina flared up in a moment of exhaustion.

Setting the binder down, I prompted, "You know that you can tell us how you feel, right? We don't have a crystal ball. We can't just guess or understand your needs. Next time, if you don't want to do something, what will you do?"

"Hmmm… Ok next time I will say how I feel and ask to have quiet time because I am tired."

"Saying that you're tired and need some rest is good enough for us to change our plans if they're not urgent." I continued, "We are a team, we all have equal voices. If you don't want to do something, the only condition is that you tell us why. Nobody is forcing anybody to agree." I gave her a big hug, thanking her for writing the story and being honest with us. I sensed that we had earned her trust, and that she'd feel comfortable expressing her needs without fear or shame in the future.

"Anything else?" I asked.

She shook her head no. "Can I go upstairs?"

"Of course," I assured, "Let us know when you feel well-rested. Maybe we can go to the Microsoft store and grab dinner afterward?"

"Ok." Sabrina nodded with her lips sealed tight. She scurried upstairs to grab a jacket.

After Sabrina went up to her room, Vick rolled his eyes at me and said, "We can't just let her get away with things. Are you sure this is going to work?" He ascribed to the belief that parents must be a united front when standing against the child. That's an awful approach! This only fosters more anger and resentment as the child would feel devalued with their point of view discounted. My purpose was for Sabrina to feel like she could collaborate with us and react appropriately moving forward. It would take time until Vick embraced this democratic resolution process in which each member of our nuclear family has equal representation and the respect they deserve.

Guide, Don't Ground.

I lay in bed that night wondering what would have happened if Vick had indeed thrown away Sabrina's dolls. It wouldn't have ended well: More chaos, more yelling, more resentment. Taking away a child's toys for yelling and screaming or taking their phone away for doing poorly on an exam are empty consequences. They are empty because they do not correct the child's behavior and hinder conflict resolution. Every parent seeks for their child to listen and to trust them. Grounding does just the opposite because it infuses children with spite and deters them from solving the problem or future ones collaboratively.

As kids proclaim independence with age, and there is less for the parents to physically take away, grounding evolves into a toxic cycle of sneaky behaviors and rebellion. These pent-up emotions can bring collateral damage to the relationship.

Parents must consider their purpose in imposing consequences. Ideally, a parent should seek three things: First, for the child to stop their bad behavior and for the arguments to stop; next, for the child to learn valuable lessons and promise to never repeat their misconduct; lastly and most importantly, for the relationship to be restored.

To achieve these goals, what would the ideal method of discipline look like? What are each person's needs? How can the disparities in each persons' needs be integrated and satisfied? How can expectations for proper behavior be established? By focusing on purpose, a parent must also consider the effective ways to instill values, principles, and solutions: This is done only with love and compassion toward the child's perspective. The nature of the consequence should always relate to the child's behavior and teach them what to do next time.

Guidance is a means of influence, just as influence is an art of persuasion. To persuade, a person must reason logically while tapping into someone's emotions. In parental guidance the process is the same, but parents must demonstrate that they care about the child's feelings to gain their trust. It is done as follows: First, the parent must sympathize with the child's feelings and ask what specifically triggered the behavior. Feelings emerge from needs, so a child's poor behavior is often a reaction to some unsatisfied need. The second step is for a parent to express understanding of the child's behavior, but also explain its negative impacts. The third step is easy— ask questions! Prompt the child to think about different ways to approach a similar problem or how to prevent a similar issue from escalating. The parent should provide clues that lead to an ideal solution, and if the child is totally clueless, propose a solution. The parent should also explain why the new solution is beneficial to everyone involved, especially why it's beneficial to the child. To conclude the conversation, reaffirm the solution in alignment with objectives, needs, and expectations.

I devoted much time to producing my parenting method. I truly cared about nurturing the relationship between my daughter and me and sought to be her role model. Stepping into motherhood made me realize that I didn't have more rights than my child, but a greater obligation to lead with compassion.

As I found writing to be my most powerful tool for reflection in my youth, I wanted to gift Sabrina the opportunity to mature through this same outlet. She'd come to appreciate it because it helped her fill a first-aid kit that could heal any wound. Parents' compassion and acceptance fosters appreciation that they seek in due time.

Part VII Motherhood: Through My Daughter's Eyes

7

The Underpinning of Winning

Y ou're not fun, you don't love me," Sabrina used to say when Vick and I would decline her persistent requests to play board games. "Just one more round of Monopoly, please," she'd beg with her big brown puppy eyes. Of course, we gave in! A small price to pay to gain her love.

As family competition grew, so did Sabrina's hunger for victory. Our cherished post-dinner ritual soon became an emotional and physical power struggle. It was game over for all of us when Sabrina's pawn fell behind: "I'm tired! I don't want to play anymore!" She'd end the game abruptly, flip the game board upside down, and throw the pieces in the air.

"Sabs, why are you doing that!? What happened?" I was scavenging for tiles across the floor.

"It's not fun! "I don't wanna play!" Sabrina exclaimed, her cheeks reddening with anger. This happened quite often, and after the third time, she still couldn't tell us exactly why. On the fourth, I pressed, "Sabrina, you told us you wanted to play. I've seen you do this three times already.

Why isn't it fun? What is going on?"

She peered down at her last few dollar bills and grumbled, "I hate losing. You always win!"

My daughter's competitive spirit had emerged by the young age of six, just as mine had. Although I admired her passion and energy, she had to understand the impact of her behavior. In family or social settings, winning is participating: The winners don't receive a prize, and the losers incur no penalty. *So what if she loses?* This was a principle Sabrina had yet to understand.

"There's no need to be upset if we win." I transitioned to explaining the purpose, "It's just about being together and having fun while playing the game. Dad and I are still proud of you whether you win or lose, ok? If you do this every time, we won't want to play with you and your friends won't want to play with you either. Is that what you want?"

She looked down shaking her head timidly, and muttered, "No."

"Ok Sabrina let's make a deal. The next time we play, no matter what the score is, we'll play to the end. Yes?"

Her eyes lifted from the floor and met mine. "Ok! Let's play again! I'm ready!"

I realized that children's competitive nature ignites many unnecessary flare-ups. My advice to Sabrina was rooted in thinking before you act, more specifically geared toward thinking about purpose prior to engaging in a certain activity: "Sabrina, if you are really in a competition, you can have a strong attitude. But you can **never ever** quit because you're losing! It shows that you are weak and it's not fun for anyone you're playing with!" Sabrina's definition of 'fun' was far off: She believed that the game was only fun if she was winning, rather than embracing the fun of the game itself. Many kids share this mentality; however, it must be debunked by a mindset shift that prioritizes fun in the game over winning. Besides, winning is a by-product of learning from your losses time and time again. Losing is a step to improving— the more you play, the better you'll get, and the more consistently you'll win!

8

She Stole My Squishies! Speak Up to Make Up

When Sabrina returned from school one afternoon, I overheard sobs coming from upstairs. She was sitting inside the shower, bawling helplessly as water splashed on her quivering body. "Sabs! What happened?"

Her cries grew louder and increasingly painful for me to listen to. I asked again. *Was it her teachers? Her friends? A hard test?* I couldn't pry it out of her. Instead of pushing, I gave her time to cool off. Fifteen minutes later, Sabrina came downstairs red-faced and puffy-eyed. She was silent.

"If something is wrong, you need to tell me. I can help you," I leaned in next to her, "We all have moments in life where something goes wrong. Even if you're embarrassed or ashamed, it's important to share your feelings so mom can help you. Bad things happened to mommy too, many times!"

Finally, she opened up: "Zoe stole my favorite squishy collection— the new one— and-and she won't give it back. We were at lunch. She took out her toys and asked to trade and I said no. But then she just grabbed mine!" The crying started again.

I embraced her with a warm hug. "I'm so sorry that happened to you. Let's make a plan to get them back, shall we?"

"Mhm. Ca-can you tell the principal?" She wiped her face.

That was too far for now. "What about you talk to Zoe first, and if she still doesn't give them back, I can help. Let's do it in stages, ok?"

"I don't want to talk to Zoe!" Sabrina refused.

"What's the worst thing that can happen?"

"Mom, she's just going to bully me more and steal more of my toys!"

"Ok, I'll make you a deal. If that happens, I'll buy you new squishies and talk to her mom or the teacher. I just want you to try."

Sabrina bobbed her head up and down. I think I had her at "I'll buy you new squishes." Regardless, I was glad that she agreed.

After dinner that evening, we brainstormed different strategies that Sabrina was comfortable with to approach Zoe. Words, body language, and timing were integral to delivering the message assertively and compassionately. I knew that Zoe had a difficult family situation, so I implored Sabrina to remain calm, cool, and collected.

"Mommy I'm scared," Sabrina confessed as I tucked her in that night. Fair: A legitimate fear for a little girl soon to confront a classmate a year older and twice her size.

"You can do it, I promise. And if Zoe bullies you again, it gives mom more of a reason to step in. Get a good rest tonight so you're ready for tomorrow." I instilled as much confidence in her as I could. She hugged her plush green dinosaur and fell sound asleep.

Sabrina was especially quiet during the car ride the next morning.

"Either way, you'll get your squishies back. I promise. Just try and talk with Zoe the way we practiced." I handed Sabrina a few of our favorite Kinder Egg chocolates as she got out of the car. "Here, Sabs, for good luck. Love you!"

Sabrina ran into the house with a beaming smile. "Mom! You won't believe it! Zoe and I are friends again! And I got my squishies back! She was so nice in class today too!" She placed her beloved squishy collection on the kitchen counter jumping with joy.

"I'm so proud of you! I told you that you could do it!" I picked her up and twirled around. "What did you say to her?" I asked.

"Well," she started proudly putting her elbows on the countertop, "Before class I asked if we could talk. I just said that she really hurt my feelings because I thought we were good friends, and she said no. Then I said my mom will call yours or Mrs. Reina if you don't give them back. Then she gave them back."

"That's my girl!" We high-fived.

When children face adversity, the way a parent communicates makes all the difference in helping them grow. Aside from the advice itself, its delivery determines how the child interprets and later manifests it. Giving Sabrina time to cool off first, and then supporting her through framing the right message with comforting body language, a compassionate tone, and appropriate timing, infused her trust in me and in herself.

Elementary school opens many opportunities to help kids navigate adversity. They can experiment with confronting and resolving conflicts with minimal risk in a protected environment. The issues they face may seem trivial, but in fact do present struggles, fears, and expose vulnerabilities to young kids. If not properly addressed, these issues can leave lasting detrimental impacts on a developing mind. Once they're older, issues increase in both severity and consequence, which is why it's essential for kids to gain basic conflict resolution skills at a young age.

A parent's role involves empowering their children beyond their fears. A child's fears are always valid because kids are new to the world of problems and must be equipped with tools to overcome them. But what does empowerment mean? Telling your child to "just stand up for yourself" is meaningless. It's empty. Authentic empowerment is substantiated by three key factors: First is helping the child understand the impact of their actions on their well-being and on others. Second is providing the child with the competence and capabilities to address the situation (words and actions). Finally, kids must be infused with courage to take action; this can be done by demonstrating how to express and present an action plan or explaining effective past examples. By practicing how to resolve conflicts and learning how to say things at the right time, in the right place, in the right way, why to say them, and the impact of not saying them, kids can discover their power. This inner power instills children with confidence to advocate for themselves in any situation.

Teaching and mastering this process does not come without setbacks: Outcomes of self-advocacy are never guaranteed. When the impact on the child is deeply harmful, a parent must step in to support the child or become the child's advocate. This is when different ways to approach the situation— with specific guidance, unconditional support, and compassion— must be presented. Teaching resilience and building

496

grit through experience is the most valuable education a person can have.

Part VII Motherhood: Through My Daughter's Eyes

9

Deeds By Kids

Sabrina's friends often came over to our house for playdates, sleepovers, or Shabbat dinners. Their interactions and conversations unveiled intriguing patterns. Every time the girls came over, their chatter surrounded school drama— normal at that age, I presume.

"Did you hear about what Zoe did to Sam yesterday at recess? She called her the f-word after she beat her in wall-ball. She's so mean to everyone!" The girls would all interject, telling story after story about kids bullying each other. "Yeah! OMG! Zoe is so mean to me too! She calls me 'Nelly with a big belly' at swim practice!" Some even shared how teachers mistreated students, and some even brought up about issues they were going through in their personal lives or at home.

One afternoon, I couldn't help but pull up a seat at our kitchen counter and sit with them. "Can I listen-in too? Maybe I can help you girls solve these sticky situations! They sound crazy!" I began to intervene with questions to better understand certain incidents: "What do you think you could have done differently to get Zoe to stop earlier? How did you react or communicate with Zoe when she hurt you? Did you tell your parents or a teacher when it happened?"

Their answers led them to 'ah-ha moments,' where we were all bouncing ideas off of each other. With vanilla ice cream all over her face, one of the girls proposed, "Yeah! Try to make a joke when Zoe is being mean! What about 'Hey Nelly, want some jelly from my belly?!' That would be so funny!" We all laughed. Nelly pledged to try this strategy at her next swim practice.

Astounded by particular anecdotes, I began asking some of the girls if they'd write their stories down so I could guide them more thoroughly. Most were happy to do so. I used Sabrina's diary template (the template where Sabrina would write her personal stories) to help the girls organize their thoughts.

Overtime, more reports of success came my way: "Mrs. Lea! Your advice helped me so much! Thank you!" But can you help me with something else? I'm having a hard time with another friend of mine." There was nothing more gratifying to me than working through the girls' issues with them. Almost every time, the tools I equipped them with made miracles. *So,* I thought, *if my strategies are so effective, why not publish these stories with my advice included to help hundreds of children?* Sure enough, I would oversee Sabrina and her friends authoring hundreds of their true stories and outlining techniques based on the method we devised, SELF-EX. The books are being finalized and will be published soon!

We named our team Deeds By Kids, a group of kids for kids, who would take on a variety of projects aimed at serving children and communities in need. These young girls' philanthropic efforts would cultivate them with strong character, ethics, and compassion. As a mom, there was nothing more rewarding than imbuing my daughter with good morals through meaningful projects and hands-on learning.

During the 2011 holiday season, Deeds By Kids gifted a local underserved community with the power of story and literature. Learning about poverty and charity in the fourth grade, Sabrina and her classmates were shocked that children just miles away from their homes did not have books to read. In just a few weeks, Sabrina and a few of her friends would sort, package, and donate over a thousand books to a local elementary school. Afternoons and weekends were spent trekking around various neighborhoods, knocking on doors, and collecting used books. The girls campaigned, "Hello, we're with Deeds By Kids. Do you have any books you don't want? We are collecting them to give to a school that needs books, we want to make a difference in kids' lives."

Successful solicitors to soulful Samaritans, the Deeds By Kids team personally delivered about twenty boxes packed with used books to Cabrillo Elementary. They would then meet the students to help them unpack and shelf the books in their library.

I recall an interaction between Sabrina and a fellow fourth grader from the day of the book drive that warmed my heart. A tender exchange of knowledge and mutual love for learning— both my daughter and I carry this memory deeply until this day:

"Do you have the Diary of Anne Frank?" A petit Latino boy tapped Sabrina on the back as she was organizing the history section.

"Here, this is my favorite, this is my book." She reached into the box just beside her to find her old copy and handed it to him.

I remembered when Sabrina ran to her room before packaging the last box of books. She brought down Anne Frank's diary, which she kept close and had read several times.

"Are you sure you want to give it away? That's your favorite, isn't it?" I asked.

"I want other people to know about her too, they need to know what was done to her," she assured, placing it inside the final box.

With admiration, I gazed at the beautiful bond emerging between Sabrina and this boy— a bond built by an appreciation for someone's life story. The librarian revealed to me that Sabrina had summarized Anne's narrative and told her new friend why she found it so significant:

"Take care of this one. I'll remember that I gave you my favorite book. But please read her story and remember it. It is so important."

"I promise, thank you." The little boy's eyes widened in admiration as they pinky promised.

The Jewish principle of Tikkun Olam was coming alive to me through my daughter's character and actions. Performing meaningful deeds of kindness to repair the world, with one person at a time, is a mission I'd pursue in her honor. I'd dedicate my life's work toward helping others become their best selves through personal empowerment, human connection, and education just as Sabrina was. Seeds of her principles, passion, and life's purpose were sprouting too.

10

Don't Let the Lie Multiply

I found a black paper bag under the couch in Sabrina's room. Inside was a lacey blue shirt with the price tag ripped off and wrapped in tissue paper. It was the shirt that Sabrina had showed me a week prior, online. "Sixty dollars for just a shirt is a bit excessive, but I'll consider it," I had said. She simply could not resist.

Sabrina was downstairs eating dinner after a full day of shopping with friends where, of course, she had bought the sixty-dollar shirt. I went down to join her but waited until she finished eating to bring up my recent discovery.

"Hi, Sabs! Did you have fun today? What did you buy? Anything?"

She looked up and shook her head, "No, but it was really fun! Maddie and Sophie found a lot of stuff though!"

I whipped the shirt out of the bag and pinched it on display. "What's this?" My anger let loose, "Where did you get this?!" Lying is an absolute no-no in my rule book. I blew up.

Sabrina stuttered and sniffled, "Mom-mommy, I'm sorry." She couldn't even look at me. She broke down in tears. Maybe I scared her, shamed her, embarrassed her— the wrong approach.

I took a moment of silence to taper my temper, then said, "Sabrina, when you're done crying, please come to my room so we can talk." I made a mental note to apologize for my overreaction once we both calmed down.

On my way upstairs, I brewed my late-night coffee and stopped by the pantry for a few pieces of chocolate. While waiting for her, I reflected on what I would say or actions I would take to teach Sabrina a very important lesson. Most parents would take the shirt away or prohibit their child from going out with her friends next time. In my mind, this would only infuse resentment and lead her to continue slithering around the truth. What a great opportunity to prevent lying from becoming a habit!

Fifteen minutes later, Sabrina's kitten-like presence appeared at the door. I put down the New York Times and invited her in. She walked slowly towards my opposite bedside facing the window.

"Sabrina, look at me. You know that mommy loves you, and I'm sorry for yelling at you." Her head turned slightly towards me. "I want to have a good relationship with you." I explained, "Lying is one of those things that makes me very upset because it tells me that you don't trust me. I don't want to have a relationship based on lies, I want one based on honesty. When we lie, we keep our brain busy with covering the lies. Is that what you want?" I paused to give her a chance to respond. She remained quiet.

I moved my coffee cup aside. "I know that when kids lie to their parents, it's because they're afraid. Is there anything I did to make you afraid of telling me you bought this shirt? I want to know if there's something I did so I can be a better mom for you to tell me the truth." I played the reverse strategy and asked again, "What is it that made you lie

504

to me?"

Now she was open ears: We finally made eye contact. She said, "You-you just said it was too expensive when I showed it to you, and you didn't really want to buy it for me. It's just that all my friends had it and I wanted to have it too."

As Sabrina entered late-elementary through early-middle school, I became more familiar with trends and peer pressure. I had also taught her that she didn't have to go along with things others did or even everything I said unless it compromised her well-being. My goal was that she learned how to challenge with respect.

"Sabrina, do you recall when I told you that you don't need to follow everything that I ask of you all of the time so long as you tell me, be honest with me about the reasons why, and give us a chance to talk about it?" She nodded subtly. I continued, "All you had to do was tell me, sweetie. You could have told me just that ahead of time, I would have understood, and this problem could have been avoided. I always want to trust you, but I think it was you who didn't trust me, right? How can we fix this and make sure that we're honest with each other? Honesty is respect for me."

Her head bowed in apologetic shame. Although this made Sabrina uncomfortable, leaving her exposed and deeply vulnerable, this was the most compassionate and effective form of guidance. "Sabs, to resolve this, all I ask is that first, you write me a story. You also must promise me that you will never lie to me ever again. You don't have to follow exactly what I say, so long as you tell me ahead of time and are honest. Do we agree?" Still silent, she extended her pinky. "Thank you. Thank you for accepting my apology and making that promise."

11

The Value of Money: UGG, Unconditional Glamor Galore

Kids and their fads— the curse of good marketing! Don't worry though: It's a craze that evolves over time and soon fades ,l;lkaway. The exposure to new, branded items that thrive in specific social circles implants the notion of 'I have to have it.' When kids are so young, they are inevitably swayed by peer pressure. 'I have to have it' translates to 'I need it!'

Some families may be unable to provide that instant gratification to their children, whether it be a choice or a financial burden. In some affluent communities, kids are branded with 300-dollar UGG boots, 900-dollar Canada Goose coats, Gucci sneakers, etc. with no questions asked. If so, it is essential that parents teach their children to spend responsibly. Even though money may be a non-issue, the purpose is to ingrain children with values so that they avoid the entitlement trap.

When money is an issue, parents preach principles to save, work hard, and reap rewards from financial gain. These same principles must be taught to children from affluent families. Kids don't learn from the typical answers of "you don't need that" or "that's too expensive." I rarely made a fuss about material objects and rather focused on teaching Sabrina to spend mindfully, responsibly, and honestly. I sought to teach her how to budget and most importantly, to work for what you earn.

One rainy November afternoon, I picked up Sabrina from the bus stop. She hopped off in a puddle beneath her that drenched her bright pink rain boots. They came up just above her ankle, capris just short of covering the patch of skin in between. She looked funny.

"Sabs, you're soaking! Come on, get in the car!" I shouted from the window. Once she settled in the car, I asked how her day was at school.

"Mommy, I want the long UGG boots. All my friends were wearing them today and they said that they keep you super warm. And they'll cover my pants!"

Unfamiliar with the UGG brand, I assured, "Sure, we can look into it." I never said no to something before evaluating it completely.

That weekend, Sabrina and I took a shopping trip to buy holiday gifts. She was lured into the shoe section, as usual, upon walking into Nordstrom.

"Mommy! Look! These are the UGGs I told you about! Can I get them? Please?" Her eyes lit up as she hugged the fluffy black boot. I asked her to check the price.

"279 dollars! For shoes? You can buy two or three pairs of boots for the price of those!" I was incredulous. There was really nothing special about them from the outside. Just fluff and buttons.

"But they're good quality and super soft! Other boots aren't that soft or as warm as those. Please, pretty please," she begged again.

"Ok, I could get you the boots, but your budget is 300 dollars total.

It's your Chanukah gift. Think about what you really want." Her lips pouted as she regretfully placed the boot down.

"Fine, I'll think about it," she murmured.

On the way home, I reiterated my reasoning with Sabrina and reminded her of the options on her plate. I didn't want her to think that I refused to buy her those shoes but wanted her to recognize that she could buy more for the same price or less.

"Since you have 300 to spend in total, I could get you the UGGs or you can get two to three pairs of other brands that are much cheaper and still have the same styles as UGG. You can get two or three in different colors for the price of one pair of UGGs. Again, I'm happy to buy you the UGGs, but I just want to make you think about something. So, which do you prefer?"

"Ok. Can we go look at other shoes tomorrow?" Sabrina glared down at her old rain boots whose neon glow had faded. I agreed.

Macy's had an array of winter boots, ranging from high-end ones to mass brands. Sabrina was drawn to a pair of long, quilted black boots by Michael Kors. They were a hundred dollars. She also found a light brown pair from Nine West on sale for fifty. Then she found another pair, fluffy all around, for another 99 dollars. Three for the price of one!

"Sabs, I am proud of you for compromising and learning this lesson. You now know how to shop smarter!" I lauded her. She thanked me and placed the bag in the trunk.

Part VII Motherhood: Through My Daughter's Eyes

12

Principles Merge a Fork in the Road

After attending three Jewish day schools from first through fifth grade, Sabrina started sixth grade at a non-Jewish private school. Her social circle would extend beyond Jewish friends to Indians, Persians, Italian-Catholics, Chinese, Sikhs, and more. Dipping into this diverse pool of friends exposed our family to a wide array of events— from Diwali festivals to Christmas dinners, and New Year's parties to Halloween gatherings. This fresh network of parents with unique personalities, cultures, and beliefs was refreshing for Vick and me too. However, different beliefs often translate to gaps in values which can cause rifts in relationships.

I have always encouraged Sabrina to socialize freely and engage that with diverse sets of friends from all cultural backgrounds. By this age, she had a strong sense of her boundaries and freedoms to make value-based decisions. I took no issue with anything she did or anyone she hung out with so long as her safety, education, hygiene, and health were intact. If these boundaries were crossed in any way, it was an opportunity for me to reinforce priorities and better decision-making skills.

By seventh grade, kids and parents had formed tight-knit groups in the school community. We got together almost weekly for dinner, going to the movies, and relished in an array of holiday celebrations. At the tail-end of October, a couple of Sabrina's close friends (whose parents were also friends of ours) organized a trick-or-treating outing. She came home one day after school with the invitation just a few days before Halloween.

"Mom, can I go? It starts at 7:30 on Friday, and Veronica said I could sleep at her house after. Our whole friend group is going too, it's not just us."

I scanned over the golden card that she handed me. The pamphlet read that parents were invited for dinner that night while the kids explored the haunted houses. I couldn't imagine a parent allowing twelve and thirteen-year-old girls to roam around in an ungated, not-so-safe neighborhood late at night. It was perched on a hill and minimally lit at night, nestled among towering pine trees and curvy, narrow streets.

"Is there a chaperon or any adult going with you?"

"No, I don't think so," said Sabrina.

"I'd love for you to go and have fun, but I'll call Veronica's mom tonight just to make sure there will be an adult there," then explained, "I don't want you girls out alone when it's dark, especially in that part of town. What if someone grabs you? If you're a group of ten girls and someone goes missing, nobody will notice! You're going to be in costumes, and so will everybody else. You never know who's who. I only want you to be safe, trust me."

Sabrina rolled her eyes with the classic teenage "Ok, mom," and plopped on the couch to do her homework.

Before giving Sabrina a definitive answer, I had to evaluate the entire situation. I called Veronica's mom that same evening. We were close friends with the family, seeing each other almost every other week and even took ski trips together.

"Hi, Andrea, how are you?" I engaged her in a bit of small talk before prompting the conversation. "I'm just calling in regard to Halloween night, Sabrina showed me the invitation Veronica gave her at school today."

Andrea spoke, frazzled, as usual. "Yes, yes, um, of course, we can talk, uhh, while girls plan to go out, I-I plan on seeing you and Vick for dinner, that is, along with the other parents too."

"Yes, we'd love to be there, but I do have one question. Will there be a chaperone tagging along with the girls? I just get concerned about them going alone in the dark."

"Well, uhh yeah, I understand your concern, but, um, there will be more than ten of them in the group. They'll be safe. They've been doing this for the past few years. Many many years now." Andrea's hesitant tone eliminated any bit of confidence I had in her.

"Andrea, I am not comfortable with sending Sabrina with the girls to trick or treat on their own. It's not safe that late at night with so many people out, especially in that area."

"Veronica organized it, so it must go through her first. Yeah, I'll have to let you know about that— she's in charge."

What? A twelve-year-old girl in charge of a decision revolving around the safety of ten girls? "Ok, thank you. Please let me know. Our children's safety is my priority. We need to be mindful of taking responsibility for other kids' safety and making other parents comfortable too. I just want what's best for our kids."

My conversation with Andrea reaffirmed my long-standing principle, that you can't change people's minds, you can only influence them. When influence fails, you can only change yourself, your reaction, or your approach to the situation. I couldn't change Andrea's beliefs or principles, so I'd alter my approach by giving Sabrina an opportunity to influence her friend. I went to Sabrina's room to inform her of my conversation with Andrea.

"Why don't you try and talk with Veronica tomorrow to see what she thinks about having chaperones? She may be more open to the idea if it came from you instead of her mom," I suggested, knowing that teenagers tend to resist their parents.

"I don't think she'll want that," Sabrina replied, "But I can call her right now so I don't have to worry about it at school. She just helped me with math, I know she's still awake." She filed her packet away in her binder.

I stepped outside of Sabrina's room to give her privacy. I also wanted her to practice persuading her friend. Failing to give Sabrina the opportunity to influence Veronica would do her a disservice: A parent who steps in for their child without giving them the tools and the chance to advocate for themselves prevents them from acquiring essential life skills and maturing independently.

I could overhear Sabrina while relaxing on the sofa across the hall from her room: "But how does having just one adult behind us make a difference? That neighborhood isn't safe at night. Don't we have to think about the risk instead of being annoyed about just having an adult there?" Also, with so many people in costumes we would have no idea if some random stranger all dressed up was dangerous! Common, V, what's more important? Like they won't even be near us, just a block behind us to make sure we're safe!" She was trying to reiterate this point again and again, explaining what I had to Andrea. As the call progressed, Sabrina's voice was intensifying. She barged out minutes later.

"Mom! Veronica told me not to come! I knew this was going to happen!" Tears streamed down her cheeks. It was understandably a true embarrassment for a teenage girl to be disinvited due to an overprotective mother.

"I know it's not safe to walk in that neighborhood at night without an adult! I'm just mad that she doesn't want me to come anymore!"

I tried to calm her down, "It's ok, you did everything right. Just think about that when it comes to your safety, nothing else matters. I'll call her mom again, I'm sure we can work things out." My mind raced to brainstorm alternative methods of influence. Aha! "I'll also talk to Sammy's and Liv's parents to see if they are aware of this, ok? I think they would want supervision too."

Sabrina nodded her head and wiped her eyes with the blanket wrapped around her.

On Wednesday morning, I called Andrea back with the same question. Her response was unchanged: "It's Veronica's decision, it's her party. She's in charge, so-so-sorry Lea, but uhh, Sabrina can find another group to trick-or-treat with."

I hung up. I was unnerved by her rudeness and lack of responsibility to put her foot down for our children's safety. Dealing with Andrea directly was no longer my game plan. I reached out to three other parents. "Are you kidding me? I had no clue!" One mom, Shandra, was absolutely outraged. "I'm going to call Andrea right now, this is ridiculous!" I was glad that at least one of them shared my concern.

My phone rang just before picking up Sabrina from tennis practice that evening. It was Andrea: "Lea, hi. So, a few other parents called me today and were also hesitant about the girls going out alone on Halloween night. And, w-well, I talked to Veronica, and she agreed to have a chaperone, but they have to be far behind them, you know, so they don't interfere."

"Great, thank you!" The word had spread. My game plan worked.

Coordinating logistics went smoothly. Vick and a few other dads teamed up to walk in the girls' shadows. I took the evening for myself and invited a few old friends over for tea. "Sorry I won't be able to make it to the dinner, Andrea, I really would have loved to, I feel like I need to skip on this one." I knew that removing myself from the parent dinner that night was the right choice, far too disturbed by Andrea's behavior. It wouldn't have been pleasant for me or anybody else if I was there. This much needed breather is something I like to call 'get air.'

When annoyed with friends, it is best to take a break from them until we've cooled off because it benefits the relationship in the long run. Be honest if they ask why you seem to be ignoring them; they'll understand— it's normal. And there's nothing wrong with it.

While enjoying my company at home, Vick texted me photos of the girls in their superhero costumes, unbothered by parents whatsoever. The kids were given the freedom to wander the spooky streets and the parents were satisfied knowing that their children were safe. These are the lines that must be drawn so that both parent and child can respect each other's needs and boundaries.

With boundaries in place, kids often feel like their parents are trying to control them. But it's not always about control, and more about safeguarding, care, and love. Where parents fall short is in their explanation of these boundaries: The 'what' is given but the 'why' is missing. This style of communication may be subconscious, inherited from their upbringing. It's time to reverse this cycle by expressing reasons behind certain rules to your children, even if the rule seems obvious. Tell them that the boundary has been drawn for their benefit, whether it be to enrich their quality of life or to protect them. The more sensible and compassionate a parent is, the more they'll listen and understand.

Sabrina and I share a common understanding that her values, education, hygiene, health, and safety, are non-negotiable. Although she was upset when I pushed her to demand that a parent accompany the group, I was glad that she agreed with me deep down. When the relationship between parent and child is tied by a knot of common principles, issues about rules are easy to remedy. When conflicts are outside the household and/or increase in severity, parent and child can easily work together to solve them. These little bumps in our lives foster personal growth and ally us closer to those we trust and share core values with. What resides at our heart's center— our purpose, values, and character— stays with us no matter the external forces pushing and pulling us into pits of adversity.

Despite frustrations with Andrea, it was important for me to keep my purpose in mind: maintaining my friendship with her family. To achieve my purpose, I had to set my gripes aside and find a solution so my daughter could enjoy Halloween night with her friends. Meanwhile, this problem could have been entirely avoided if Andrea had fulfilled her parental duty. It wasn't my role to hold her accountable for this. Needless to say, disinviting someone by saying, "go find another group because my daughter is in charge" is flagrant and immature.

Adults have the responsibility to ensure the safety of their own kids and **especially** the safety of other kids in their company. But I was not going to try and change Andrea. Well-aware that she was not as vigilant a parent as I was, I'd take precautions when sending Sabrina to her home moving forward. I would inquire about the details of each event she or Veronica would organize to make decisions that secured my daughter's safety.

13

A Crash from Whiplash:
A Healthy Path to Greatness

Aweekly family ritual of ours involved an evening at the movies and an après-film dinner discussion. One Friday night, Sabrina, Vick, and I attended the debut of Whiplash, a movie about a conservatory musician discovered by a top-tier instructor who used abusive tactics to shape elite students. While the student endures tremendous misery, he becomes the best of the best. He sacrificed his well-being to achieve excellence.

As we stepped out of the theater, Vick said, "You see, that's how you get to be great!"

Sabrina and I looked at each other open-mouthed. "Seriously? You've gotta be kidding, dad."

Then, I tagged on, "Yeah, come on! What are you saying? Great is great, but not at the cost of your sanity! There has to be a way to mold someone's success by inspiring and encouraging them in a healthy way!"

Vick didn't realize it then, but the consequences revealed in the film would forever change his attitude toward Sabrina through her academic, musical, and athletic careers.

When Sabrina was in preschool, Vick and I caught her banging on a grand piano in one of the practice rooms. We shouted internal cries of joy, both intent on our daughter beginning music lessons when she was the right age. Sabrina's magnetic attraction to the piano made it easy enough. Lessons would begin at age five.

Piano became Sabrina's biggest nightmare. It became ours and her teachers as well. Between Sabrina's resistance— "I don't want to play this song! I don't want to practice!" — and Vick's insistence— "Sabrina sit down! Do it now!" — many evenings turned sour. Sabrina's teachers received the same treatment, making their turnover rate high. While we fired some, most of them fired Sabrina. She even made one of her teachers cry and go home in the middle of a lesson! This same woman— brave, compassionate, and patient as can be— would stick by Sabrina's side for the next nine years.

Disciplining Sabrina when it came to piano practice was necessary. Vick's methods, however, were making her not only resent her dad, but hate playing the piano entirely. He demanded that she practice exactly what the teacher had instructed exactly when he wanted it done for thirty minutes or more. Sabrina would gently ask, "Can I do it later?" to which Vick would declare, "Nope! You must do it now!"

As tensions escalated, a mediator had to intervene: Me. "We cannot continue like this. Sabrina, you know that piano is not an option. It's only for your benefit. And Vick, you know that yelling at Sabrina is not an option either. It doesn't work. How about we make a schedule?" I suggested, "What about penciling in a certain time for piano practice that you can agree on?" I asked Sabrina for her opinion: Empowering her to create her own schedule was key here.

"Sure." Motion resolved.

I created a planner template inside of Sabrina's binder where she could pencil-in her daily activities. While drawing sharp checkmarks of completion may have incentivized her, she'd soon find great satisfaction in managing her own time. She began taking initiative to complete her daily requirement or simply dabble around the keys. Sabrina still resisted here and there, and Vick sometimes retreated to his directive tone, but both were aware of their responsibilities and the rules within them.

With her maturity came Sabrina's acknowledgment that piano was a pillar of her education— one of the five non-negotiables along with her values, safety, hygiene, and health. This "musical girl," as her piano teacher would say, grew hungry for challenges. She sought to push her small hands and short fingers to play pieces beyond her level. Despite many tantrums, she never gave it up. During a holiday dinner when Sabrina was sixteen, a friend of ours asked Sabrina, "Why didn't you quit?" She said, "That would've been a waste, I'm too good to quit now."

Today, Sabrina finds serenity in learning pieces that move her or composing arrangements to her favorite pop songs. She can sit at the piano in our dimmed home-library for hours, experimenting with combinations of different melodies and harmonies. Our goal as parents has been accomplished.

Excellence is a product of practice, passion, and resources. However, the approach to practice can make or break the passion and performance. When a child is pushed to the brink, passion can crumble because practice becomes a chore, executed with rage, or morphs into a toxic obsession with perfection. Both can foster unhealthy habits or tragic outcomes. Regardless of excellent performance, what good is it if it's not sustainable? Nothing is worth more than a child's well-being.

If children refuse to participate as Sabrina did, or if a parent notices declining trends in their practice or declined performance, they need support to voice their feelings. A way that parents can do this is by asking questions about their resistance. Based on the answer, a parent can determine the next steps forward: First is to empower children with values of hard work that surround enjoying the practice, even if obstacles present immense challenges. Next steps are to help them to create a healthy, balanced routine. Consistent success— which lead to peak excellence— is a product of trusting children to do their best with utmost support.

Not Good Enough

Music wasn't the only area where Vick held high expectations for our daughter. School, of course, was most important. Coming from Jewish day schools, Sabrina struggled with her transition into sixth grade at an elite college prep academy. Like most parents, Vick expected her to be a model student with high test scores all-around. Math was particularly challenging for Sabrina, but it happened to be a subject where her dad had expertise. He tutored her.

"You can do better, you need to practice, you're not working hard enough," and would print packet after packet until she completed a mock exam flawlessly in record time.

"Can I get a break? I've been working for five hours already!" Sabrina would whine, dropping her pencil and shaking her wrist.

"Nope, not until you get above 95% in under forty-five minutes!" he'd respond, "Your test is in two days, this is your priority."

Each time Sabrina resisted, Vick would blow up: "You're so disorganized, this is why you don't do well! Your head is like cement! Nothing gets to you! You're too messy! Look at your handwriting!" He'd threaten to punish her by taking away privileges or leisure time. I refused to accept this style of parenting, knowing that it would hurt more than help her.

Please take it easy on her. Give her a break and explain it to her nicely. Yelling at her isn't going to make her better," I intervened.

Instead of taking my advice seriously, I was blamed. Vick would shout, "When you defend her all the time, she thinks she can get away with slacking off! It's your fault she doesn't listen! This is why she doesn't take me seriously and doesn't do well!"

Inevitably, I'd often inherit Sabrina's fights with Vick. I could not allow him to demean her, especially since she was trying her best. Sabrina confided in me, "I can't work or do well when he yells at me like that." A few years later, she confessed that his comments made her feel incompetent and discouraged her from wanting to try at all. An erosion of self-esteem often leads one to the cliffs of surrender. And surrender doesn't always mean giving up: It may mean unnecessarily surrendering yourself to certain standards that are not authentic to who you are as an individual. And worst of all, surrendering on yourself as a human being entirely.

Hair Pulls

That Saturday morning kicked-off the weekend with pure hysteria. It was as if I had seen a ghost. This ghost: a quarter-sized bald spot-on Sabrina's scalp.

"Stop! It's nothing! Don't touch me!" she yelled, slapping my shoulder.

"No! I saw what I saw, now let me see that!" I tilted her head toward me and examined it, proceeding to dig through her thick, wavy auburn hair looking for more spots.

"I promise, that's the only place!" Sabrina cried, "Get off of me!" She ran to the bathroom.

Vick hopped on google and typed in 'hair pulling.' I followed him to the office. Google search spat out 'trichotillomania,' an anxiety-induced hair-pulling disorder. Sabrina later admitted that she would pick at her scalp during exams, while she was studying alone in her room, and even as she was falling asleep. She wasn't even aware of her own behavior or its root cause.

All I knew was that Vick's tutoring methods weren't helping. Such tremendous stress and pressure would make me want to pull my hair out too! Despite offering Sabrina all the resources she needed to stop, she adamantly refused therapy. Many high-achieving kids like Sabrina find a stigma around therapy, ashamed of needing professional help to overcome their emotional pain, let alone needing help at all. But emotional pain is just as legitimate as physical pain, just as mental illnesses lead to physical ones.

Sabrina came out of the bathroom, still wiping her face. "I promise, I'll stop. Trust me," she implored. So we did. But this was the wrong decision. Health is one of the five non-negotiables— and I failed to put my foot down right away.

Around this time was when we watched the movie Whiplash which revealed dangerous impacts of extreme anxiety. It was then that Vick connected the dots and realized that his parenting style, remarks, expressions, and over-all disciplinary methods were contributing to Sabrina's deteriorating well-being. He finally started to change, and slowly but surely, her hair began to grow back.

But this journey was far from over. Sabrina only stopped the hair pulls for a short while, only until anxiety manifested itself in her life once again. Like conflicts, stressors are inevitable, which is why reactions to stress and stress management are essential tools. They are deeply personal, requiring self-discovery of triggers and coping mechanisms. Children should be encouraged to seek help once they notice themselves spiraling downwards, whether it's from a parent or an outside source that they trust. Since parents can control the dynamic at home, it is their duty to nurture a comfortable environment whereby the child can express their feelings and/or reach out for help.

Part VII Motherhood: Through My Daughter's Eyes

14

Turn You and Take Your Journey

That same stressful year happened to be Sabrina's Bat Mitzvah. It is customary for Jewish boys and girls to undergo this coming-of-age ceremony at twelve or thirteen. A Bar or Bat Mitzvah is the ritual associated with a child taking responsibility for their actions and fulfilling righteous deeds, called mitzvot. The child traditionally reads a portion from the Torah, analyzes it as relates to personal life, and performs a community service project. This is all symbolic of incubating the Jewish mission of Tikkun Olam in new generations.

"Turn you and take your journey" is the first line of Sabrina's assigned Torah portion, Deuteronomy I. For biblical context, Moses prepares the Israelites to take their journey into the promised land of Israel. He endows them rules and responsibilities to fulfill upon entering. While Moses was a great leader, he was prohibited entrance into Israel because he resisted a command from God. Moses's legacy is marked by accepting the consequences of bold leadership and maintaining an unwavering commitment to his people. Moses's promise to the old generation was to prepare their children for a future abundant with milk and honey— richness of life. Richness is not merely a measure of assets and resources but a measure of one's ability to maintain relationships, spark new connections, discover passions, and seek purpose. This is what brings sweetness to one's soul, inspiring individuals to forge ahead based on values and objectives. After studying the text as a family for hours, we would finally agree on "The Journey" as Sabrina's theme.

On the night of her Bat Mitzvah, Sabrina delivered a speech that related this biblical story to her life: "My parents, like Moses, have prepared me to assume responsibility and pursue my own journey," she remarked. Sabrina also committed to living by thirteen core principles which would guide her along the windy roads of life. Many of these core principles are associated with her childhood experiences and are mentioned in this book whereas some are closely tied to her education and projects. She begins with my number one principle, which is to establish purpose in every situation, and follows with listening attentively and never hesitating to ask questions or voice your need for support. Next is to take ownership,

sabs principles

turn you, and take your journey

principles derived and interpreted
from sabrina's torah passage
in honor of her bat mitzvah

23 july 2015

1 establish purpose

2 listen attentively

3 explore and inquire

4 plan and prepare

5 ask for help

6 accept responsibility

7 take ownership

8 recognize and appreciate

9 speak assertively

10 honor your word

11 treat all with respect

12 lead with confidence

13 hope always for a better tomorrow

" these are the words which moses spoke— turn you, and take your journey, dread not, neither be afraid..."

" אלה הדברים, אשר דבר משה; עלו, וסעו את־הדר, לא־תיראו, ואל־תערצו, ואל... "

deuteronomy 1: 1-3:22

to lead with confidence, then to recognize and appreciate. The principles conclude with hope because with no hope, there is no purpose, and with no purpose, future aspirations are dimmed.

Sabrina's speech was also complemented by the idea that our different journeys paint our individual characteristics and unique life tracks. Each of our journeys are marked by past experiences which can be reflected on in the present and employed as lessons for the future. Sabrina's community service projects wove a tapestry of these concepts, her passion for writing, and curiosity about Jewish history.

Sabrina's Passion Project

The year prior, we embarked on our annual summer vacation to Israel. That trip was a bit different than routine family visits and casual exploration. Sabrina's preliminary Bat Mitzvah ceremony would be held at the Davidson Center, the only portion of the Western Wall where women are allowed to read from the Torah. Her Bat Mitzvah celebration was held back home, in San Diego, a few months later.

Packaged with Bat Mitzvah age are many responsibilities: Vick and I considered our daughter's acquaintance with her Jewish roots an important one. Our month's stay was dedicated to touring various sites out of religious and historical lenses. We knew little that our visit to one of the most heart-wrenching memorials would inspire Sabrina's sequence of projects and ignite profound, lasting passion. Yad Vashem, the Holocaust memorial museum in Jerusalem, is where all of this happened.

The harrowing premise of the Holocaust left our innocent teenage girl exposed to an insolvable puzzle, whose pieces composed a horrifying image of our world and human capacity. "Why didn't other countries do something? How could people do this to other people?" she'd ask, "Could something like this ever happen again?" No answer would quench her ravenous appetite to understand what, how, and why the world could stand by this tragedy in silence.

Answers that Sabrina uncovered in books and films only propelled her to dig deeper. Eager to learn from primary source accounts, she began searching for local survivors to interact with. Their stories of survival kindled a fire in Sabrina to preserve their legacies. One survivor implored, "If this generation doesn't know what happened to us, nobody will, because we will all be gone. Please tell our stories." Another told her, squeezing her hand, "This is how I learn now: be active, do something." Sabrina manifested this practice— be active, do something— and sealed her promise to carry the torch of survivors' stories by documenting, posting, and spreading them online to educate her peers and community. Unbeknownst to us all, Sabrina's Bat Mitzvah project was born: Endless hours of research and writing didn't even phase her. It was a never-ending cycle of curiosity: True passion.

That spring, we traveled to Europe so Sabrina could immerse herself in history and extend her survivor outreach to abroad. This project's coalescence with her thirteen principles authored her rule book to life. Sabrina's most treasured principle is inspired by Holocaust survivor Elie Wiesel's famous statement, "Never stay silent. Neutrality helps the oppressor, never the victim. Silence encourages the tormentor, never the tormented." [10] While I had raised Sabrina to speak up, her understanding of standing up in the face of injustice was shining through a different light.

---

[10] Wiesel, Elie. "Acceptance Speech." 10 Dec. 1986, Award of the Nobel Peace Prize. Oslo City Hall. Speech.

Coming of Age with Maturity and Wisdom

The ability to make connections between pieces of knowledge and derive their greater meaning demonstrates maturity and wisdom. Sabrina's presentation of these two qualities in her activities, relationships, and behavior granted me a novel outlook to what maturity and wisdom truly mean. That is precisely the reason why my greatest gift is being able to see the world through my child's eyes, and why I encourage each parent to do the same.

Sabrina has been not only my masterpiece, but my master. She has not only guided and empowered me to be a better mom but inspires my principles toward others and shapes my passions. My daughter is the mirror I continue to look through for each decision, adventure, or endeavor I pursue in my personal and professional life.

Concluding With Purpose

Final Remarks

1

My Life's Mission at Work

On my 50th birthday in 2017, Sabrina and Vick asked me what my wish would be for this new chapter in my life. Around the same time, the #MeToo movement had peaked with Larry Nassar's case. I was glued to the trial's progress as the story unfolded, unable to comprehend how victims were silenced, attacked, dismissed, and ignored. The institution's behavior, although to a lesser severity, reminded me of how Sabrina was betrayed: The patterns were clear. My determination to bring about or be part of the change to this perverted culture was sparked. To Vick and Sabrina's question I replied, "I want to be their voice." These words would immediately become actions. Like my daughter discovered her passion project, I found mine.

Discovering the scale of these cover-ups repulsed me. I researched the hundreds of cases nation-wide, country-wide, and in the local school district. Talking to parents and students got me involved with our community's local politicians and various agencies. As my knowledge base grew, so did my understanding of education codes, federal laws, and state statutes regarding school safety, bullying, sexual harassment, and the fiduciary responsibility of administrators. I reached out to the District Attorney, Department of Education, Department of Justice, and Office of Civil Rights. My findings revealed that the many laws and codes made to protect children go unenforced. Failed accountability perpetuates bad behavior and emboldens abuse.

Hours of research culminated in my extensive report, The Cover-Up Practices that Normalize Child Abuse. My heart bled with the victims' endurance of harassment and deprivation of justice. To ensure that our local administrators act responsibly was my first aim at spurring change. At school board meetings, I was outspoken and advocated relentlessly on behalf of parents and students. They called me "the Pitbull."

After questioning the relationship between policies and their lack of enforcement, I was stonewalled by all but two board members. The remaining two offered me a deep insight into the Triangular Conflict of Interest. This model displays the relationship between unions, local schools, and the public system who prioritize institutions over children's safety and well-being. Unfortunately, these practices are ubiquitous, normalized nation-wide and in every industry.

Outrage fueled me to build Let's Speak Up (www.letsspeakup.org) in 2018. I was focused on educating, empowering, and advocating for student's rights and their well-being. A student at the local public high school at the time, Sabrina became a first-hand testament of what was going on in the district. Our team developed a web application where victims could anonymously report any misconduct or wrongdoing they had experienced on campus. We became an instrumental voice for students, receiving hundreds of complaints from across the country. My influence within the district grew as I became more vocal and audacious.

Inevitably, my supporters, friends, and team members encouraged me to run for a school board position. Hence my career in activism.

During my campaign, I realized that victims are not the only ones hurt by coverup practices. While victims suffer from trauma, anxiety, and depression, offenders are denied a path to treatment. Cover-ups legitimize the offender's behavior to repeat their misconduct, which jeopardizes their emotional, mental, and physical freedom long-term. They are ridden with shame, anxiety, and silence because the institution holds secrets surrounding their crime(s). Further, an offender's situation exacerbates when the irrefutable pattern is presented in court. Their lives are destined to ruin rotting behind bars.

I began exploring recidivism rates in our juvenile and criminal justice system. I discovered that rehabilitation significantly reduces rates of recidivism and concluded that offenders are likely to stop perpetrating if they are held responsible from the onset. Through constructive therapy and relevant projects, they gain potential to understand their impact. By understanding the harm that they inflict on their victims, society, and most of all, themselves, brings an awareness that can shift their mindset.

Additional research revealed that cover-ups are detrimental to the institutions themselves, too. Hundreds of millions of dollars in settlements result in financial demise, sometimes to the extent of bankruptcy. Considering the detrimental impacts of cover-ups on victims, offenders, and institutions, my team and I realized that inspiring a culture that holds everyone accountable from the onset can protect each stakeholder: Remedying misconduct cases in the short term prevents abuse in the long term. Breaking the cycle of abuse would also restore trust and confidence in each affected party— leaders and organizations included. Administrators are guaranteed protection only when fulfilling their fiduciary duty, whereby their organization can avoid years of secrecy, legal chaos, and financial crisis.

In 2019, The Let's Speak Up team expanded. We resolved that the solution had to be holistic: Technology without a culture-change is a mere part of the whole. So, rather than advocating solely for victims and students, we pivoted to the paradigm of protecting people, organizations, and society. Our new vision became ICIARA. This Independent Complaint Investigative Assessment Resolution Application aims to educate all stakeholders of their responsibility to address misconduct constructively, compassionately, and collaboratively. We created an AI algorithm that immediately links incidents with their severity to address complaints before they worsen and mitigate liability. To market our mission, our team constructed a website, wrote blog posts, and reached out to influential people in the area to pitch our platform.

ICIARA is currently working on publishing a book called Act Responsibly. Much of its content and materials are derived from my expertise in developing and delivering leadership workshops. The unique methodology, the 7E's to Effective Training, is what I used to engage and empower participants. Through IQNet Interactive, I developed a total of 12-unique workshops including e-LEADERSHIFT to Cross-Cultural and Collaborative Communications, Elements in Building Trust and Confidence, How to Cure the Cancerous C's, 7-Ways to Stand Up to Bullying, and 7-Simple Ways to Mend Differences. Prior to IQNet, I spearheaded Iclique-in Technology, Inc. (www.haychamba.com), a platform that connects blue-collar and manual workers to corporations via bilingual text messaging. I had formed a partnership of similar nature shortly after Sabrina was born. Innolink, Inc. to commercialize Israeli technologies in America.

The combination of my technical skills, global awareness, diverse cultural background, passion for public affairs, and human development initiatives were the path to my purpose and mold my profession. Many of my project ideas sparked from demands I deemed necessary by the community, the market, and of course my daughter. My entrepreneurship, however, emerged from the need to hone my skills while being a mom. I am so grateful to my husband who allows me to explore my interests and pursue them with unbridled freedom. Through each of my endeavors, I am determined to never lose any facet of my identity while contributing to my family. Acknowledging that my relationship with myself is the only one I cannot escape, my life's purpose will forever surround self-development and helping others grow.

Knowing Thyself

I had yet to appreciate my journey through cultural extremes. Through my twenties and thirties up until motherhood, I always deemed each culture shock as contradictory to the last, each as another layer of confusion to my identity. Today, I find these cultures as complementary connectors to one other, molding me into a diverse, critical thinker with a firm sense of self. Each layer upon my identity is built with integrity and tenacity as I define purpose in everything that I do. Seeking, setting, and striving toward purpose with grit and courage is the recipe to radical confidence.

Over the past thirty years, I've been able to strike the balance between my role as a mother, wife, entrepreneur, and friend. While accomplishing the goal I set at age twenty-three has been ever-so rewarding, it took tremendous commitment: When we commit, we care, and when we care, we become vulnerable, and when we become vulnerable, we become fragile. Naturally, humans are prone to cracking, but knowing myself has enabled me to glue a mirror that shatters into a million pieces back together. I narrate my story to empower anybody, no matter how lost and broken they feel, to become confident in their own skin.

When I look in the mirror today, there are no tears streaming through cracked glass. Through the cracks I see light, through challenges I gain knowledge, and through obstacles I find opportunities. Rather than a shattered woman in agony, I see a woman smiling proudly back at me. My reflection is the catalyst through which I exhibit resilience and radiate it onto others. My reflection is a daily reminder to continue living by my principles and my purpose, with a daughter who can draw from them just as I do from her.

Epilogue

To my mother on her birthday

January 7, 2020.

Lea Wolf, _____?

It was at a dinner party we hosted a couple of months ago where a discussion surrounding identity prompted my thoughts. The question that was raised was as follows: "Who do you see yourself as in a single word? How do you want to be remembered?"

You were perplexed, unable to define your complexities in one word. "Maybe a social entrepreneur," was your instinctual response. You explained that to do so, it would depend on the relationship and context of a certain situation. I found this valid but surprised at your inability to recognize the single quality that emerges, regardless of external factors.

You often ask why people can't just do the right thing. You are someone who, when injustice exists, never fails to protest. You are a soldier who battles until the very end— until morals, ethics, and humanity have triumphed. Driven by wounds that may leave indelible scars, perseverance and resilience crown you with victory. The word **'warrior'** is your answer.

Today is the day I tell you that the impact you've had on me is beyond tremendous: Strokes of brilliance in your parenting have shaped me into the person I am today. Born to a beautiful woman who is bold, smart, and vivacious, I could not ask for anything else in a mother. Our relationship is truly, one of a kind. When I tell others about you, I express that even more than my mom, you are my **very** best friend. The intimacy we share is irreplaceable; I find comfort in your warmth, humor, and wit. With every strange conversation we engage in, we continue to tie knots in our unbreakable bond. Even more so, the past couple of years connected us on a different level. Before these past two years, I was only acquainted with myself at a mere surface level; in other words, I did not really 'know myself.' But, as you say, when you learn to "deal with adversity," it makes you stronger. And so, in this instance, as stress and anxiety completely changed my life, your guidance brought me closer to not only you but myself. Helping me experiment with different diets, lifestyles, workouts, activities, friends, and even the possibility of changing schools mid-year, you lingered in my shadow as I stumbled through challenges:

"Mom, I hate this school." Then came, "Mom, my stomach hurts," and afterward, "Mom, I'm having a panic attack," followed by streams of tears and episodes of anxiety.

You are a fabulous listener and counselor, better than any therapist or doctor. With the sharpest of minds, your thoughts are unique, and creative. Drawing from your personal experiences to teach me about your shortfalls and successes is the most valuable advice— authentic, meaningful, inspirational. Every day, your optimism and confidence in yourself have driven me to strive toward a similar goal: To "lead life with a smile, purpose, and just do what you feel like you need to do."

Doing what you feel that you need to do embodies who **you** are: A leader, born and unstoppable. Unlike many, you lead with virtues and compassion rather than power. Growing up, you never sought control over me. Instead of grounding me when I misbehaved, you tasked me with writing essays that forced me to learn from my mistakes. Instructed to analyze my actions and solutions for the future, I developed my problem solving and decision-making skills from a young age. Only in urgent causes or risky situations, your aggression comes from love, passion, and the need to protect. Navigating me through the choppy, unpredictable waters of life has engendered my maturity and growth. You have instilled qualities of leadership within me, teaching me that you cannot change others, but can influence them through how you present yourself, express your thoughts, and convey your message.

Exerting great influence on those you already know; you also leave an impression on everyone you meet. With the beauty and charisma of a princess— whether it be on the snowy streets of 42nd Street Manhattan or mid-serve on the tennis court— people are drawn to you. Your effervescent smile is magnetic, and your confident voice is captivating. In a society where many mask their true identity behind blotches of make-up, fake smiles, and checking boxes, this world is in dire need of more people like you. Uplifting and humorous, you're real and genuine, focused whole-heartedly on your goals, passions, and those you love. Through the bridges you build, and never burn, you have demonstrated to me the importance of human connection. I credit you with steering me in the right direction along the windy roads of friendship, teaching me that everyone in my life— whether they befriend or betray me— has their purpose.

Most importantly, you preach the significance of family. "Friends are temporary, and the only people who will always stick by you and love you unconditionally are those in your nuclear family" are your words; and with no doubt, they are true. Disappointed by those I consider to have my back, you embrace me with open arms and leave me emerging

542

stronger from my pain. Obstacles aside, you fulfill my many desires and go miles beyond what is needed to ensure my optimal health and happiness. From buying me Pandora at least once a month to organizing dinner parties whenever dad 'feels like cooking,' these continued small gestures are ones that I will surely pursue in my family: It's been ingrained in tradition. That spark of authenticity that many families lack primarily comes from you, extracting the soul and meaning out of every experience.

No one can ever seem to take the soul out of you: You are 'meaning,' personified. Your meaning in life is your family, your purpose, and your mission. As your daughter, I could not be more grateful that you fight for this every day, like a warrior.

To my inspiration, my role model, and a masterpiece in **my** life, never stop being you. Never stop fighting for what you love like the warrior that you are.

Lea Wolf, <u>Warrior.</u>

To my mother on her birthday, *January 7, 2020*

To a woman who stands tall

Perched upon the highest of mountains

Above it all

Overlooking the island's widest ocean

To ensure her most precious treasures

Fulfill her heart of devotion

Sounds of waves

Crashing and breaking on the shore

She notices conflict emerging

Her actions prove nothing more

In the stream-split valley just below

Witness to those in fight

Refusing to stand by the river's flow

Descending from the heights

Reverberating within her soul

Is a visceral call

To abate all malice, she is summoned

And with compassion and love

All for its pure cause

Despite the natural world's rules and laws

She is a warrior

With Love, ~ Sabrina

Connect
With Us

Invite us to share our transformational stories and
life changing paradigms to help you be your best self.

These lessons, tools, and techniques are a source of inner-
power and inspiration to better relationships.

Our speaking engagements can be focused on a specific topic
or audience upon your group's request. Here are some
suggestions:

Self-Growth, Adolescence, Dating, Intimacy, Parenting, Motherhood,
Marriage, Trust and Confidence, Self-Discovery, Self-Fulfillment,
Purpose, Be Your Own Advocate, Cultural Inversions and Diversions

If you have questions or suggestions,

we would love to hear from you

858.255.0207 ◆ MMM@bysabs.com
www.bysabs.com/mymothersmirror
Instagram: @mymothersmirror.memoir

Sabrina

Made in the USA
Monee, IL
13 June 2025

19063716R00305